THE
SOUTHERN
BAPTIST
HOLY
WAR

THE
SOUTHERN BAPTIST HOLY WAR

JOE EDWARD BARNHART

TexasMonthlyPress

Texas Monthly Press, Inc.
P.O. Box 1569
Austin, Texas 78767

A   B   C   D   E   F   G   H

Library of Congress Cataloging-in-Publication Data

Barnhart, Joe E., 1931–
   The Southern Baptist holy war.

   1. Southern Baptist Convention—Doctrine.
2. Baptists—Doctrines.   3. Church controversies.
I. Title.
BX6462.7.B37   1986   286'.132   86-5988
ISBN 0-87719-037-2

Book design by David Timmons

For Quentin and Reve Perreault

Contents

Preface

had looked forward to listing the names of all who helped with this book and even to indicating how they helped, but the list is too long. I hope I am not short on gratitude, for without the patient assistance of Southern Baptists on both sides of the controversy that is steadily tearing them apart, this book would have died in its fetal stage. With rare exception, the individuals interviewed were uncommonly straightforward and, I believe, as honest as humanly possible in offering me various ways of looking at what is happening to the Southern Baptist Convention, the largest Protestant denomination in the nation.

In marriage and divorce counseling the counselor must keep in mind that there are often more than two sides to marital conflict. As Southern Baptists face the possibility of divorce, some of their leaders are struggling to keep in mind that there are many sides involved and many interests at stake, with staggering material losses and gains to consider. In 1985 alone, Southern Baptists gave $3.6 billion through their churches and institutions. The total value of Southern Baptist Convention churches and agencies approximates $20 billion. No one is going to pronounce the final truth about Southern Baptists—certainly not I. But perhaps I have gained some insight into both their exceedingly complex organizational life and the tragedy that is rocking this great denomination on its heels. This book reflects much of what I saw, heard, and felt while interviewing a large cross section of these people and what I learned over the years by reading an enormous amount of their literature.

It has been a deeply moving experience for me to write and rewrite the chapters that follow. Perhaps the reader who journeys through them will sense some of the compelling adventure that I felt in writing them.

Responsibility for the shortcomings of this book falls on my own shoulders. Mrs. Kay Prewitt, by detecting and correcting numerous flaws in various versions of the manuscript, has saved me considerable embarrassment. Warmest thanks go to her, to Mrs. Betty Grise, and to the library staff of North Texas State University for helping to make my research and writing enjoyable. Because the story contained in the book is so serious, I have profited from the efforts of my wife, Mary Ann, to remind me of its pleasant and humorous side. It was she who helped me laugh at the fact that her fallible husband was writing a few chapters on the infallibility controversy.

Those who do not know Baptist ministers personally may not realize that they are often a very funny lot, sometimes teasing one another unmercifully. Of the many whom I interviewed at length, some seemed to be, in my judgment, geniuses, only a few came across as crazy, and none was boring. Interviewing them was for me an education.

Joe Edward Barnhart
Denton, Texas

1.

A Noise of War in the Camp

"A preacher who doesn't believe that the
Bible is the whole Word of God ought to go
sell aluminum siding."
The Reverend Bailey Smith
February 1985

THE POWER AND THE GLORY

Well over fourteen million strong, Southern Baptists number a million and a half more than all the Jews throughout the world. America's most popular church historian, Martin Marty of the University of Chicago, has described Southern Baptists as the Catholic Church of the South. He had in mind their bigness, their power, and their semiestablishment status. As America's largest Protestant denomination, they have stepped over the Mason-Dixon line to establish conventions in 38 states. With financial help coming from the Southern Baptist Convention Foreign Mission Board, Canadian Southern Baptists have already purchased 150 acres near Calgary, Alberta, for a theological seminary campus scheduled to open in the fall of 1987. In the United States six Southern Baptist seminaries, including the largest seminary in the world, will receive a total of more than $25 million in the current year from the Convention's Cooperative Program alone.

Southern Baptists are an assertive people with a diverse heritage reaching back at least into seventeenth-century New England and Europe. Today these dynamic people are caught in a tortured marriage of primarily two parties that make one another miserable. Like a wolf and a bear chained together, they snarl and battle ceaselessly. And yet somehow they have managed to survive as a thriving denomination. Thus far!

Louis Moore, formerly religion editor for the Houston Chronicle, could be given the title "war correspondent." Since 1979 he has followed at close range the Battle of the Baptists. For a while he kept reporting that nothing would come of this ecclesiastical civil war. He even gave plausible explanations of why and how the gigantic denomination would avoid an irrevocable split in twain. But on October 13, 1984, Moore reversed himself, asserting that the Southern Baptist Convention (SBC) had passed the point of no return en route to disaster.

No doubt many Southern Baptists of each warring party would like to see their enemies (formerly mere opponents) leave and form a separate denomination. Concerned outsiders keep asking why the parties cannot sit down together and work out an amicable divorce to their mutual satisfaction. Jimmy Draper, the winsome and popular president of the Southern Baptist Convention in 1982–84, thinks that his fellow Southern Baptists are caught in the strange predicament of having no feasible method for separating. For some, there is the will to split but no means, no modus operandi.

In some crippling marriages, husbands and wives, either too rich or too poor to make a divorce practical, are compelled by circumstances to remain together despite the cruel wounds they inflict upon each other year after year. With more than fourteen million members and billions of dollars at stake, the Southern Baptist parties appear to be locked together in sadomasochistic matrimony, in sickness and in health, for better or for worse. Apparently for worse—and richer. In the last eight years, the bittersweet arrangement that weds the Moderate Party to the Inerrancy Party has grown increasingly bitter. The Inerrancy Party insists that the Bible is inerrant, that is, wholly and absolutely free of all error in its "original autographs." Memphis pastor and current Convention president Adrian Rogers (he also served as president in 1979–80) states this position crisply: "The Bible is either absolute or it's obsolete. There can be no in-between." Leaders of the Inerrancy Party are committed to weeding the in-betweens out of every position of influence within the Southern Baptist Convention. Convinced that the other party has changed and violated a thousand times the terms of their arrangement, each speaks glowingly of its own integrity and castigates the intimate enemy for losing its integrity.

Outside observers have advised these fierce Baptists either to divorce (and the sooner the better) or to come together in fervent prayer. But there has been considerable praying by both sides already. And the more the members pray for each other, the more it seems they prey upon each other. In 1984 Roy Honeycutt, Moderate Party champion and president of the prestigious Southern Baptist Theological Seminary at Louisville, Kentucky, declared holy war on the Inerrancy Party, whose leaders he decried as in league with "unholy forces" within the Convention. In retaliation, the embattled patriarch of the Inerrancy Party, white-haired W. A. Criswell of Dallas, fired back at Honeycutt by calling for his immediate resignation. As one woman said, "For years we Southern Baptists played softball. Now it's hardball."

In 1984 several trustees of the world's largest seminary, Fort Worth's scholarly Southwestern Baptist Theological Seminary, warned the seminary's president, Dr. Russell H. Dilday, Jr., to keep quiet about the Baptist controversy. Instead of heeding, Dilday issued his own public warning, charging that one group in the Convention had set out on a course to seize control of the Convention's six seminaries as well as the Convention's numerous and complex agencies, some of which reach around the world. In March 1985 President Dilday announced, "Unless this takeover movement is put aside, in another three or four years Southern Baptists will lose Southwestern Seminary."[1]

High drama almost always involves a cast of major characters. In the Convention's high drama red-haired Paige Patterson stands conspicuously upstage, looking like a wholesome version of Norman Mailer. Sitting in Patterson's large office and listening to his hoarse voice, I could not help noticing two large wall portraits of W. A. Criswell, undisputed major character and leader of the Inerrancy Party. In one portrait, Dr. Criswell was standing on a mountain overlooking the Holy Land. Both Criswell and Patterson believe that one day the same Holy Land will literally flow deep with the blood of those fighting in the great and final Battle of Armageddon. They are sometimes called biblical literalists, Criswell having published a book with the title *Why I Preach the Bible Is Literally True*.

On a prize piece of real estate in downtown Dallas stands Criswell's gigantic First Baptist Church across the street from the Baptist bookstore and the Criswell Bible College and Graduate School of the Bible. On page two of the school's bulletin and beside Chancellor Criswell's picture are his words: "I am a literalist and not a liberal."

Dr. Paige Patterson, president of the Criswell Center for Biblical Studies, looks upon Criswell as his spiritual father. What is sometimes forgotten is that Paige is the son of Dr. T. A. Patterson, who has held positions of highest influence in the Texas Baptist Convention and still serves as a major force behind Paige's attack on what he regards as widespread liberalism within the seminaries and the Southern Baptist bureaucracy. An articulate and gifted tactician of the Inerrancy Party,

Paige insists that he and most of those with him do not want to seize control of all six of the Southern Baptist seminaries. They want only half of them. "We're being generous," he said in a February 1985 interview, "when we make this proposal, since ninety percent of the Southern Baptist people are theologically on our side."

In June 1984 the Inerrancy Party candidate, Charles Stanley, minister of Atlanta's First Baptist Church, was elected Convention president. The position is endowed with the power to make key appointments to the crucial Committee on Committees, and the Inerrancy Party has had a grip on the office since 1979.

After graduating from Southwestern Baptist Theological Seminary in 1971, Stanley became the first minister of the First Baptist Church of Fruitland, North Carolina, and a faculty member of the independent Fruitland Bible Institute. Later, after moving to Ohio, he returned to the South to become founder, principal, and pastor of a fundamentalist school. Eventually, he became the minister of the First Baptist Church of Atlanta, where he established two popular satellite TV ministries. A bitter controversy erupted in his Atlanta church, and a few hundred members left to join a church whose minister at the time was Russell Dilday. In 1979 Charles Stanley helped the Reverend Jerry Falwell (who is not a Southern Baptist) found Moral Majority, Inc. Having his own TV audience, Stanley preaches to more people than any other Baptist minister, with the exception of Pat Robertson of the 700 Club. (Even though Robertson is a Southern Baptist and a potential candidate for the U.S. presidency—with Jimmy Draper's support—he could not get elected to high office at the Baptist convention because he speaks in tongues and professes to be a faith healer, two practices that most Southern Baptists decidedly frown upon.)

In June 1985 angry members of the Moderate Party arrived in Dallas by the thousands, determined to unseat Stanley and deny him the traditional second term as Convention president. "He's an outsider and an interloper," many of them charged. Although Southern Baptist seminaries train nearly one fifth of all Protestants enrolled in institutions accredited by the Association of Theological Schools, Charles Stanley had urged his own children to stay away from Southern Baptist seminaries and to attend the fundamentalist and independent Dallas Theological Seminary.

Founded in 1924 and noted for the way it divides the whole of human history into a sequence of dispensations, the school has the policy of employing only faculty members who subscribe to biblical inerrancy. (To say that the Bible is inerrant is to say that it teaches no error and contains no false statement that is not corrected within the Bible itself.) The Dallas seminary is an indoctrination center primarily for fundamentalist and evangelical ministers committed to the doctrine of inerrancy. In fact, students entering this seminary are asked to sign a document to certify their belief that the Bible is free of all error of any and every sort. Hal Lindsey, author of the best-seller doomsday book *The Late Great Planet Earth,* learned much of his dispensational theology and apocalyptic scheme while attending Dallas Theological Seminary.

Dr. Norman Geisler, who teaches at the Dallas seminary, testified on behalf of the creationists in the 1981 evolution trial in Arkansas. Under questioning by an attorney, he admitted that he regarded Noah's flood not as a sea of water but as the appearance of a universal ice age, a view that contrasts sharply with that of most of Geisler's fundamentalist and creationist colleagues. Knowing that Geisler professed to believe the Bible to be inerrant, the attorney asked him if he believed in a personal devil.

"Oh, yes," Geisler answered.

"Are there, sir, any other evidences for that belief besides certain passages of Scripture?"

"Oh, yes," Geisler replied, "I have known personally at least twelve persons who were clearly possessed by the devil. And then there are UFOs."

"The UFOs?" the attorney asked. "Why are they relevant to the existence of the devil?"

"Well, you see, they represent the devil's major, in fact final, attack on the earth."

"Oh," said the attorney. "And, sir, may I ask you how you know, as you seem to, that there are UFOs?"

"I read it in the *Reader's Digest.*"

On March 1, 1985, Harold Lindsell, formerly editor of the influential *Christianity Today,* said in an interview with me that despite the excessive dispensationalism at Dallas Theological Seminary, he as a Southern Baptist prefers its faculty to that of any of the Southern Baptist seminaries. Lindsell has written several articles and books, including "The Battle for the Bible," attacking the rise of what he calls theological liberalism in Southern Baptist schools. His explicit goal is to eliminate from the faculties all who do not subscribe to the doctrine of biblical infallibility and inerrancy and to replace them with professors like those at Dallas Theological Seminary. When asked if he would fire Russell Dilday, president of Southwestern Baptist Theological Seminary, Lindsell replied, "Dilday should be relieved of his responsibility."

"Is there any difference between that and being fired?" I asked.

"We have to be careful in selecting our words."

"I repeat. What's the difference, Dr. Lindsell, between firing these seminary presidents and faculty members and relieving them of their responsibilities?"

"There's no difference. But 'firing' is such a negative, nasty word."

"Would you fire the entire faculty and administration at the Southern Baptist seminary in Louisville?"

"If they don't believe the Bible is the inerrant word of God, then yes. Of course, each school has a charter and trustees."

"How many at Southern Seminary would you fire if you could?"

"Look, Lewis Drummond is on the Southern Seminary faculty. He says he doesn't know anyone but himself at Southern who believes in the inerrancy of the Bible." (Dr. Drummond, Billy Graham's close friend, teaches evangelism at Southern Seminary.)

"Then all but Dr. Drummond should be fired?"

"Well, only after there has been a careful investigation by the trustees to determine if each faculty member believes that Adam and Eve were historical figures, Moses wrote the Pentateuch, and the Book of Isaiah has only one author. I'd ask about twenty questions. . . . You know, many people will tell you big, fat lies. . . . And there are Bible-believing, evangelical trustees on Southern Baptist seminary boards who don't have any guts. I'm on the board of trustees for Gordon-Conwell Theological Seminary in Massachusetts. I can tell you now, we'd remove from our faculty anyone who uses redaction criticism on the Bible or anyone who didn't believe in biblical inerrancy."

In many ways Dr. Paul Pressler, a distinguished judge in Houston, deserves the title of Chief Strategist of the Inerrancy Party. It was he who studied the Southern Baptist Convention constitution and by-laws for the purpose of offering Paige Patterson and other defenders of inerrancy his counsel as to how they might gain control of the Convention agencies and institutions. The strategy is simple. As Judge Pressler noted, the lifeblood of the Southern Baptist system flows through the trustees. Most Southern Baptist institutions are under the charge of their separate boards of trustees. If new board members who favor the platform of the Inerrancy Party can be elected, then the agencies and institutions can be made to run in accord with the convictions of the new trustees as soon as they constitute a majority on each board. In urging his colleagues to go for the jugular, Judge Pressler pointed out to them the following critical facts: The newly elected president of the Convention appoints new members each year to the Committee on Committees, which in turn nominates members to serve on the powerful Committee on Boards, Commissions, and Standing Committees; on the shoulders of this second committee falls the responsibility of nominating to the Convention the trustees and overseers authorized to determine to a great extent the makeup of the agency or institution under each board's charge. Clearly, if a president is so inclined, he can appoint to the Committee on Committees only those in agreement with his theological persuasion.

Since 1979 the Inerrancy Party has elected its own president without fail. This year, 1986, the party elected fundamentalist Adrian Rogers. Before that, it was Stanley. And in 1983 Jimmy Draper was reelected without opposition. A protégé of W. A. Criswell's and for two years an associate pastor at Criswell's First Baptist Church of Dallas, Draper originally spoke of unity among Southern Baptists. In 1985, however, he threatened to advise his church, First Baptist of Euless, Texas, to withhold money from the Southern Baptist Cooperative Program if Charles Stanley was not reelected to the Convention presidency.

Even though the Inerrancy Party is nationally dominant, Judge Pressler was doubtless correct when he told a group of ministers in Knoxville, Tennessee, on April 29, 1985, that Southern Baptists have developed a two-party system. That is another way of saying that a new polarization has set in, bringing with it an increasing bitterness. Writing in the June 1983 issue of an Inerrancy Party publication, The Southern Baptist Journal (not an official SBC publication), the editor expressed the unmitigated longing to rid Southern Baptist institutions of what he and his comrades labeled as liberals.

> The liberals and their supporters tried very hard to prevent some of the conservative nominees from being elected to the trustee position. However, Dr. Charles Stanley, Chairman of the Committee on Boards, along with the other conservatives, were able to elect all 110 nominees for trustee positions.
>
> This is the third year we've had a chance to elect a large number of conservative trustees. . . . Thus, we have elected more

than 300 "conservative" trustees out of a total of 937 trustees. We
are now on the verge of having a real majority of conservatives
on a few of the key boards.

   If we elect another president next year at Kansas City—we
should have a majority of conservatives on a few of the key
boards.

The editor, after urging his readers not to slow down, went on to express his hope that the liberals were reading the handwriting on the
wall and that they would be able to "find jobs without going through
the agony (for all of us) of being fired by our trustees."

Judge Pressler, a distinguished-looking man in his fifties and a
graduate of Princeton University and the University of Texas Law
School, does not like to speak of firing professors. He insists that he
wants a radical change in the hiring policy of Southern Baptist schools
so that only teachers who hold that the Bible is inerrant will be appointed to the faculties. Those already on the faculties who do not
subscribe to the inerrancy doctrine would be permitted to remain provided they change their way of teaching to meet the new demands of
the new trustees. Opponents of Pressler's plan contend that the demands would turn the schools into narrow indoctrination centers
rather than centers of education. Professors not giving public allegiance to the strict Inerrancy Party line would be intimidated and manipulated to the point of rendering their teaching ineffectual.

TORNADO ON THE HORIZON

The leaders of the Inerrancy Party say the people in the pews do not
know what is being taught in at least four of their Southern Baptist
seminaries. If the secret were made public, the Inerrancy Party leaders insist, the people in the pews would be appalled. Increasingly
there has been talk of "exposing the truth about the seminary faculties" on the floor of the annual meeting of the Southern Baptist
Convention.

Many testers of Southern Baptist political winds believe that a
terrible ecclesiastical tornado has formed and is on the verge of shattering the more than 37,000 Southern Baptist churches. They believe
that the great Baptist purge will hit hard before the end of this century. Paige Patterson and the Inerrancy Party are already demanding
parity at the seminaries. Bob E. Patterson, professor in Baylor Univer-

sity's Department of Religion and president of the National Association of Baptist Professors in 1981–82, contends that "parity is nothing
more nor less than the prelude to purging our Southern Baptist educational institutions."

Although denying any interest in a "wild-eyed witch hunt whereby
we charge into our schools and agencies and lop off heads right and
left," a former Convention president insists nevertheless on a litmus
test for employees of the Southern Baptist Convention agencies and
of the schools run by Southern Baptists. Euless, Texas, pastor Jimmy
Draper writes, "In other words, we need to have a consensus among
Southern Baptists as to the irreducible minimum theology that a person must subscribe to in order to be acceptable as a professor at one of
our schools, or as a worker, writer, or policymaker in one of our agencies." [2] When asked in February 1985 if he would have fired Professor
Dale Moody from the Southern Baptist Theological Seminary years
ago, Draper answered without hesitation, "Yes!" When, however,
Dale Moody sent a long and carefully outlined letter on September 10,
1982, asking Draper to show him where he had misconstrued the
Bible on the question of apostasy, Draper replied in a very short letter
dated September 15, 1982, that unfortunately he did not have time to
show him.

The point here is that Professor Moody was relieved of his position
not because he denied the infallibility of Scripture but because his interpretation of Scripture did not agree with that of large groups of
Baptist ministers in Arkansas and elsewhere. Pressler was unquestionably sincere when he stated in Knoxville, Tennessee, in 1985, "The
conformity we seek is never the conformity of interpretation." But it
was unclear whom Pressler thought he was speaking for when he said
"we," for many of the Inerrancy Party clearly do think the question of
conformity of interpretation is crucial to Southern Baptist life and
identity.

The story of the failure of the Southern Baptist Theological Seminary in Louisville to renew Moody's contract in 1983 is revealing.
Moody has been charged with lacking political acumen when he gave
public addresses on a controversial topic that he knew would provoke
a number of Southern Baptist preachers to demand that he be fired
from the seminary. A few Baptist colleagues have even volunteered
their half-hearted, armchair psychological insights into what they take
to be his recent subconscious motive of self-destruction. What those
colleagues fail to see, though, is that Moody has not changed. Rather,

the Inerrancy Party leaders are correct in saying that the political climate among Southern Baptists has changed. Since 1945 Moody has been teaching his controversial interpretation of the Hebrews 6:4–6 passage on apostasy. In the sixties a group of preachers in Oklahoma tried to get him fired on the grounds that his view of apostasy was contrary to what most Baptists believed, but the attempt failed largely because Southern Baptists two decades ago were reasonably tolerant of diversity of theological opinion, especially in their institutions of higher learning.

At the Southwestern Baptist Theological Seminary in Fort Worth, Dr. John Newport for decades gave his students a wide theological spectrum in the classroom. More recently, a group of preachers has been trying to build up enough momentum to fire him from the seminary. As vice president of academic affairs and provost of the world's largest seminary, Newport undoubtedly has considerable influence on Southern Baptist theological education, although scarcely the sweeping control that some have imagined. For years, Newport has been a member of a society of scholars dedicated to studying the theology of Paul Tillich, whose abstruse style of writing has generated wide speculation as to what he really means. Almost everyone agrees, however, that Tillich was not orthodox. Furthermore, Tillich was an adulterer. For some reason Newport has been blamed for not emphasizing that in his little book on Tillich. Newport has also failed to reveal in print the names of orthodox preachers and evangelists who are adulterers, but the critics seem not to condemn him for that bit of discretion. As a scholar, Newport did not use the recent adultery of Jerry Falwell's fundamentalist preacher friend as a mark against fundamentalist theology.

THE POLITICAL PLOT THICKENS

The Battle of the Baptists is studded with ironies, one of which is the case of the theological war-horse, Dale Moody. Amid all the furor created by the Inerrancy Party regarding the alleged liberalism infecting each seminary faculty, a controversy suddenly exploded over Moody, who was one of the two or three most theologically conservative members of Southern Seminary's faculty at Louisville.

Baptized in 1927 at the age of twelve in Grapevine, Texas, and ordained at the age of seventeen, Dale Moody can today braid a rope of scriptural texts and arguments quicker than most of his challengers can draw their theological six-shooters. His great-grandfather was a pillar of the old Lonesome Dove Baptist Church, founded on the day that Texas became a part of the United States in 1846. The church still exists in Tarrant County. While teaching at the seminary in Kentucky Moody was invited to become the first Baptist to teach Protestant theology at the famous Pontifical Gregorian University in Rome. He has also devoted years to the study of Jewish theology. In 1981 Duke K. McCall, while still serving as president of Southern Seminary, knew that he was headed for trouble when he received news that Moody had stirred up a swarm of angry preachers of Arkansas' Little River Baptist Association. McCall received the following letter:

Dear Dr. McCall:

The saints in Little River Baptist Association send greetings to you and to the staff of Southern Seminary. We are proud of the rich tradition that Southern has in training men for the ministry.

There is one matter, however, that has caused us great alarm and dismay and has caused us to question the integrity and the credibility of the school.

Have you and the Board of Trustees been aware of Dr. Moody's position on apostasy? Will you please explain to us how you have justified retaining him in your employment? Do you plan to let him finish his contract at the school without a reprimand for his heresy and for his sowing of discord among brethren? Your immediate response to our letter will be appreciated.

Dated December 11, 1981, the letter was signed by David Miller, director of missions for the Little River Association, and by Bill Williams, the association's moderator. The controversy became public in August 1982 at the Executive Board of the Arkansas Baptist State Convention. Doubtless no match for Moody in a moderated debate either before his fellow ministers or in a book, fundamentalist David Miller chose to make a political move against Moody, denouncing as "lily-livered, gutless, and pussyfooting" those ministers who refused to join him in his crusade against the seminary professor.

The story of the indomitable Moody's trip to face the heated Baptists in Arkansas is filled with still more drama and ironies, the reports of which would fill a large book. The Moody controversy had scarcely lifted off the ground when Roy Honeycutt succeeded Duke McCall as seminary president in February 1982. Honeycutt began his presidential career wedged into a corner, forced to decide whether to keep on the faculty a man perhaps more theologically conservative than himself. In a November 18, 1982, letter to President Honeycutt, Moody observed, "As I calculated, a thorough examination of the 20 articles of the Abstract of Principles [of Southern Seminary] would leave me with a grade of 99. Do you know of any person who could make a higher grade on the Abstract of Principles than I can? Can you make a higher grade than that yourself?"

ONCE SAVED, ALWAYS SAVED

It was primarily seventeen pages in Moody's new book, *The Word of Truth*,[3] that triggered the theological thunderstorm centered in the land of the Razorbacks. In those seventeen pages Moody argues unequivocally that it is possible for Christian believers to apostatize and lose their salvation. Those who understand Southern Baptist preachers will recognize at once that Moody's words on apostasy were nothing less than a theological scandal. (The SBC Broadman Press did not publish his book.) Most Southern Baptist ministers hold dearly to the doctrine of eternal security, popularly known as Once Saved, Always Saved. According to the doctrine, once sinners become Christians, they are sealed forever and can never thereafter apostatize or lose their salvation. Their place in the Kingdom is guaranteed once and for all. It was God's unearned grace that brought them into the Kingdom, and it is God's grace that will keep them there. Once saved, Always saved! The profound comfort and joy that the doctrine has brought to Southern Baptist people struggling heroically against temptations and defeats can perhaps never be felt by those outsiders who have not known such unshakable security.

It has been alleged that when the angry Arkansas Baptist ministers threatened to carry their fight with Moody all the way to the annual convention of Southern Baptists, President Honeycutt and the trustees declined in the spring of 1983 to renew Moody's contract, preventing the furor surrounding Moody from engulfing the entire seminary. The Convention's Foreign Mission Board then withdrew its invitation to Moody to teach for a year in Hong Kong. Moody's service as a distinguished faculty member at the seminary since 1945 was swept overboard in the emotional storm.

The termination of Moody at the seminary was more complex than some of the state Baptist papers have been able to show. It was certainly more complex than I will be able to show. But the details of it should, and doubtless will, one day be explored in depth in a book devoted exclusively to them. Suffice to say here, Moody did not make the job of the new president of the seminary easier by pressing for a critical review of the seminary's Abstract of Principles, which every Southern Seminary professor is required to sign. Of course, Moody believed that more important matters were at stake than the president's job, and in genuine modesty Honeycutt would have agreed. Today, however, the question of the seminary's Calvinistic Abstract of Principles still remains unresolved. No one maintains that all the principles are inerrant, but there is no broad consensus regarding how to go about revising them, if they need revising at all. According to Moody, one of the seminary's most distinguished and honored professors, A. T. Robertson, signed the Abstract of Principles every year of his seminary teaching career even though he apparently was aware of standing in strong disagreement with at least one of its many highly technical articles. Although most institutions have a right to seek to maintain their historic identity and integrity, an institution of higher education is unique in that it offers its scholars an implicit contract to encourage them in their earnest quest for truth, including their right to revise their conclusions. That contract is as binding as any Abstract of Principles and cannot easily be revoked without violating the institution's integrity and historic commitment to remain a citadel of higher learning.

A number of Moody's colleagues at the seminaries and colleges are angry with him. They also feel guilty for failing to come to his aid and frustrated because, they still believe, no rational option was open to them. They were trapped. My point in bringing up the Moody case, which seems on the surface to be an anomaly, is to indicate that teaching in a Southern Baptist institution of higher learning requires a special and extraordinary political acumen. Many professors believed that Moody's desire to bring the seminary's Abstract of Principles to the national convention floor sometime in the eighties for review and revision by convention vote would have created a firestorm of political controversy, leaving the seminary's academic life scorched and charred for decades to come. By contrast, Moody believed in perfectly good faith that the convention would have set the seminary on a better course of academic freedom and given it clearer direction into the next century.

There is no question that many of those Baptists with either axes to grind or legitimate complaints to make against the seminary would have used the opportunity to get at the seminary. It is still impossible to determine which prediction would have come to pass—Moody's or most of his colleagues', if either. In the end, it was a question of friends and colleagues finding themselves in strong and critical disagreement. To this day, there are professors who wish they could tell Moody how much they respect him as a scholar and for the decades he devoted to the seminary. But it would be too embarrassing and awkward to do so. More time is needed. One thing remains: Moody's impact on the seminary for good is already an enviable legacy. He will have to accept it.

It is unfortunate that none of Moody's opponents in the Southern Baptist Convention have found time to accept his open invitation to engage in a systematic debate on the issue that sorely vexed the Arkansas ministers—not even Jimmy Milligan, the professor at Mid-America Baptist Theological Seminary in Memphis who convinced a number of Arkansas preachers that they did well to oppose Moody. If Southern Baptist ministers who know Moody were the kind to make bets, they would not lay down money that his open challenge to Roy Honeycutt, W. A. Criswell, Jimmy Milligan, Paige Patterson, or Jimmy Draper will be accepted by any one of them. And the ministers know down deep in their hearts that lack of time is not the real reason the challenge will remain unaccepted. The real reason is that they know that his opponents will need to find better arguments than they have previously advanced if their position is to survive Moody's painstaking scrutiny.

As the theologians and biblical scholars among both the school faculties and the ministers are quite aware, several articles and commentaries have been written on apostasy. Believing that it is indeed possible for a Christian to commit apostasy that cannot be forgiven, Moody felt strongly that it was morally wrong and dangerous for the scholars to let the people in the pews rest comfortably with the impression that they were completely immune to irreversible apostasy. Hence, he took his case directly to the ministers to try to persuade them to warn the people. Some of Moody's colleagues in the seminaries and colleges interpreted his behavior differently. To them, he was generating an anger-filled controversy, especially among the ministers who could eventually make serious trouble for the seminaries, for there are indeed always those who want to take potshots at the seminaries. Many of Moody's colleagues failed to consider, in my judgment, two crucial factors so simple that they were often overlooked. Moody actually believed in eternal damnation and thought that the threat of damnation for some of his fellow Baptists loomed so great that he had a moral imperative to do what he did. If those two factors had been given more sustained weight, it is likely that Moody's colleagues would have been more understanding of his efforts while still disagreeing with him.

The truth seems to be that a large number of Southern Baptist theologians and biblical scholars simply did not believe in eternal damnation, at least not Professor Moody's version. Even though admitting that Moody's exegesis of the five apostasy texts in the Epistle to the Hebrews was on target, they differed radically with his whole conception of what salvation and the loss of salvation really were; his warnings against apostasy were, they believed, ill-founded though conceived in goodwill.

By contrast, those who agreed substantially with Moody's view of salvation and eternal damnation have remained quite unable to counter his exegesis of Hebrews point by point. W. A. Criswell seems to have endorsed Simon J. Kistemaker's 1984 commentary, Hebrews (Baker Book House), which, ironically, supports Moody's rather than Criswell's exegesis of Hebrews 6.

Whatever else may be said about the Moody case, it has laid to rest the innocent-sounding contention of some in the Inerrancy Party that the entire current controversy about the Southern Baptist institutions is over the nature of biblical authority and inspiration rather than the question of biblical interpretation.

CAN THE WAR BE CONTROLLED?

The Southern Baptist war has many battle lines. Paul Pressler and Harold Lindsell appear to want to confine the war to the question of the inerrancy of the Bible rather than plunging into skirmishes over interpretations of various biblical texts. Lindsell is not certain that Moody should have been relieved of his position at Southern Seminary, at least not because of his interpretation of apostasy. It is highly unlikely that the war can be confined to the inerrancy issue alone, even though it is clearly the most pervasive issue. Draper, Pressler, and Paige Patterson go so far as to say that they will not insist on the word "inerrancy." A careful study of the controversy, however, reveals that at least Pressler and Patterson mean inerrancy. In the final analysis, the question of the Bible's inerrancy is the primary battle, with questions of interpretation serving to make the war more widespread, uncontrollable, and unpredictable. Pressler recently told a group that only minor surgery would be required to cut the cancer out of Southern Baptist institutional life. The moderates, however, take a more politically conservative approach. In the first place, they are not even sure that Pressler's diagnosis is correct. In the second place, they have no great faith in the surgical methods of men like Pressler, Lindsell, and Paige Patterson.

2.

The Power and the Money

The Reverend Sun Myung Moon may have been sent to prison partly because he was a conspicuous foreigner who had set up a not-too-subtle lobby in Washington, D.C. But that in itself was not illegal. The other and technical reason he went to prison was that he had played too fast and loose with the money that people had entrusted to him. There are many Lone Ranger evangelists and TV preachers whose way of juggling contributions is less than admirable. Billy Graham once said that some of them make him climb the wall. Senator Mark Hatfield, a born-again Christian and Baptist who served as lay preacher in the Navy and later at Stanford University, grew deeply concerned about proposed legislation that would have been the first step toward government auditing of church-related finances and taxation of church investments. Calling a meeting of key evangelical leaders, the senator suggested that they had better begin regulating themselves if they did not want the government to do it for them. Out of the meeting grew the Evangelical Council for Financial Accountability in 1979. Hatfield persuaded his close friend Billy Graham to bring his organization into the new council dedicated to financial integrity. Jerry Falwell was also convinced of the wisdom of joining. Later, however, Falwell's organizations pulled out after coming under severe criticism from a number of sources about the cloud of mystery surrounding his finances. A major disagreement also developed between Falwell and Art Borden, executive director of the council. To maintain council membership, Falwell's religious organizations would have to do what all the other groups were required to do, namely, reapply from scratch every year and provide audits. Falwell pulled away instead.

Earlier, in 1973, the U.S. Securities and Exchange Commission had charged Falwell's church with "fraud and deceit" in the issuance of $6.5 million in unsecured church bonds. Eventually, the church finances had to be placed under the control of a group of five businessmen selected by the court.[1]

In 1982 Perry Deane Young wrote a book on preachers and politics in which he makes the following charge:

> Jerry Falwell has fooled a lot of people for quite a long time. They believed him when he said there were children starving to death in Cambodian refugee camps, although they didn't read the details that explained that none of their contributions would ever reach those children.

Young charges that Falwell is an artist at juggling funds and "borders on illegality."

> In early 1980, Falwell launched the "Liberty Missionary Society" with an appeal for funds to help "thousands upon thousands of small children . . . dying from starvation and malnutrition in refugee camps around the world. . . . " The first project of this society was to aid the Cambodian refugees in Thailand. As usual, Falwell covered himself by saying this was only "one of" the projects he needed money for. But when he published the projected two-million-dollar budget for these new "missions," $450,000 was earmarked for construction projects at Liberty College and another $450,000 was to go for training missionaries. Not one penny had been designated for food, although the appeal connected with this projected budget carried this message from Falwell: "In order to minister to starving people, we must first feed them."[2]

By contrast, there are numerous Southern Baptist denominational leaders who become positively jubilant if cross-examined about Baptist finances. Talking about the SBC Cooperative Program budget as if it were a new grandchild, they are eager to show off booklets, charts, budget pies, and records, and their openness would defy anyone to find a financial scandal or shady method in their midst. One Baptist in her fifties told me that the Cooperative Program is to Southern Baptists what the child Samuel was to Hannah. "We conceived it by the grace of God, and we give it back to God as an offering."

Despite the intense battles among them, Southern Baptists today are justly proud of the financial integrity of their many institutions. In the history of Christianity few churches have been more open about their finances than the contemporary Southern Baptists. That has not always been the case, however; in September 1928 the Convention's Home Board discovered what appeared to be an embezzlement of $909,461, which at once increased the Convention's indebtedness to $2.5 million. The struggle of Southern Baptist people to pay their debts during those lean Depression years was nothing less than heroic. Already in 1921 a catastrophic drop in cotton prices had caused missionary enterprise to be slashed in half over a period of seven years. Baptisms had fallen from 56,164 in 1921 to 17,649 in 1928.[3]

Given the Convention's new organizational structure after the humiliating scandal of 1928, it is all but impossible today for a major financial scandal to happen within it. A local minister might run off with either local church money or the church organist, but since 1928 there has not been a truly big-time church crook among Southern Baptist denominational leaders. As several Roman Catholic investigators have suggested, Cardinal John Cody of Chicago may have taken more Catholic money in one decade than all the embezzlers and thieves among Southern Baptists have filched from their churches since that baleful year of 1928. The new openness among Southern Baptists means that they usually know what is going on in their denomination or can easily find out.

In the 1984–85 fiscal year, Texas Baptists alone gave $1.5 million to combat world hunger. With carefully monitored foreign mission posts established around the world, Southern Baptist people can give their hard-earned money with the assurance that it will be spent efficiently and will not end up in the pockets of corrupt politicians at home or abroad. In 1984 Southern Baptists gave $58.5 million to the Lottie Moon Christmas Offering for foreign missions. An additional $25 million was raised for the Annie Armstrong Easter Offering for home missions, an increase of 10 percent over the 1983 contributions. Those two designated offerings were above and beyond the Cooperative Program, which is the regular annual SBC budget. Staggering as the sums may seem, the missionary offerings are collected every year. Furthermore, the Cooperative Program budget represents only a small percentage of Southern Baptist monetary giving.

The story of Lottie Moon, the remarkable missionary of the 1880s, is as gripping and suspenseful as any romance-adventure novel. Although engaged to a professor at the Southern Baptist Theological Seminary in Louisville, she sailed to China as an unmarried missionary, breaking off her engagement with the man she loved. In one of her letters home she wrote that she hoped no other missionary would have to endure the loneliness that she had endured. Lottie Moon toiled heroically in China for many years, finally dying, on a Christmas Eve, of malnutrition, along with thousands of the Chinese to whom she had devoted her life in the hope of converting them to Christianity. Southern Baptists' sustained commitment to foreign missions is indicated by the fact that one half of the denomination's regular Cooperative Program budget goes to the Foreign Mission Board.

In the June 1984 Kansas City annual meeting of the Southern Baptist Convention, the messengers from the churches approved a Cooperative Program allocation goal of $130 million for its agencies for the period of October 1, 1984, through September 30, 1985. That meant that the Foreign Mission Board received from the Cooperative Program $59 million in one year alone, the Home Mission Board $24 million, and the six seminaries together more than $24 million, or almost one fifth of the Cooperative Program money.

According to Earl Kelly (1984 president of the Association of Baptist State Executive Secretaries), the SBC Cooperative Program

is basically a simple system: each [local] church votes on a percentage of its income to be sent to the state convention for all causes outside the local situation. Each state then decides how much of these funds should remain within the state to support joint efforts in Christian education, medical care, children's homes, assemblies, mission work among ethnic groups, evangelism and church planting, specialized help for churches in programming and planning, etc. The balance is then sent to Southern Baptist causes for home missions, foreign missions, and numerous agencies which operate on behalf of all Southern Baptists.[4]

Consider also that most Southern Baptist gifts of money—almost $3.5 billion in the fiscal year 1983–84—go not to the Cooperative Program but to other projects, each local church designating how this money will be spent. Roughly speaking, the typical SBC local church sends 10 percent of its money to its state Baptist convention office, some sending more, some less. This is Cooperative Program money. Each state convention then determines what percentage will go to the Southern Baptist Convention office in Nashville and how much will remain with the state convention. Normally, almost 40 percent goes to Nashville and 60 percent to the state convention to run its many agencies and institutions.

Many people will be surprised to learn that Southern Baptists are much larger than the Southern Baptist Convention. Each state's denominational machinery is invested with its own responsibility and power. Hospitals, children's homes, colleges and universities such as Samford in Alabama, Furman in South Carolina, Mercer in Georgia, Baylor in Texas, Carson-Newman in Tennessee, Oklahoma Baptist University—these represent but a few of the institutions under the auspices not of the Southern Baptist Convention but of each state convention and the institutions' governing boards. (The six seminaries receive money from the Southern Baptist Convention's Cooperative Program budget, and their trustees are appointed through that convention's organizational procedures.)

In 1983–84 the state conventions received $181,724,700 as their share of the Cooperative Program, while the Southern Baptist Convention received $108,835,732 as its share. The Cooperative Program total of the almost $3.5 billion that Southern Baptist people gave was $290,560,432. Cooperative Program money represents the steady support that stabilizes Southern Baptist agencies and institutions year after year. It represents the way the state conventions finance their programs within each state and the way they cooperate routinely on sustained interstate goals.

From 1845 to 1925, Southern Baptists had no Cooperative Program. Before the program came into being (on May 13, 1925, in Memphis, Tennessee), Southern Baptist preachers and institutional presidents spent a lot of their time traveling from church to church to raise money, sometimes begging, year after year. Today, no one has to beg for the elderly preachers' annuity fund; the money comes in through the Cooperative Program. One minister recently told me that Southern Baptists are held together by three bonds: the Holy Spirit, a burning sense of mission among the people, and the Annuity Board. At the 1985 convention in Dallas I overheard another minister tell his friend jokingly, "If the Convention splits, I'm going with them." He was pointing to an Annuity Board sign.

Jack Sanford, editor of *Western Recorder*, the state paper of Kentucky Southern Baptists, reflects the feelings of many Southern Baptists about their Cooperative Program:

> When you separate the facts from the show-biz emotion of religious giving, some interesting results come to light.
>
> Joseph R. Estes, Kentucky pastor, has done just that and his separation of fact from fiction should be an encouragement for all Southern Baptists.
>
> Estes points out the seven leading religious programs on national television (Oral Roberts, PTL Club, Jerry Falwell, 700 Club, Rex Humbard, Robert Schuller, the Armstrongs) received $293-million in 1983 from television viewers.
>
> With the $293-million they supported: four churches, one hospital, seven weekly TV programs, and five schools.
>
> By contrast, the 14 million Southern Baptists sent through the Cooperative Program and regular mission offerings $230,565,113. These gifts were used to support: six seminaries with 10,000 students; 67 colleges with more than 200,000 students; Baptist student ministers on 1,100 campuses; 32 weekly TV and radio programs; 3,700 missionaries in all 50 states; and 3,600 missionaries in 105 countries.[5]

The conclusion that Estes and Sanford drew is clear. If Baptists want the best deal for their money, they would be wise to stay with the tried and proven Cooperative Program. (It should be noted that most Southern Baptist institutions are free to raise money in addition to receiving Cooperative Program contributions. The seminaries have endowments. The Lottie Moon and Annie Armstrong offerings are above and beyond the Cooperative Program.)

At each annual state convention, the messengers from the local churches determine how the Cooperative Program funds are to be divided in that state. After each state keeps its share, it sends a piece of the pie to the Southern Baptist Convention's Executive Committee, which proposes how the program receipts will be distributed to the national convention's numerous agencies. Each June, at the SBC annual meeting, the churches' messengers vote on the Executive Committee's recommendation, either approving or amending. Within the 1985–86 Cooperative Program allocation budget of $130 million, the six seminaries were allocated nearly $25 million, the Foreign Mission Board $61 million, and the Home Mission Board almost $25 million.

In 1984 the SBC Annuity Board paid more than $36 million in retirement and protection benefits. Insurance benefits amounted to $40.5 million. The Southern Baptist Foundation offers a wide range of investment and estate planning services to the Convention and its churches. In Washington, D.C., Southern Baptists are among the nine Baptist bodies making up the Baptist Joint Committee of Public Affairs, which generates support in that city, for church-state separation.

Neither the gigantic Baptist Sunday School Board nor the Woman's Missionary Union receives money from the Southern Baptist Convention's Cooperative Program. Instead, each contributes money by selling its literature. Southern Baptists have so many agencies and organizations at various levels that it would be impractical to list them all here. A few examples will perhaps give a picture of their diversity. Crosspoint, a new project of the Church Recreation Department, is a children's sports camp. There are 62 Baptist bookstores and mail-order centers. The two national conference and resort centers that millions of Southern Baptists have attended over the years are Ridgecrest in the Blue Ridge Mountains of North Carolina and Glorieta in the Rocky Mountains of New Mexico. The Family Ministry Department of the Baptist Sunday School Board provides resources for marriage enrichment, parent enrichment, single adult, and senior adult ministries. Unfortunately, the stirring stories of the Baptist Telecommunications Network (BTN), the Radio and Television Commission (with its fascinating network of underground rooms, equipment, and highly dedicated personnel in Fort Worth), and the American Christian Television System (ACTS) are too long to be told in this book.

The brilliance of the Cooperative Program has been clouded by the Convention's troubled future. There is no point in denying that if Southern Baptists split in twain, the process will take many painful years to complete itself, bringing prolonged economic and operational turmoil to each of these agencies and institutions and to every level of Southern Baptist life. There are indications that the holy war will reach the Foreign Mission Board. If the Inerrancy Party succeeds in blackballing the missionaries that the Moderate Party approves, then the missionaries favored by the Inerrancy Party will eventually be blackballed by the Moderate Party. Whatever else will be said about Southern Baptists if they split, it will surely not be said that they had a friendly divorce. If they continue to live together, they will not long be a denomination at peace with itself.

A Texan and a graduate of North Texas State University is the president of the SBC Foreign Mission Board. Keith Parks is unapologetic about his grand dream of fulfilling the aim of what Southern Baptists have recently titled Bold Mission Thrust. Their dream is to bring the Christian gospel to every human being on the planet by the year 2000. Parks favors what he calls career missionaries, people who know the language and understand the mores and customs of the people with whom they are working. Unlike some big American churches of various denominations that pick up missionaries for peanuts and send them out untrained for a short period, Parks emphasizes the long-term effects that missionaries can have. For the Foreign Mission Board, missionary evangelism entails involving new converts in indigenous churches. By "indigenous" is meant churches that are not simply pockets of Americanism on foreign soil. The goal is to have the churches operated and ministered to by natives of the country so that the new churches can become Christian in character rather than a religious version of American McDonald's or Kentucky Fried Chicken in Africa, Asia, and Latin America.

Currently there are more than twelve thousand Southern Baptist churches that are self-supporting in foreign countries. In 1984 there were 156,326 baptisms recorded, or about 45 baptisms per missionary. It is necessary to keep in mind that Southern Baptists do not baptize infants automatically upon birth. Ideally, candidates for baptism must be old enough both to understand what they are doing and to commit themselves of their own choice. In the drive to train nationals to lead the new churches, the Foreign Mission Board is training 9000 students in seminaries and theological institutes, and another 7800 are enrolled in theological education by seminary extension. There are 63 dentists and physicians, 72 missionary nurses, and 50 other missionaries engaged in health care services under the auspices of the Foreign Mission Board—all working closely with hundreds of national physicians and nurses.

Increasingly, the printed page and other mass media are becoming powerful tools of missionary endeavor. A hundred missionaries are working in 31 publication centers around the world to help publish more than twenty million translated books, periodicals, curriculum pieces, and tracts.[6]

Plans have been made by the Foreign Mission Board to develop long-range methods for ministering to those suffering from natural disasters, wars, and various human tragedies. Keith Parks emphasizes that Southern Baptists through the Foreign Mission Board have been able to do foundational work over the decades that will bear fruit in the years to come. In 1984 the board received $55,639,000 through the Cooperative Program and $58,529,000 through the Lottie Moon Christmas Offering. For years the Woman's Missionary Union has been educating many Southern Baptists in a global outlook and has been the major instrument in making both the Lottie Moon Christmas Offering and the Annie Armstrong Easter Offering a practical reality. Indeed, without the union, the Southern Baptist mission dream would likely have remained just that—a dream.

Some of the Inerrancy Party leaders among Southern Baptists have made it clear that they want to employ no missionaries and no officers of the Foreign Mission Board who fail to subscribe to the inerrancy of the Bible. One way of looking at the conflict among Southern Baptists is to view it as competition for jobs. There are limits to the employment opportunities even within the vast Southern Baptist network. In April 1985 William Powell, Sr., one of the most strident warriors of the Inerrancy Party, made the following revealing complaint:

> There will be many good SBC people hurt and "spiritually killed" because of the trustees of the seminaries, colleges, and universities and the presidents of our SBC campuses permitting the liberals to come on our SBC campuses just for interviews for jobs. . . . The trustees could have fired the liberals—but they did not. The trustees fired 12 teachers at Southern seminary in one night in the late 50s—but the battle was: "Who was going to run the seminary?" Duke McCall [the seminary president] or the professors.[7]

Just before retiring in 1985, Powell pointed out that according to a report from an SBC agency in Nashville, about 2500 pastors and church staff members are fired or "pushed out" every year. There is no question that Powell is among those who want the so-called liberals fired and their own inerrancy advocates hired. He labels his theological enemies not only as liberals but also as a cancer to be cut out of the Southern Baptist body. Only the naive believe that Inerrancy Party leaders like Powell want their longed-for purge confined to the schools.

Southern Baptists of his persuasion believe that the cancer of liberalism resides in every part of the Southern Baptist body.

THE POWER OF THE SBC PRESIDENT

The president of the Southern Baptist Convention is empowered to appoint members directly to the Committee on Committees. He (there has never been a woman SBC president) is instructed by the SBC bylaws to make those appointments in conference with the Convention's vice presidents. Charges were made that Charles Stanley did not consult with each vice president as required during his 1984–85 term as president. The Committee on Committees is responsible for nominating members to the exceedingly powerful Committee on Boards. The latter group nominates the trustees, directors, or boards of institutions of the Convention. In addition, it nominates members of the general board, all standing committees, the Christian Life Commission, the Education Commission, the Radio and Television Commission, the influential Executive Committee, and several other commissions.

Dallas's W. A. Criswell is quoted as saying that when he was SBC president in 1969–70 he did not realize that the office had so much power vested in it. In recent months there has been considerable talk among Southern Baptists about diluting the president's power by giving each of the presidents of the 38 state conventions a vote in appointing members to the Committee on Committees. At the state conventions the moderates seem to win the presidential office more often than does the Inerrancy Party. At present, the Inerrancy Party is weaker at the local and state levels than at the annual convention.

POWER OF THE TRUSTEES

The role of the trustees of Southern Baptist institutions can be shown by telling the story of the Battle of Lexington Road. The Southern Baptist Theological Seminary is located on beautiful grounds on Lexington Road, Louisville, Kentucky. It is across from the rolling green of Cherokee Park, whose magnificent trees were uprooted by a tornado in 1974. The tragic story of this seminary battle is important because it makes vivid what Paul Pressler meant when he said that the lifeblood of the Convention flows through the trustees of its institutions. In telling it—or, to be more accurate, in giving one account of it—I will try to show that it is unnecessary to attribute knavish motives to any of the participants. The trustees realized in the fifties that the seminary had grown to be one of the largest in the country. Previously the faculty had had a great deal to say about how the seminary carried out its responsibilities. For better or worse, a number of trustees began to think that the president's hand in running the school should be strengthened, thus allowing the trustees to deal directly with one person rather than a large number.

President Duke McCall, who had proven to be a competent administrator in denominational politics over the years, either agreed with the trustees' judgment or thought he was simply accommodating both trustees and faculty by serving as a mediator. Understandably, some of the faculty began to feel that they were no longer a part of the tradition that had shaped their great theological seminary but were instead being viewed as hired hands (or heads) at the factory.

Unlike such previous seminary presidents as John R. Sampey and E. Y. Mullins, Duke McCall was perceived by many of the theological faculty as a professional administrator rather than as a fellow scholar filling a temporary administrative position. He was regarded as a man who saw himself not as one among equals but as the company executive. In fairness to some of the faculty, McCall did appear increasingly remote from them, as the new executive of the type identified more with Ford Motor Company than with the Southern Baptist Theological Seminary. In fairness to McCall, he could not become what he was not. It takes years to maintain oneself as a serious scholar, and he had spent his years as a faithful denominational executive. In fairness to the trustees, a number of them did perhaps share a professional kinship with Duke McCall the executive. They could speak the same language, the language of the organization, of big money, public image, public relations, and salesmanship. McCall had, after all, been the executive secretary of the Executive Committee of the Southern Baptist Convention. He had earned the trustees' respect and admiration. It was only natural that the many administrative personalities among the trustees turned to him when problems arose.

In addition, there were rumblings that the seminary professors were introducing ideas and methods foreign to most Southern Baptists. In itself, that could be either positive or negative news to the trustees, who had not arrived at their positions of responsibility by turning their backs on new ideas and methods. Not being knowledgeable in biblical studies and theology, however, most of the trustees were genuinely uncertain as to what to make of the charges that the professors were introducing not only new but also subversive ideas. The nation had just recently gone through the Joe McCarthy trauma, and it was still popular to attack professors as subversives, in this case as subversives of the denomination.

Quite naturally, the trustees turned to McCall for help. He was, in the first place, astute about denominational shifts of wind and Southern Baptist backstage politics. In the second place, he had earned a theological doctorate. He was no theological innocent. It was assumed that he could speak the language of the theological faculty in particular—the way E. Y. Mullins and John R. Sampey had years earlier. Apparently, some of the faculty came to believe that McCall was no longer a colleague who shared in the give and take of theological, biblical, and historical exchange. Rather he had, in their eyes, distanced himself to become their boss. They in turn, in self-defense, became his judge.

That is a crucial point to make, a point that those who are not inside the world of academic research must struggle to understand. A dedicated scholar must have freedom, air to breathe, room to toss new ideas before his or her academic peers so that those ideas can be scrutinized and rigorously criticized on their own merit. Ideas are presented inside the scholarly circle, not always because the presenter believes them but because they might prove fruitful despite their flaws and defects. Often a scholar will set forth ideas he does not believe simply to elicit the best possible criticisms from his colleagues.

That is not to imply that Duke McCall was lax in his duty to protect academic freedom at the seminary. It is unlikely that he understood why he was so feared and resented. The bitter truth is that over the years some denominational colleges had been run by administrative bullies who intimidated the faculties and made a mockery of academic freedom. The far-reaching structural shifts at the seminary brought out fears that the faculty would lose its power to help shape the seminary's future.

Unfortunately, the Battle of Lexington Road was too often explained from a psychological rather than a sociological perspective. Had the latter predominated, the controversy might have been controlled and the showdown avoided. Dr. Clayton Sullivan, who was a graduate student at the seminary during the battle, is doubtless correct to conclude that it was fought by good and competent men under conditions that, spinning out of control, developed their own perverse momentum.[8] It was the sort of battle that no one truly wanted and that few at the time clearly understood. It served only to bring out the worst on both sides and stands today as a chilling reminder of how unpredictable even justifiable power plays can be for even the strongest of Southern Baptist institutions.

In any case, thirteen scholars of the theology faculty communicated to the trustees that they did not regard McCall as truly representative of them. They were profoundly correct on that score. Indeed, it has become a pressing question on all campuses: "Who truly represents the faculty?" Whether the thirteen professors were correct in thinking that it was possible to be represented by any president under the new structure is a question that deserves serious consideration.

To make the entangled story short, the showdown between McCall and the thirteen faculty members ended with the departure of twelve of the faculty, one professor choosing at the last moment not to leave. Dr. J. J. Owens, seeing that his colleagues and he had lost, chose to remain at the seminary he loved. Duke McCall stayed on as president until 1982, when another crisis arose just in time for the new president, Roy Honeycutt, to feel its scorpion sting.

Today, Inerrancy Party zealots long for still more purges at the seminaries. Those who can overlook theological differences momentarily, however, will probably agree that the unparalleled loss of scholarship at Southern Seminary was unquestionably the worst blow that had ever befallen any of the seminaries. It has taken years to build up an academically respectable faculty since those bleak days in the late fifties. One popular Bible teacher was brought into the New Testament department at once to help fill the gap, but he was not of the caliber of Professor T. C. Smith or Professor Heber Peacock.

But then, if the disaster had to strike the seminary, it could not have arrived at a more opportune time. Because Southern Baptists were not then sharply divided into two parties, the trustees and McCall were relatively free from outside political skirmishes while they tried to restore the seminary faculty to its former splendor. If McCall and the trustees had seemed incompetent to deal creatively and fairly with the faculty members who left, they seemed quite able in the sixties and seventies to learn from their costly previous mistakes.

Today, there are many who think the seminary would have fared significantly better had McCall left and the twelve professors remained. Was one good president worth twelve good faculty members? Fortunately, after three decades, the air of scholarship is clear at

Southern Seminary for three reasons. First, despite Honeycutt's mis-handling of the Moody case, he has fought hard for freedom of re-search on campus. Perhaps no president in the history of the semi-nary has been as bold and relentless as he in defense of freedom of expression on campus. Some university presidents begin to think that they alone are somehow the public image of the institution and that they alone should speak to the news media and the public on behalf of the faculty. It is to Honeycutt's credit that in the age of image building, he has not presumed to be the Big Daddy of the seminary. In his sup-port of the right of the faculty to speak out, he has endeared himself to the faculty. Most see him as a fellow scholar who personally under-stands their need for freedom of inquiry.

The second cause of the clear air of scholarship at the seminary is the willingness of the faculty members to publish their research ideas despite the anti-intellectual hawks within the Convention. Rather than debate those ideas on their own merits in an open forum, the hawks want to use them to make political war against the faculty. The third reason the climate of freedom is bright and clear at Southern Seminary can be found in the enlightened dedication of the trustees. Despite their fumbling of the Moody case, they have faced up to the fact that without them as defenders of freedom there can be no aca-demic life at the seminary worthy of the name and worthy of the school's great tradition of scholarship and training.

The Inerrancy Party sees with crystal clarity that the six seminaries are going to play a more critical role in the Southern Baptist life than ever before. And if the Foreign Mission Board and the Home Mission Board become still more significant as the Southern Baptist Conven-tion moves beyond Dixie into new territory, the Inerrancy Party zeal-ots will seek to purge them, too. There are big Baptist dollars at stake, gigantic and influential institutions to win or lose, and agencies to control. Jimmy Draper is only one among many in this relentless Southern Baptist battle who have said that they are tired of the con-flict. But battles do not begin or end because the warriors and generals are tired or vigorous. They go on because social, political, and other forces are at work. The purpose of the rest of this book is to examine some of those forces and to look at some of the interesting person-alities involved in this strange and tragic Southern Baptist holy war.

3.

Inerrancy and the Bible

nable to grasp what the inerrancy controversy among Southern Baptists is about, a number of reporters have assumed that it is really over power and money and little more. All that is lacking to turn the Baptist battle into a racy Sidney Sheldon novel, they seem to think, are scenes dripping with the details of evangelists committing adultery under the big tent. The more seasoned reporters, however, know that Southern Baptists are at war with each other about something more profound than power for its own sake. No one can seriously deny that the power struggle is going on, but the critical question is why? What is to be gained and what is to be lost? With some notable exceptions, the secular news reporters cannot answer those questions because they are not trained to probe deeply into religious motivations and issues.

On page one of the November 11, 1985, issue of the *Los Angeles Times* John Dart reported on a fall 1985 seminar of biblical scholars in St. Meinrad, Indiana, whose purpose was twofold. First, the scholars quietly debated and discussed their research on the roughly five hundred sayings attributed to Jesus in the New Testament and nonbiblical sources. (Some of the latter have been discovered and translated only in recent years.) Second, they used the ballot box to vote secretly on which of those sayings were authentic and which were inauthentic or doubtful. The results would have stunned most American Sunday school teachers, for the overwhelming majority of the scholars concluded that comparatively few sayings attributed to Jesus, including the beatitudes, came from his lips. Among the thirty scholars was a Southern Baptist Theological Seminary professor.

In April 1985 I attended and reported on a conference of biblical scholars meeting on the campus of the University of Michigan, a conference devoted exclusively to professional papers on the question of the historical Jesus. Professor G. A. Wells of England presented a paper in which he flatly denied that Jesus ever existed. He had written three books in defense of his view. Another scholar delivered a paper on the Gospel of Thomas. Still another defended his book *Jesus the Magician.* Anyone who attends the meetings of the Society of Biblical Literature or the American Academy of Religion will leave with one settled conclusion: Contemporary biblical scholars not only are involved in highly technical studies but also are presenting theses that were scarcely imaginable at the turn of this century. For good or ill, a sweeping revolution has come about in the world of biblical scholarship, a revolution about which the majority of the people in the pews know next to nothing.

DID JESUS EXIST?

Will schoolchildren in generations to come be taught that "Jesus" was the name of a man-god once earnestly believed in but subsequently viewed as merely another mythical divinity? Zeus, Mithra, Cybele, Dionysus, and Orpheus are but a few of the defunct gods whom men and women once claimed to serve. In the back of the minds of many Christians lies a disturbing question about Jesus: Will he, too, join the long list of extinct gods?

The answer that most evangelical Christian scholars give is clear and simple. It is impossible for anyone of the twentieth century to observe the Jesus Christ of the first century in the flesh, and the Bible is the sole remaining account of Christ's teachings and activities. It and it alone bridges the gap of almost twenty centuries of history. If the Bible's historical trustworthiness were undermined, not one single fact about Jesus could be established with reasonable certainty. At best, anyone still interested in Christianity would become totally dependent upon scholars' exceedingly tentative reconstructions of the earthly Jesus of two thousand years ago. Already there exists, among the scholars who question the inerrancy and absolute reliability of the Gospels, a bewildering diversity of conjectures of what the real Jesus was like, what he taught and did, if indeed he existed in the first place. One such scholar, James Barr, admits forthrightly, "There will now probably never be sayings of which we can say with certainty that Jesus of Nazareth actually spoke these words."[1]

One does not need to agree with believers in biblical inerrancy to understand why they think they have the only realistic option available for those who wish to remain in the Christian tradition. Only a person out of touch with recent New Testament research could believe that most biblical scholars have reached a consensus regarding who Jesus was. It is understandable, therefore, that many believers fear that without flawless Scriptures to support it, Christianity may eventually be regarded as just another ancient mystery religion doomed to fade into the night.

Some among the Inerrancy Party charge that the rank and file, bill-paying Southern Baptists have not the faintest notion of what is being taught behind the walls of their seminaries, especially at the doctoral level. The charge has substance and deserves to be taken seriously. But the Inerrancy Party has devoted little effort to exposing publicly in any meaningful detail what the seminary professors are in fact teaching about the Bible. There remains the strange impression that the informed members of the Inerrancy Party prefer to keep their fellow Southern Baptists ignorant of all but a sensationalized and fuzzy sketch in fifty pages or so of what the professors are introducing in the Baptist seminaries.

There is more than one motive for keeping the bill-paying Baptists uninformed about the intricacies of biblical scholarship. First of all, many of the critics of the seminaries are not biblical scholars and so are not equipped to criticize in detail without exposing themselves as amateurs. Zig Ziglar, the popular Sunday school teacher at Dallas's First Baptist Church, typifies those in the Inerrancy Party who are reluctant to plunge into the thick of the battle apparently because they lack the academic training for it. What Ziglar lacks in biblical scholarship and training, however, he makes up for in political skill. His name is well known outside the Baptist community because of his speeches and books on motivation and popular psychology. He was elected first vice president of the Southern Baptist Convention in 1984 and has contributed significantly to the how-to-get-ahead philosophy among many contemporary Americans. One reviewer of his book *Steps to the Top* makes this observation: "They used to be called inspirational books, and in the 1930s they were represented by titles like *How to Win Friends and Influence People,* by Dale Carnegie, and *The Power of Positive Thinking,* by Dr. Norman Vincent Peale. . . . Vaulting some forty years in time, we find high up on the 1974 nonfiction bestseller charts, Zig Ziglar's *See You at the Top,* a motivational book for the times that was to sell more than a million copies."[2]

In criticizing especially the religion department of Baylor University, Ziglar wants a report on how many converts the professors have won each year. Having lectured extensively on ways to close the sale in the secular market, Ziglar seems now to be calling on Southern Baptist professors to sell Jesus Christ more effectively in the classroom.

Another motive behind the reluctance to discuss theological scholarship is shared by the Moderate Party and the Inerrancy Party. It is fear of the consequences. From 1978 to 1982 the Broadman Press published 24 small volumes under the general title of Layman's Bible Commentary. Except for a few notable pages, the commentaries could have been written a hundred years ago, as if the authors had no knowledge of the last fifty years of biblical research. In reality, most of the authors were quite informed, which was why they were selected to write the volumes. But they failed to give their lay readers a commentary series worthy of their intelligence and religious maturity.

With a show of elitism that Inerrancy Party leaders often attribute to liberals, Dr. Joe T. Odle, editor of Mississippi's *Baptist Record* in the seventies, made the following statement to a group of prominent Convention leaders in Denver:

> A second trend which is just as disturbing is the tendency to *allow questions of Biblical criticism* to creep into the [Convention's] curriculum materials. This has not happened very often, but many question whether it should appear at all. No one will deny that Biblical criticism, when carefully and wisely used, has a proper place, but many would question whether that place is in quarterlies which will be used by the rank and file of Southern Baptists. Most of them know nothing about Biblical criticism, are not prepared to use it, and probably could care less.[3]

As editor of the *Baptist Record* Odle did everything he could to see to it that Mississippi Baptists in the pews would remain unprepared to make use of biblical criticism in their study of the Bible.

In 1984 Paige Patterson, president of the Criswell Center for Biblical Studies of Dallas, challenged Roy Honeycutt, president of the Southern Baptist Theological Seminary, to a public debate on the issue of the Bible's authority. Honeycutt declined the challenge and offered, in substitution, to discuss the issue with Patterson in a published book. Patterson did not accept the invitation.

That bit of artful sidestepping by both men is symptomatic of an alarm prevalent within the two warring camps. The moderates are exceedingly reluctant to let the people in the pews see for themselves just how wide the gap is between the Sunday school and other materials published by the Convention and what the professors are teaching, especially in their advanced courses. The moderates seem to fear that if the church members do see how far the professors have advanced into biblical criticism of every type, they will rise up in revolt and demolish academic freedom at the seminaries.

Ironically, many members of the Inerrancy Party seem just as fearful of what may happen if the people in the pews discover that for decades they have been spoon-fed a theological diet of scarcely more than inspirational pabulum. Many of the bill-paying Baptists might even demand more of the fruit of critical biblical scholarship. If the moderates fear a backlash that would turn the seminaries into centers of indoctrination on the order of Jerry Falwell's school in Lynchburg, the Inerrancy Party fears that a growing number of Southern Baptists will acquire an insatiable appetite for something far different from the restricted diet they have been consuming.

The controversy over the inerrancy of Scripture is not about remote abstractions. Plainly stated, it is about the extent of the Bible's authority and accuracy. An inerrant document is by definition free of all erroneous teaching, and an infallible revelation does not mislead. Those who embrace the principle of the Bible's inerrancy and infallibility raise an interesting and crucial question for those who hold that the Bible's accuracy is limited: If the Bible is in error about some of the details of Christ's life and teaching, is it in error about all the details? The question faces head-on the issue of ultimate authority. If Christians are left to sift through the Bible to separate the credible from the incredible, will the Bible no longer be the Christian's final court of appeal? Will there be any final court of appeal?

JOHN HENRY NEWMAN'S TURN TOWARD ROME

The nineteenth-century Anglican theologian John Henry Newman converted to Roman Catholicism because he demanded a faith with final, unquestioned authority. He did not turn to the Baptists, Methodists, or the other nonconformists because, he said, their faith lacked a firm foundation. For the benefit of those who regarded the Bible as the sole authority, Newman pointed out that the Church was established by Christ himself and that it was through the Church that the

Scriptures were inspired in the first century. Furthermore, it was through the Church that the Scriptures were preserved over the subsequent centuries. Newman argued that since the Church was appointed as the infallible and final court of appeal on earth, it alone could prevent believers from going astray in their interpretations.

While not denigrating the importance of the churches, Southern Baptists have never been impressed with Newman's arguments. Like Southern Baptists, Roman Catholics harbor numerous historical ironies, as the following episode from Newman's life will show: After becoming a cardinal of the Roman Catholic Church, Newman found himself thrown into a bitter and scandalous controversy regarding papal infallibility. Pope Pius IX insisted that papal utterances were free of all error whenever delivered ex cathedra. With iron determination and a talent for bullying others, he called the cardinals and bishops together in an ecumenical council to declare formally the dogma of infallibility. Cardinal Newman opposed the move with all his strength, asserting that infallibility resided in the Roman Church as a mystical community of special bishops and cardinals, not in the pope per se. To Cardinal Newman's dismay, the bishops and cardinals of the 1870 Vatican Council voted to institute the dogma of papal infallibility. Later, Newman did a complete turnaround by announcing that he would embrace the new dogma, now that the mystical community of bishops and cardinals had established it.

Distraught by the proliferation of new denominations and the seemingly endless interpretations of Scripture, some of the Catholic bishops joined Pius IX in search of a way to turn back the rising tide of religious confusion. Unfortunately, the First Vatican Council took the wrong turn, Protestant scholars argued. Instead of installing the papal office as the final appeal, Catholics would have been better advised to return to the Scriptures. Rather than consult himself if he wishes to learn what Christ taught and did, is not the pope finally compelled to consult the Scriptures? And do not Catholic scholars likewise turn to the Scriptures, not to papal visions, when they wish to clarify a point about Christ's life, teachings, and saving work? While admitting that the early churches were the agencies through which the Scriptures were delivered, the Baptists and other Protestants did not leap to the conclusion that a church had to be infallible. On that point, Newman was judged to be in error.

Newman had, nevertheless, placed his finger on a sore point for evangelicals: the bewildering diversity of interpretations of the Christian Scriptures. If the Creator has given the human race an authoritative Scripture free of all error, would he fail to give believers a trustworthy agent or a reliable method for interpreting his written revelation? What is accomplished if the original documents of the Bible remain accurate while the interpretations proliferate like rabbits?

Two responses are given by members of the Inerrancy Party. The first, which is little more than a circular argument and a bluff, argues that there exists a greater consensus among believers on the major points than appears on the surface. The second answer is that since God gave his human creatures free will, willful self-delusion has generated most of the confusion and error.

The second answer in particular has been used to rationalize a high degree of intolerance and even persecution among believers, since it seems to deny the possibility of honest disagreement—a point to be considered later, when it is time to examine the rising pitch of alarm and acrimony among leaders of the two warring Southern Baptist parties.

THE MODERATE PARTY AS A COALITION

The Moderate Party of Southern Baptists is a coalition of principally three branches. The first believes that the Bible is both infallible (unfailing in accomplishing its purpose) and inerrant (errorless). The second branch believes that the Bible is infallible but holds that it contains errors. The third regards the Bible as authoritative but rejects inerrancy and infallibility. The members of this branch think the word "infallibility" has been so stretched and twisted that it no longer carries a standard meaning among Southern Baptists. They have dropped the word, preferring to spell out their own view of the Bible's authority.

If the first branch holds to the infallibility and the inerrancy of the Bible, why are its members with the moderates instead of the Inerrancy Party? Chiefly, they are driven by two goals, namely, to win converts and to establish their converts in local Southern Baptist churches. Though they would like all the converts to subscribe to biblical inerrancy, that is not, they insist, a goal to be pursued at the expense of the two primary goals. With a certain political astuteness, they have concluded that few evangelistic and missionary endeavors in the world can equal those of the Southern Baptist Convention, with its Cooperative Program and efficient organizational machinery. Hence, they have chosen to work within the Moderate Party so long as they are personally free to embrace and preach inerrancy. Also, they fear that if the Inerrancy Party should gain control of the Convention, it would spawn endless inquisitions, slanders, and power plays that would severely weaken the Convention and most likely either divide it down the middle or fragment it into several ineffective denominations fighting one another bitterly in the courts into the twenty-first century, thereby disgracing the name of Christ and rendering Baptists laughingstocks in the news media.

INERRANCY VERSUS INFALLIBILITY

A large percentage of Southern Baptist moderates seems to hold the Bible to be infallible but not inerrant. How large a percentage? That is unknown and will likely never be known. Southern Baptist agencies possess a variety of sophisticated resources for statistical studies and surveys, but they are notoriously reluctant to poll their members in rigorous detail about their doctrinal beliefs. A scattering of professors have polled and surveyed Baptists at a modest level. But the act of taking a detailed Convention-wide sampling of what Southern Baptists believe would spark a furious uproar. There is only a remote possibility of creating survey questions that would not be perceived as either biased or superficial to the various Convention leaders.

Drawing a hard line between inerrancy and infallibility, adherents of the Moderate Party's second branch insist that the line is crucial. They charge that the excessive claim of inerrancy detracts from the more important claim of biblical infallibility, and they state the distinction between the two concepts crisply. Inerrancy asserts that the Bible in its original documents is totally without error. Infallibility stresses that the Bible is unfailing in accomplishing the purpose that God intended. The moderates who hold only to biblical infallibility believe they would be personally dishonest should they fail to admit that the Bible contains errors and discrepant passages that cannot be perfectly harmonized. The purpose of the Bible, they argue, is not to provide the churches with a document that they can boast of as flawless in every respect. God apparently does not require flawless vessels and instruments to accomplish unfailingly his purpose. In their insecurity, human beings may be tempted to demand an error-free document, but God is under no obligation to yield to their demand. Humility lies in accepting what is revealed without demanding that it come in a preconceived form.

In a flash of indignation, one noted proponent of inerrancy, Edward J. Young, insisted that he could have little respect for a God who allowed inaccuracies to enter the Bible. A revelation that contained flaws would be "insulting," said Professor Young: "What kind of God is He if He has given such an untrustworthy Word to mankind?" If the Creator cannot prevent his special revelation from being cluttered by errors and flaws caused by human agents, then "such a God is no God at all!" He is not even "worth knowing."[4]

Those who reject inerrancy are not impressed by Young's indignation; they feel no compulsion to adjust their view to his private moods. They suggest that he and those like him adjust their moods and withdraw their subjective demands on the Creator. Granted that errors exist in the Bible, it is a colossal error to demand that Scripture be completely error free in every respect.

THE SLIPPERY SLOPE

The argument of the slippery slope is one of the most powerful and fruitful ever advanced by advocates of biblical inerrancy. It not only forces every alternative of inerrancy out of its cocoon of naivete but also exposes the inerrancy theory itself to an unanticipated and morally shocking implication. Before the slippery slope can be examined, however, something needs to be said about what is at stake in the battle over the Bible. What is to be gained or lost? What lies at the foot of the slippery slope?

If no case can be made for the Bible as a trustworthy revelation of the Creator, can a case be made for any of the other scriptures of the world? Proponents of the inerrancy of the Christian Scriptures are united in believing that the hundreds of millions of people around the globe who accept the Qur'an, the Upanishads, the Bhagavad Gita, the Book of Mormon, or Divine Principle as divine revelation are one and all deluded.

A modern alternative to belief in God and resurrection is evolutionary naturalism, which agrees that the hundreds of millions of Hindus, Muslims, and others are deluded, but no more deluded than Christians boasting of the divine origin of their Scriptures. Without a touch of sentimentalism, evolutionary naturalism asserts that the human species arrived in the universe with neither a purpose behind it nor a lasting future before it. Void of all cosmic meaning, human existence is scarcely a snap of the finger in cosmic time. In some respects, the human organism is simply a gene machine, a medium by which genes are purposelessly perpetuated from generation to generation. According to most evolutionary naturalists, the human species is a terminal case, its ultimate extinction inevitable, so that in time all the wondrous achievements of art, music, and literature will perish forever, leaving the universe to roll on in its blind way as if Bach, Mozart, Van Gogh, Isaiah, Gandhi, Dostoevsky, and the rest of the human race had never enjoyed their piteous instant of glory in the cosmic scheme of things. Human devotion and kindness are real, according to evolutionary naturalism, but they have no more cosmic significance than has a sneeze or the rusting of a piece of iron. Whether people perform acts of kindness or simply scratch an itch, neither activity has any lasting importance. All is temporal and fleeting. If struggling parents sacrifice to send their children to college, they have no more eternal reward than if they had plunged a knife into their offspring. The life of Martin Luther King, Jr., will prove to be of no more lasting value to the universe than will the life of Charles Manson.

Those who cannot accept evolutionary naturalism must struggle with some perplexing questions. Is there a Supreme Intelligence who has designed this vast and complex universe? And if there is, has this Being communicated in some way with mortal humans who occupy a tiny pocket of the universe? Does this Supreme Intelligence care that the human race suffers quiet despair or that it fears death and longs for meaning? If so, how can human mortals know about this Being unless there is clear and special revelation?

Most Southern Baptists of influence in the Convention are united in agreeing that there is a God who has revealed himself through nature, human history, and the Scriptures. They are divided, though, over the details and the content of that revelation. Numerous Southern Baptists are quick to admit that certain parts of the Bible not only fail to reveal God's character but are downright immoral and slanderous as well. On this, there is no compromise. An example is found in the chilling story of Abraham. According to Genesis 22:2, God said to Abraham, "Take your son, your only son Isaac, whom you love, and go to the land of Moriah, and offer him there as burnt offering upon one of the mountains of which I shall tell you." At the end of the story, God blessed his faithful servant because he had been willing to carry out the command without question. Indeed, Abraham, taking the knife in hand, had prepared himself to plunge it into his only son and set him aflame upon the altar.

Among Southern Baptist moderates, many flatly refuse to take this story at face value. They argue that Abraham only thought God had commanded him to slay Isaac and make of him a burnt offering. When Broadman Press published the Southern Baptist commentary on Genesis in January 1970, a storm broke. The commentator, an English Baptist, asserted that God could not in fact have commanded the killing of Isaac. Eventually the volume was officially removed from the bookstores, and the the task of writing a new commentary on Genesis 22 fell into the lap of Southern Seminary's Clyde Francisco, one of the more conservative members of the faculty.

In the furor over the story of Abraham and Isaac, the champions of inerrancy charged that the liberals had trapped themselves in self-contradiction by embracing the very arbitrariness and subjectivism that they professed to abhor. In other words, if those who reject inerrancy are free to pick and choose what is acceptable and not acceptable within the pages of Scripture, then they are setting themselves up as the final judge of what God can and cannot reveal about his own purpose, character, and acts. Mountain climbers sometimes come upon vast sheets of ice or slippery slopes that lead downward thousands of feet to disaster. Experienced climbers step back, knowing that if they step out on the slippery slope, they may lose their firm footing. Similarly, when a reader of Scripture concedes even one error in the text, has he not stepped out on the slippery slope? To advance even one yard on that slope, say the defenders of inerrancy, is to take the fatal step that will lead to the bottom in ruin.

According to the Gospel of Mark, when Jesus came upon a certain fig tree that had nothing but leaves, he cursed it. Never again would it produce fruit. When C. H. Dodd, an esteemed New Testament scholar, examined this curious little story, he concluded that the modern Christian knows by "instinctive criticism" that Jesus could not have cursed "a harmless fig tree because it failed to satisfy his craving for fruit out of season."[5] To be sure, the Gospel of Mark does not say that Jesus craved figs, but it does say that "it was not the season for figs," which for Professor Dodd raised the question of why Jesus would even expect to find fruit. (In telling the same story, the Gospel of Matthew deletes the notation that "it was not the season for figs.") Still, the question remains as to how Dodd concluded that Jesus did not curse the tree or cause it to wither at once.

To employ the historical-critical method is to read the Bible or any literary document with an interest in tracking down the literary and oral predecessors that fed into it. Usually it entails also an openness to the possibility that the biblical author might have slanted or reworked the material drawn upon.

Dodd argued that the discipline of historical criticism leads the Christian to reconstruct from biblical records, admittedly imperfect, a Jesus whose character simply would not allow Him to cause the fig tree to wither.[6] Hundreds of books by biblical critics and scholars such as C. H. Dodd are bought by Southern Baptist money and placed in the seminary libraries for the Baptist seminary students to read. Furthermore, many of those students are required to read books containing the same historical-critical method used by Dodd. Even though members of the Inerrancy Party are divided among themselves regarding whether such books should be urged upon seminary students, they stand united in their complaint that Professor Dodd and similar scholars do a destructive scissors-and-paste job on the Scriptures by selecting passages that suit their biases and by rejecting passages that do not. If Professor Dodd rejects the Mark and Matthew accounts of the fig tree incident, where is his stopping point on the slippery slope of picking and choosing biblical texts? If readers cannot accept all of the New Testament statements about Christ, then the Gospel accounts become little more than inkblots used in a Rorschach test, revealing more about the reader's biases than about the earthly Christ. All of which raises the question "Why should people read the New Testament in the first place if it is merely a stimulus for their subjective responses and biases?"

THUNDERSTRUCK AT THE SEMINARY

When earnest men and women leave their colleges and home churches and move to one of the Southern Baptist seminary campuses, many of them are thunderstruck by what they read in the required books and are shattered by what they hear in the classrooms. It is as if they had stepped into an alien world. New doors swing open and strange doubts rush into the mind, attacking like swarming wasps. Some students find themselves haunted so relentlessly by their new doubts about the Bible's authority that they begin to wonder if their ministers at home have been honest with them. Critics of the seminaries are doubtless correct to charge that much of the biblical criticism taught in the seminary classrooms exacts a heavy toll from these Baptist men and women. For many students, once the door of doubt is opened, it is impossible to shut. Still more questions storm in: Is the Bible in the last analysis an overrated book? Are at least portions of the Bible as irrelevant to modern life as the Egyptian Book of the Dead?

Many people look upon the Bible the way they look upon Aristotle's *Ethics and Poetics* or Plato's *Republic,* namely, as classical literature that can sometimes throw light on human experience but in no way as divine revelation. Though such ancient works may be read with great profit, they must nevertheless be read with discrimination. Aristotle and the Apostle Paul, for example, attribute to women a status inferior to men, a view that surely must be rejected in the name of human decency. (Many advocates of inerrancy deny that Paul denigrates women in any way, which is a point to be considered later, when it is time to discuss the place of women in Southern Baptist life.)

Most leading defenders of inerrancy concede that some passages in the Bible pose serious problems in either of two ways. Some appear on the surface to strain our moral sensibilities, and others appear to strain human rationality. When those same defenders must reject the theory of evolution in favor of a more or less literal interpretation of the Genesis story of creation, they realize that they appear blindly irrational to the scientific community, the overwhelming majority of which subscribes to the theory of evolution. The defenders of inerrancy know full well that they pay a dear price for holding that the Bible cannot be in error even in matters of science, for such noted Harvard scientists as Edward O. Wilson (formerly a Southern Baptist from Alabama) and Stephen Jay Gould regard fundamentalists as closed-minded obscurantists. Furthermore, most Southern Baptist biologists are evolutionists. But better to suffer the disdain of contemporary biologists and other scientists, contend the defenders of inerrancy, than to step out onto the slippery slope. If the Genesis account of creation is conceded to be mythical, who is to say that the biblical teachings on forgiveness and resurrection are not also rooted in mythology? There can be no compromise with the slippery slope!

4.

Stepping into the Baptist World

TAKING THE ROLE OF A VISITING ANTHROPOLOGIST

n one way, certain kinds of missionaries, espionage agents, and anthropologists are alike. While living within a society whose worldview they do not embrace, they must nevertheless gain some understanding of that society. Each group has a different motive for understanding something about the people they live among, but none can work without taking the risk of stepping inside the alien worldview and looking at life if possible from the natives' perspective. The readers of this book who are not Baptists are invited to take the risk of stepping into the Southern Baptist world and thinking like Baptists, becoming vicariously members of that proud tribe for one purpose only: to understand what this worldview means to those who live and breathe it and to feel some of what they feel with all their heart.

Those readers who are Southern Baptists are invited to journey through these pages alongside an author who has lived inside and outside the Baptist worldview. They are invited to note many of the reports gleaned from Southern Baptists themselves and some of his reflections on these remarkable people and their special view of reality. There is probably no better place to begin this adventure than with the doctrine touched on earlier, the doctrine known among Baptists as eternal security. By exploring this strange and fascinating belief, readers will quickly gain insight into the role of the Bible in Southern Baptist life. They will see at once why the Bible is for Southern Baptists a book of both solutions and problems.

As was mentioned in Chapter 1, most Southern Baptist leaders agree on the doctrine of Once Saved, Always Saved. According to this doctrine, since salvation is a gift of divine grace, it cannot be a reward earned by works or spiritual brownie points. On the question of good works and deeds, the average Southern Baptist minister will respond immediately that the Christian does good works not to earn salvation but because he already enjoys it as an unearned gift that can never be nullified or revoked.

The anxiety-ridden struggle to keep oneself inside the pale of salvation day after day belongs to some denominations, but it is no part of the Southern Baptist way. Even though Christ in the Gospels condemns sexual lust as adultery in the heart, Jimmy Carter as a Southern Baptist felt no need to pretend that he was free of all such lust; he openly admitted it, not in pride but in simple honesty. He could afford to be honest because he believed that not even adultery in the heart could cause God to revoke the gift of salvation to one who had already received it by trust. Grasping the meaning of eternal security, Baptists may breathe freely and confidently, fearing nothing and no one regarding their unshakable place in the Kingdom.

Unfortunately, there is one passage of Scripture in particular that now and then comes to the surface of Southern Baptist consciousness to create its own terror and doubts about eternal security. If Southern Baptist ministers were asked to name the one New Testament passage most difficult to reconcile with that cherished doctrine, they would with few exceptions turn to the deadly Chapter 6, verses 4–6, of the Epistle to the Hebrews.

A former president of the Southern Baptist Convention, Dr. Herschel Hobbs, admitted from the start in his commentary on the disturbing Hebrews 6 passage that it "presents grave difficulties."[1] No one knows who wrote the Epistle to the Hebrews, and the circumstances that prompted its writing are difficult to reconstruct. Furthermore, Hebrews 6:4–6 is somewhat awkwardly styled, but the RSV translation is fairly readable: "For it is impossible to restore again to repentance those who have once been enlightened, who have tasted the heavenly gift, and have become partakers of the Holy Spirit, and have tasted the goodness of the word of God and the powers of the age to come, if they then commit apostasy, since they crucify the Son of God on their own account and hold him up to contempt."

FACING THE CRISIS

Within the Southern Baptist tribe can be found the following four major interpretations of that unnerving passage:

1. Christians who commit apostasy—who publicly break their covenant with the Son of God—can never be restored to the point where they will repent of their treachery. Their betrayal is like a personal contribution to the crucifixion of the Son of God, holding him up to contempt. Professor Dale Moody defended this position for forty years at the Southern Baptist Theological Seminary. The famous seventeenth-century Baptist John Bunyan also seemed to hold to the same interpretation: "Then I saw there was a way to hell even from the gates of heaven, as well as from the City of Destruction." When some of the Baptists in Arkansas protested that Moody's interpretation could not be correct because it denied the alleged apostate the opportunity to repent and be restored, Moody replied, "That's no argument, Brother. If Scripture says it, then I believe it. Whether or not you or I like what it says is irrelevant." According to Moody, such stalwart Southern Baptists as A. T. Robertson and W. T. Conner believed it possible for a Christian believer to apostatize irrevocably.

2. Some Baptist scholars have argued that the passage is entirely hypothetical so that it applies to no one—raising the question of why the author of the epistle would bother to solemnly warn readers of something that could apply to no one. (See also Hebrews 10:26f.) This interpretation has only one advantage. It allows the cherished doctrine of Once Saved, Always Saved to stand without being contradicted, at least not by the Epistle to the Hebrews. W. A. Criswell and Paige Patterson hold to this interpretation, but two former Convention presidents, Jimmy Draper and Herschel Hobbs, have discarded it as insupportable.

3. The third interpretation is one that, again, allows Baptists and Calvinists to cling to Once Saved, Always Saved. It goes as follows. The passage is not referring to Christians at all but to people who, while associating with the church and Christians, remain nevertheless as unbelievers. If such unbelievers fall away or fall back, they cannot be brought to the door of repentance again. In short, if they fall back after almost entering into the full benefits of salvation, then it is impossible to offer them a second chance. They have joined those who crucified Christ by turning away in final, irreversible rebellion.

According to the third interpretation, since the subjects under discussion are not yet believers, their falling away is not a case of the truly saved losing their salvation by committing apostasy. Although fundamentalist scholar H. A. Ironside and a number of Southern Baptists have embraced it, Moody and Draper reject this interpretation, too, as does E. Y. Mullins, one of Southern Seminary's most recognized scholars and presidents.

4. The fourth position is formulated by a former Convention president, Herschel Hobbs. He contends that the controversy over the Hebrews 6 passage has met a dead end because it took the wrong road initially. The critical question, he says, is not who is the intended recipient of the warning of Hebrews 6 but rather what is at stake? What is to be lost? His answer is that growth in Christian living, not salvation, is at stake. Hebrews 6, therefore, warns Christians that they are in danger not of damnation but of falling back from the full maturity of their faith. Hobbs's interpretation puts a great strain on the text. One must search far and wide to find a commentary that will unequivocally agree with it. All but a few scholarly commentaries side with Dale Moody's interpretation, not Hobbs's.

Hobbs exercises great ingenuity in making this exceedingly troublesome passage square with his quasi-Calvinistic belief that no Christian can fall from grace into eternal damnation. In trying to justify his interpretation, he resorts to two lines of defense.[2] First, he makes his own translation of certain pivotal words from the Greek in which the epistle is presumed to have been originally composed. Second, he reaches beyond the immediate content of the epistle to import a context that will lend weight to his unique interpretation. By importing supportive contexts that favor their biases, the leading defenders of inerrancy reveal that they are masters of the art of picking and choosing. To justify the practice, they rely upon several pragmatic slogans: "The Bible is its own interpreter," "Our interpretation of any one passage must fit with the whole context of Scripture," "Every passage must be understood in light of the perfect unity of Scripture."

The slogans are general, flexible, and vague enough to give exegetes enormous discretionary powers in selecting supportive contexts from within the covers of the Bible and using them to strengthen their theological biases. Predictably, Hobbs writes, "Our conclusion must be in harmony with the whole teaching of the gospel."[3] That is but another way of saying that he has resolved not to let this threatening passage in Hebrews 6 contradict his belief in Once Saved, Always Saved. Indeed he has, he believes, already found "an abundance of New Testament teaching" outside the Book of Hebrews that weighs heavily against the notion that a Christian can commit apostasy.[4]

Inside Hebrews are five other texts that Moody emphasizes and Hobbs plays down, which forces Hobbs to step outside the biblical borders to marshal support for his case. He turns to the Greek language and etymology, which antedate the New Testament. (There was once a time when many biblical exegetes believed that "Holy Ghost Greek" was a pristine language divinely preserved to guarantee the diligent students of Greek the reward of discovering the pure meaning of Scripture that inferior languages would contaminate. Thanks to Greek scholars, among them the Southern Baptists' own A. T. Robertson, that notion has been exposed as a piece of romantic lore.)

Hobbs, confident that he can gain support from the ancient Greek language, concludes that the infamous, threatening word of Hebrew 6:6 need not be translated as "apostatize" but rather is used in the sense of "breaking the terms of a contract." Hobbs fails to see that to apostatize is to break the terms of a contract. The author of Hebrews 6 goes out of his way to warn that the violation is permanent, irrevocable, and without possibility of reinstatement. Against almost all other interpreters, Hobbs de-emphasizes what the biblical author goes to great lengths to emphasize. Whatever interpretation finally carries the day, one conclusion stands out like a red flag: The art of biblical exegesis has become a scholarly discipline that leaves the untrained layperson with comparatively little significant contribution to make to the study of the Scriptures. It has long been a part of Baptist tradition that each individual is free to interpret the Scriptures for himself. That is still true formally, but in actuality the people in the pews are relying more and more on ministers and teachers to interpret the Scriptures for them.

BACK TO THE ORIGINAL GREEK

Southern Baptist seminaries were once at the forefront in requiring their ministerial students to study ancient Greek, the language in which all or most of the New Testament documents were originally written. Some students enter this study with the innocent expectations of a bride or groom, believing that by learning to translate from the original Greek, they will eventually arrive at the exact meaning of each verse of the New Testament. In reality, the opposite often comes about; instead of gaining the exactitude longed for, they discover that

one Greek word may have two or many alternate meanings from
which they as new translators must choose. If anything, their task of
interpretation becomes more complicated, and the range of legitimate
options and shades of meanings from which to select grows more
sweeping than they had imagined.

I can recall my own thrill when, as a young Greek student and a
Southern Baptist, I first saw that the troublesome Acts 2:38 passage
could be translated in such a way as to outflank the Church of Christ
assertion that baptism is essential to salvation. Most members of the
Church of Christ and most Southern Baptists believe that Presby-
terians, Methodists, and many others have never been truly baptized.
(Being sprinkled as an infant does not count.) Unlike most Church of
Christ traditionalists, however, Baptists do not hold that baptism is
unconditionally essential to salvation. Unfortunately, the King James
translation of Acts 2:38, as well as the Living Bible and the Revised
Standard Version, makes it appear that baptism is necessary for salvation, from which it follows that Presbyterian Ruth Graham (Billy
Graham's wife) and everyone else who has been sprinkled in infancy
are doomed to hell unless they get immersed. The King James Version
reads as follows: "Then Peter said unto them, Repent, and be baptized every one of you in the name of Jesus Christ for the remission of
sins, and ye shall receive the gift of the Holy Ghost."

Unlike my Church of Christ friends, I could never as a youth and a
Southern Baptist rest comfortably with that injunction. And the marginal note in my Scofield Reference Bible, like the American Standard
Version, served only to reduce the passage to ambiguity by replacing
the word "for" with the word "unto."

The gloom lifted when I realized that the King James Version might
be wrong. Billy Graham's wife wasn't doomed to hell after all, even if
she hadn't been truly baptized! Later I discovered that the Baptist
translator E. J. Goodspeed had made parenthetical the troublesome
baptismal injunction of Acts 2:38 and that another Baptist translator,
Charles B. Williams, had used a footnote and a free translation to
eliminate any hint that baptism was essential to salvation. The Lord
and the Baptist translators of the Greek text had delivered the Church
of Christ into our Baptist hands!

For some students, such flexibility offers an exhilarating new freedom, but others find it disillusioning and confusing. Several meanings of a word often compete with one another, and the student may
discover that the selection of one legitimate meaning or cluster of

meanings is conditional. Far from making the interpretation process easier, the attempt to translate from the Greek turns out to be colored by biases. Each translation is already an interpretation conditioned by the framework in which it is couched. Instead of finding a neutral or unbiased framework from which to choose the precise translation, the developing Greek student gradually understands that there is almost always more than one perspective from which to make his choice. One meaning is appropriate only if seen from perspective A; another is more appropriate if viewed from perspective B, C, or D. (A survey of commentaries on chapters 9 and 11 of Romans will illustrate this point vividly.)

When Hobbs chose to reject "commit apostasy" as the appropriate meaning of the troublesome Greek word in Hebrews 6:6, he was doing so because to some extent his own bias demanded it. That is not to condemn him, however, since it is impossible to interpret without biases. One may exchange one bias or perspective for another, but it is impossible to shed all biases. Only the epistemological primitive thinks he has a neutral framework.[5] The complex practice of picking and choosing meanings of the text is not a practice that the translator can learn to overcome with increased discipline, as if it were a human weakness. Rather, it is an objective necessity and, ironically, the result of intensive training and education in biblical studies.

This all leads to the following observation: Even if there were in existence an inerrant set of biblical texts, no set of inerrant meanings of the texts could ever come into existence. The fine art of etymology-chasing alone would guarantee that. Under the delusion of getting back to the ultimate root of a word, some etymology hounds create meanings by selecting a stopping point along the trail that leads backward into the word's lineage of meanings. The justification for stopping at one point rather than another must come from a thick theoretical framework already in play. Anyone who claims simply to "read the text itself," as if reading bathroom scales, is resting on the naive presumption that the human mind can be turned into a blank sheet (the tabula rasa) across which truth simply writes itself so long as the mind remains innocent. Doubtless, some holiness Christians imagine that the Holy Ghost wipes their sanctified minds free of all biases and restores them to a sinless, errorless state of innocence. But from such people most Southern Baptists quickly run, believing that their professed innocence usually betokens fanaticism.

Among the Southern Baptists who do not hold to inerrancy is a group whose members assert that the Bible has no consistent position on apostasy. These Baptists openly admit that some biblical passages line up on one side while other passages line up on the other side. They contend that a forced harmony does violence to the integrity of each passage. Better, they say, to accept that the biblical passages do not ring with one clear, consistent voice on every doctrine than to force a superficial harmony. It also turns out that among inerrancy defenders there is a great diversity of opinion as to what the perfect unity or harmony of the Scriptures really is. In fact, numerous subunities are posited, each competing for status in the putative highest unity.[6]

5.

Every Context has a Context

It seems so innocent to say that a biblical passage sits in darkness, void of all meaning, until illumined by its contexts. But once we admit that every text requires contexts to baptize it with meaning, there can be no turning back, for there is no end to the ring of contexts, each evoking a new shade of meaning from the text while simultaneously imposing its own external meaning. All Southern Baptist seminary students learn that a biblical text has a context. Not all of them learn, however, that every context has a context. An example of the interplay between texts and contexts can be found in the way Christians have dealt with Romans 9:11–21. The prima facie meaning of this text seems to be as follows: God elected some people and rejected others wholly because he willed to do it. He chose to love Jacob and hate Esau not because something in Jacob appealed to him or something in Esau repelled him. Indeed, the text says plainly that God chose Jacob over Esau before they were born, which emphasizes that Jacob was no more virtuous than Esau. This text is well known as the major source of strict predestinationism. To soften its hard line, some Christians have encircled it with imported contexts that imply a doctrine of free will in opposition to strict predestination. In response, the defenders of hard-line predestination import a still wider ring of contexts to restore to primacy their original doctrine of predestination. Some hard-liners even reverse the process by turning Romans 9:11–21 into the key interpretive context through which they interpret all the texts of Scripture.

A large strand of Christian history traces the gerrymandering of theologians' favored contexts around Romans 9:11–21. One evangelical Christian writer grew so frustrated with the process that he broke with some of his colleagues and exclaimed, "I do not know how to reconcile Paul's teaching on election with the Bible's apparent commitment to the notion that people are free and morally responsible agents. Nor do I claim to know how to reconcile Paul's statement that 'there is neither male nor female . . . in Christ' (Gal. 3:28) with some of his apparently sexist teachings."[1]

When the Baptists and the Church of Christ disagree fiercely over the translation and meaning of the text of, say, Acts 2:38, they do so partly because each must engage in the exegete's unavoidable context shifting and gerrymandering. To be sure, the right wing of the Church of Christ imagines that it "simply reads the Bible" as if the entire process were an exercise of childlike transparency. But an increasing awareness of the elements that affect the exegetical process drives translators and exegetes toward the following conclusion: It is no longer possible for informed translators and exegetes to pinpoint the meaning of most given texts. There remains always and inescapably the element of exegetical relativism. It must not be confused with absolute relativism, which denies that the given texts and contexts exercise any limitation on the range of meanings. To set significant limits on what a text can mean, nevertheless, is a far cry from specifying what the text finally and irrevocably does mean. All assigned meanings to texts are conjectures, some tested, others untested.

Diverging from the majority of biblical scholars, the evangelical writer John Wenham asserts that the accounts of the physical resurrection of Jesus Christ can be fully "harmonized." However, the arguments he makes in closing his case appear less than impressive and will disappoint most earnest evangelical and fundamentalist believers. Even the publisher's promotional statement regarding Wenham's book *Easter Enigma: Are the Resurrection Accounts in Conflict?*[2] has the sound of an apology: "A measure of reasoned conjecture and historical imagination is unavoidable in an effort like this, and the book does not claim to be more than a possible reconstruction."[3]

BAPTISTS AND THE MILLENNIUM

After being defeated in his reluctant bid for the Convention presidency in Dallas in June 1985, Winfred Moore was elected as first vice president over Zig Ziglar. In an interview shortly after his election, Moore was asked about troublesome passages in the Bible. He answered with his dry wit, "The ones that trouble me are the ones I do understand—like love of neighbor—and don't do much about."

The doctrine of the millennium (Christ's return to reign on this planet for a thousand years) became a troubling source of controversy for Southern Baptist ministers and teachers in the twentieth century. Today, they seem unable to find a common understanding of the doctrine beyond the belief that it is important. Most of them hold that the Bible is the sure guide to correct doctrine, but after working systematically through the Bible, shifting contexts both ingeniously and clumsily, they have emerged with sharply divergent views of the millennium.

Anyone who studies Southern Baptists patiently will observe that their worldview contains no way to deal consistently with the fact that seemingly sincere believers who read the Bible diligently often fail miserably to resolve their differences. Some of them are tempted at times to embrace the holiness explanation that a pure heart can filter out error, which suggests that erroneous beliefs are lodged in the impure hearts of their opponents. Since Southern Baptists are not of the holiness movement, they are uncomfortable with that simplistic explanation. On the question of the millennium, Southern Baptists have disagreed sharply and then suffered the bewilderment that sometimes comes over them when they realize they have no settled way of accounting for their disagreement. Others take pride in the Baptist tradition that gives individuals the right to interpret Scripture as each person's conscience and study dictate.

In the South and the North, Baptists have undergone considerable context shifting regarding the millennium. Before the Civil War a high percentage of Baptists, along with other Christians in the United States, were optimistic postmillennialists. Encouraged by the revivals and widespread conversions in the early 1800s, postmillennialists came to expect sensational results from their expanding missionary and evangelistic efforts around the globe. They believed that Christianity would win the hearts of most of the human race, thus bringing in the millennium. After that victory, in the postmillennium, Christ would return to earth. As E. F. Kevan notes, many of his fellow evangelicals have been postmillennialists.[4] Into the twentieth century Benjamin B. Warfield was still advancing a postmillennial view, as Harold Lindsell and the Warfield scholar Samuel G. Craig acknowledge.[5] The founder of Southwestern Baptist Seminary, B. H. Carrol, died a postmillennialist.

Among Southern Baptists in the forties and fifties the premillennial
view came close to becoming a new orthodoxy. Many of those who
turned toward premillennialism were the kind of fundamentalists
who saw the modern world as rapidly surrendering to secularism. According to their scenario, events would grow steadily worse until
Christ came, not as a climax to the successful conversion of most of
the human race but because the redeemed had to be snatched out of
an increasingly wicked world and transported via the rapture to be
with Christ.

Because of the rising intensity of their battle with those who reject
the doctrine of the Bible's inerrancy, many within the Southern Baptist
Inerrancy Party seem to have been forced to make peace with those
amillennialists who also happen to embrace inerrancy. (The amillennialists tend to view the reign of Christ as a social and spiritual phenomenon, not a political reign on earth.) The Inerrancy Party cannot
at present afford internal battles over the millennium. The point here
is that whereas many Southern Baptists once regarded the premillennial view as the only clear and obvious interpretation of biblical
prophecy, for now they are willing to make room for different opinions. Paul Pressler says he has many friends who are amillennialists.
The compromise suggests that the Bible teaches either one view or the
other, depending on how correctly it is read by devout believers.

What the believer in inerrancy cannot believe is that the Bible might
actually contain both views! Believers in inerrancy like Paige Patterson
and Jimmy Draper must hold that the Bible teaches one and only one
view even if there are now legitimate differences as to what that view
is. Among those who reject inerrancy, most hold that the Bible provides no single, coherent picture of the millennium. Currently, there
are at least three popular views, for the simple reason that no exclusive view of the millennium can be found in the Bible without
doing considerable violence to its diverse texts and contexts.

It is interesting that the rapid decline of nineteenth-century optimism, the outbreak of World Wars I and II, and the Great Depression
all seemed to cause the evangelicals and fundamentalists to read the
scriptural texts in light of the context of world events. That would
seem to be a 180-degree turnaround for some proponents of inerrancy, who have insisted tirelessly that it is the Scriptures that throw
contextual light on world events but not the other way around.

One noted evangelical Baptist, Bernard Ramm, says that the battle
among Southern Baptists over their seminaries has to do primarily

with one question: "How can believers maintain their Christian stance while attempting to face the rise of modern knowledge?"[6] Twentieth-century fundamentalism found in world events a context for radically reinterpreting those portions of Scripture having to do with the end of the earth. At the same time, other Christians found in the new world of biology and biochemistry a context for radically reinterpreting those portions of the Scripture having to do with the beginning of the earth and the species. Each group sincerely believed that it was "rightly dividing the word of truth." And their heirs will continue to believe those and many other reinterpretations in the decades to come, as long as there remain the endless circles of contexts to throw new interpretive light on each text of Scripture.

The Bible is itself an inexhaustible supply of texts and contexts, all casting their lights, reflections, and refractions in countless directions. The play of interpretive lights on and within the Bible will continue with such bewildering speed that it will never be possible to determine precisely where Scripture as a self-contained entity begins and its imported contexts end. Currently, there seems to be a new and surprising turn in interpreting the millennium. Once again, the fundamentalists are reading Scripture in light of current events. A politically oriented postmillennialism has begun to infiltrate the premillennialism of Jerry Falwell and Tim LaHaye. These two men appear to believe it is possible to turn back what they see as the tide of secularism in the United States. As John Heinerman and Anson Shupe show in their new book *The Mormon Corporate Empire*,[7] Jerry Falwell has reached out to join hands politically with the postmillennial Mormons to help advance the vision of "America for God." LaHaye has moved to Washington, D.C., to establish a fundamentalist lobby.

1983 HERESY TRIAL IN DALLAS

No New Testament scholar, including evangelicals, will deny that Christians of earlier centuries attributed a number of sayings and deeds to Jesus that are not mentioned in the New Testament documents. According to one extracanonical Gospel, an ox and a donkey worshiped the baby Jesus. "Then that which was spoken through Isaiah the prophet was fulfilled: 'The ox knows his owner and the donkey his lord's manger.' . . . Thus that which was spoken through the prophet Habbakuk was fulfilled: 'You are known between the two animals.'"[8] In addition, a tree bends down at the feet of Mary and

Jesus, who gather its fruit for their refreshment.[9] In the canonical Gospels, Jesus does not converse with animals, although he does order the wind to be still, and the wind obeys. If evangelicals balk at the thought of an ox or a donkey worshiping Jesus, they do not balk at the Old Testament story of Balaam's ass conversing with her master. For centuries rabbis have told stories in which animals think and speak, to drive home a moral point. Speaking before the June 1985 Pastors' Conference in Dallas, inerrantist Adrian Rogers told the following story of a woodpecker: "I heard of a woodpecker down in south Florida pecking on a pine tree, and about that time a bolt of lightning hit that tree and split it right in two. That woodpecker flew off and flew back later on with nine other woodpeckers. He said, 'There it is, gentlemen. Right over there.'" Like the woodpecker, people sometimes take credit for things they did not bring about. No one at the Pastors' Conference stood up to denounce Rogers for telling a yarn that was false. No one called him a liar, because everyone assumed that the yarn was not intended to be taken at face value.

The Gospel according to the Hebrews, Gospel of Thomas, Gospel of Philip, Gospel of Truth, Gospel to the Egyptians, Secret Books of James, Apocalypse of Paul, Letter of Peter to Philip, and Apocalypse of Peter offer various stories and statements about Jesus that are not in the canonical Gospels. Professor Helmut Koester of Harvard University suggests that the Gospel of Thomas, although compiled around 140 C.E., may include traditions older than the Gospels of Matthew, Mark, Luke, and John.[10] Unfortunately, many documents were burned by Christians who called themselves Catholic and orthodox. Around 447 C.E., Pope Leo the Great not only forbade the reading of the Acts of John but also ordered them entirely destroyed.[11] In 326 C.E., the emperor Constantine ordered that the books of heretics (Christians who held minority opinions) should be searched out and set to flames. Theodoret, bishop of Cyrrhus in Syria, about 450 C.E. admitted that more than two hundred heretical books were revered by the people in the churches of his diocese. He credited himself with doing away with them and then introduced the four Gospels that had been labeled canonical.[12]

The Jewish literary genre called midrash embroidered putative historical events with imaginative additions of dubious historical accuracy. Billy Graham used the genre effectively in his sermon on Daniel in the lion's den when he put words into the mouth of Daniel. "Move over, Leo," said Daniel, according to the preaching of Billy

Graham. Preachers today still use the midrash rather freely. The nineteenth-century Baptist preacher Charles Spurgeon of London felt it necessary to scold his fellow ministers who invented sermon illustrations. Most biblical scholars believe that the authors of Matthew, Mark, Luke, and John used the midrash. In a dramatic heresy trial, members of the Evangelical Theological Society met in Dallas at the Criswell Center for Biblical Studies on December 17, 1983, to consider the case of one of their own. Dr. Robert Gundry, the erudite professor of New Testament and Greek at Santa Barbara's Westmont College, was rebuked for writing that the author of the Gospel of Matthew employed the genre of midrash. In his thick book *Matthew: A Commentary on His Literary and Theological Art,*[13] Professor Gundry steps beyond most evangelical scholars by arguing that Matthew changed some of the historical details about Jesus' life and even invented events. Gundry does not, for example, believe that the wise men actually visited Jesus. Most scholars, except for evangelicals and fundamentalists, agree that the story, like so many stories of other ancient heroes and gods, is mythical.

Myths often sprang up around great men of antiquity. In *The Life of Pythagoras,* Iamblichus contends that it is only a rumor that the god Apollo was the biological father of Pythagoras.

> "However, the soul of Pythagoras came from the realm of Apollo, either being a heavenly companion or ranked with him in some other familiar way, to be sent down among men; no one can deny this. It can be maintained from his birth and the manifold wisdom of his soul. . . . He was educated so that he was the most beautiful and god-like of those written about in histories. After his father had died, he increased in nobility and wisdom. Although he was still a youth, in his manner of humility and piety he was counted most worthy already, even by his elders. . . . He was considered by many to be the son of a God."[14]

Spearheading the drive to force Robert Gundry out of the Evangelical Theological Society, Norman Geisler of Dallas Theological Seminary insisted that the method of redaction criticism could not be tolerated by evangelicals. Harold Lindsell, at the forefront of the move to expose Southern Baptist professors who had not embraced inerrancy, was one of the first to raise the question of Gundry's membership in the society.[15] Evangelist R. L. Hymers, founder and president of the Fundamentalist Army, joined Geisler. An ordained Southern Baptist minister and a graduate of Golden Gate Baptist Theological Seminary (one of the six Southern Baptist seminaries), Hymers casti- gated Gundry on TV and through ads in the *Los Angeles Times,* charg- ing that he was worse than the liberal professors, whom Hymers had already classified with prostitutes and murderers. In a December 1983, sermon delivered in Los Angeles, Hymers exclaimed: "The liberal theological professor, the prostitute, the drug addict, and the mur- derer—all agree on one thing. . . . All agree that the Bible is not the word of God. Have you ever noticed that? Did you ever wonder why? They're all sinners. I love to say that. I know it's true. I've been around, baby. I've been on Hollywood Boulevard. And I've been at Golden Gate Seminary—a marked similarity. . . . Have you ever met a pros- titute who believes in the inerrancy of the Bible?"

Hymers did not indicate how extensively or scientifically he had surveyed prostitutes to determine their views on Scripture. Nor did he reveal his methodology or the data base used in his survey. Con- tending on TV that the human race has arrived at the last days of apos- tasy, Hymers denounced Gundry as the worst of the apostates, worse than the liberals themselves, and as the fulfillment of the prophecy in II Thessalonians 2:3—the final sign to come before the rapture, when all true believers will be caught up in the air to be with the Lord. Over and over Hymers contended that it was not education or learning that caused scholars like Gundry to forsake the doctrine of biblical iner- rancy. The cause, he asserted, was sin in the lives of the scholars. In his TV sermon entitled "Liberalism at Westmont: A Sign of the End Times," Hymers exclaimed with rising fervor, amid the applause of the audience, "If you reject the authority of the Bible, God says that you are good for nothing. . . . I do not care if you are a professor who has come here to hear my sermon in disguise. . . . You are good for nothing. Good for nothing! Good for nothing!"

It must not be imagined for one moment that any of the other mem- bers of the Evangelical Theological Society made a vitriolic and per- sonal attack on Robert Gundry. There is, however, something about the evangelical and fundamentalist framework that makes it difficult to account for honest disagreement among people of goodwill regard- ing a number of critical theological issues. It is sometimes only a short step from being unable to explain how people of equal integrity can disagree on basic issues to being unable even to recognize the integ- rity and sincerity of the people one disagrees with. In the end, ETS members voted to terminate Gundry's membership.

In an extended interview with Dr. Gundry in Anaheim, California, in November 1985, I learned that the trustees of the evangelical Westmont College have resisted all pressures to fire him and have maintained an exceedingly cordial working relationship with him. Gundry not only continues to regard himself as an evangelical Christian but also holds that the Bible is inerrant. At the same time, he contends that the Bible writers, like other ancient writers, sometimes embellished their sources and imaginatively expanded historical incidents for moral and theological purposes. He refers to the inventive expansions of the Old Testament in 1 Enoch, Testaments of the Twelve Patriarchs, Testament of Job, Testament of Abraham, Books of Adam and Eve, Martyrdom of Isaiah, and Assumption of Moses.[16]

Gundry's 1982 commentary on Matthew was debated in eight articles of the March 1983 issue of the *Journal of the Evangelical Society;* the debate cannot be summarized here, but the scholarly arguments were impressive on each side. Perhaps the following quotation from one of Gundry's articles will reveal what the majority of the society found so objectionable about his commentary:

> But we know that ancient people tended to embellish the birth stories of great men more than they embellished other parts of their life stories. We think, for example, of the embellishments on Noah's birth in 1 Enoch 106:1–19; on Moses' birth in Josephus *Ant.* 2.9. 3–7; . . . on Alexander the Great's birth in Plutarch's *Life of Alexander* 2.1–3.5; on the birth of Sargon of Agade in ANET 119. Therefore, if Matthew's habits can account for the differences between his and Luke's version of Jesus' birth, the law of parsimony works against the supposition [that Matthew drew from and made use] of another tradition. Why not say that Matthew "Gentilizes" the shepherds at the nativity as he Christianizes Pilate at the trial. . . .
>
> Close reading shows, then, the presence of many more discrepancies [between the Gospel of Mark and the Gospel of Matthew] than those traditionally recognized. Besides old and new ones we now recognize tendentiousness where formal contradictions would be hard to prove. The old problems of harmonization [of the Gospels], the new ones, and the merely tendentious items fall into patterns that permeate Matthew's gospel. Taken together and related to comparable Jewish literature of the

New Testament era, these phenomena provide cumulative evidence much stronger than did the old, isolated problems of harmonization taken by themselves—evidence that Matthew often embellished and otherwise changed the historical facts. Such changes suggest not that he was making historical mistakes (and if not, the term "discrepancies" applies only under the wrong assumption that he was always trying to write historically) but that he was taking homiletical liberties with Mark and Q [a source from which Matthew and Luke might have drawn when writing their Gospels] much as Jewish midrashists of his era took homiletical liberties with the Old Testament.[17]

What infuriated Hymers most was Gundry's suggestion that Matthew's alleged edits, embellishments, and imaginative expansions of the historical data were divinely inspired. Gundry states plainly that whatever liberties the author of Matthew took, the Spirit of Christ directed the editing flawlessly and infallibly. Filled with hot, righteous anger, Hymers exclaimed to his audience, "Thus, Dr. Gundry says that the Holy Spirit led Matthew to lie. I find that reprehensible!"

Apparently Hymers has done a little of his own embellishment and imaginative extension of Professor Gundry's words. Strictly speaking, Gundry neither said nor meant to say that the Holy Spirit led Matthew to lie. The professor's point was that Matthew and other ancient writers embellished their stories much as a stanza of an old Christmas song tells of the three kings from afar returning home by the light of the brilliant star that had earlier guided them, with their gold, myrrh, and frankincense, to the Lord of Angels.

There are problems with Dr. Gundry's position, just as there are problems with the positions of his rivals. My purpose here is not to decide which one is the most adequate but to throw light on the whole, bitter controversy. It cannot be overemphasized that Gundry's evangelical and fundamentalist opponents are genuinely and desperately worried about the slippery slope that they think he has stepped onto. With equal earnestness, Gundry is worried that the evangelicals and fundamentalists will impose unrealistic expectations upon the Bible, distorting and undermining the sacred truth they care so much about.

The following question is one that scholars like Gundry have to deal with sooner or later: Could the author of the Gospel of Matthew have incorporated the tale of the Magi if he had known that it was not a literal report of an event that happened at a specific time in a specific place? A similar question might be asked about the story of George Washington and the cherry tree. Some historians believe that a Presbyterian minister invented it for children for a specific moral purpose, namely, to encourage them to follow the moral example of the nation's founding father. Apparently, the minister honestly believed that Washington was a man who would not tell a lie even to rescue himself from shame and humiliation. The minister thought the cherry tree story was typical of a man like Washington, even though it might not have been an actual historical incident. Indeed, there is precious little historical information about the childhood of Washington, just as there is precious little about the childhood of Jesus.

In a homecoming address to the alumni of Westmont College, Gundry offered a revealing explanation of his controversial view:

> In Jewish literature written after the close of the Old Testament and up through the time of the New Testament, various authors took liberties with the data of the Old Testament. Where the text of Genesis has only God's command that Abraham take a journey throughout the Promised Land, one author creates a whole journey in order to make Abraham a good example of obedience. The author even details the particular places that Abraham visited. The first century Jewish historian Josephus includes stories about Moses' boyhood that we have no reason to think had any historical basis. He even makes the grownup Moses into the general of the Egyptian army who leads them out to defeat a horde of Ethiopians. To avoid a bad example of lying, another Jewish author changes Jacob's false statement to his father, Isaac, "I am Esau," into the truthful statement "I am your son." Yet another Jewish author of the period does what many a modern preacher does but what the biblical text neither mentions nor denies, i.e., he makes Isaac offer himself willingly when Abraham starts to sacrifice him at God's command.
>
> In fact, these and other ancient Jewish authors were doing what practically every contemporary evangelical does in handling the biblical text. They were dressing it up, changing it here and there, updating it in another place, inserting an imaginary conversation or event or detail in yet another place—all to make the text more applicable, more emphatic, more contemporary. Think of present-day preachers (and Sunday school teachers and

Young Life leaders) who have made Daniel so trustful in the lion's
den that he slept on a lion's mane all night, or who made up
whole conversations between the serpent and Adam and Eve in
the Garden of Eden or between the devil and Jesus in the temptation stories. . . .

Remember that, if nothing else, the parables show that not
everything that happened on the pages of the Bible happened in
history.

Toward the end of his address, Professor Gundry stated that the
Gospels were written the way that preachers preach, not the way
scholars do research. Apparently he meant that preachers take liberties with historical data that scholars are forbidden to take in their
journals on pain of being severely criticized.

Contemporary embellishments may be found in the preaching of
Texas evangelist James Robison. He has stated, for example, that Jesus
never drank alcohol. Most specialists in ancient Greek hold that the
translators of the New Testament were perfectly correct to translate
the word "oinos" as "wine," which is what Jesus is reported to have
drunk. According to Matthew 11:19, Jesus was accused of being an
irresponsible "winebibber" (KJV). The charge would have been pointless had Jesus been simply a grape-juicebibber. Robison, nevertheless,
did not lie when he said Jesus never drank alcohol. Most Greek ex-
perts would say that Robison was simply in error.

It is important to see how Robison arrived at his embellishment.
First, he held that Jesus was the perfect man in every way. Second, he
held that drinking alcohol cannot be a part of the perfect life. Given
those premises, it follows that Jesus could not have drunk wine. Some
biblical scholars hold that the story of Jesus' birth was deduced from
similar premises, one of which being that the perfect man would have
had a miraculous entrance into the world, such as a virgin birth. The
fundamentalist scholar J. Gresham Machen wrote a masterful work on
the virgin birth, in which he thought it necessary to show where the
accounts of Jesus' birth differ from those of the miraculous births of
such men as Plato, Alexander the Great, and Apollonius. The Jewish
writer Philo, a contemporary of Paul the Apostle, wrote a detailed account of Moses' life by drawing material from the elders of the Jewish
people and combining putative oral reports with written material.
Most contemporary scholars regard Philo's account to be full of embellishments. Philo apparently believed them to be factual, although his

concept of factual may not have been completely identical to that of contemporary critical historians.

Sportscaster John Madden has mastered the art of verbalizing what he thinks players on the field are thinking or saying to themselves during the game. Not everyone could give as plausible an account because few people have had Madden's experience as both player and coach. What he offers is a typical monologue (sometimes a dialogue) in an idealized version that edits out the profanity. Gundry believes that Matthew gives an idealized picture of the disciples, whereas Mark does not. "Throughout the gospel of Matthew the disciples look much more knowledgeable than they do in Mark, where they constantly look stupid."

Anyone who hears evangelists tell the same graphic story more than once can easily observe that some of them are quite free with narrative embellishments, not because they are liars but because they are speaking evangelistically. Instead of purporting to offer 100-percent accuracy in the story, they are attempting to make a theological or moral point that they consider more important than perfect historical detail. According to Gundry, sometimes a sermon is careful and exact, sometimes free and creative—and both preachers and audiences swing from one to the other with little difficulty. "And there are," Gundry adds, "many different degrees of exactness and creativity. . . . Inspiration and inerrancy do not rule out creativity any more than they demand scientific exactness."

The dispute over inerrancy will go on. How Southern Baptists will resolve it politically depends on the options open to them. They most certainly will not arrive at conformity of opinion on this issue. Paige Patterson, who also attended the society meeting at which Robert Gundry was expelled, has raised several useful questions at various times: If the story of the three wise men is an embellishment, then is the story of Jesus' virgin birth an embellishment too? Going a step farther, was the resurrection of Christ simply the invention of pious, goodwilled Christians? Did Christ's teaching not originate with him? In short, where is the line to be drawn between the historical core and the pious inventions of imaginative writers of the first century? Is the whole thing an embellishment? These are sane and honest questions that cannot be ignored by modern-day Christians. Equally sane and honest are the questions that Robert Gundry, T. C. Smith (one of Southern Baptists' most rigorous New Testament scholars), and a large company of other Southern Baptist scholars have raised for evangelicals and fundamentalists like Paige Patterson and W. A. Criswell to face without resorting to political ploys. A purely political answer will no longer suffice in this momentous battle about the Bible.

6.

The Resurgence of Conservative Christianity

hristianity has always had a love-hate relationship with the world. According to the first chapter of Genesis, God created the world in stages and pronounced each as good. According to II Peter and Revelation, however, the world will eventually be dissolved in flames. America's foremost early Calvinist, Jonathan Edwards (1703–1758), had a love affair with the lush woodlands of New England and from there paved the way for a buoyant optimism that saw the frontier as an extension of an ideal Christendom. For at least a hundred years after Edwards's death, evangelical preachers remained exuberant in their visions of Americans as God's new chosen people. Pulpits rang with the praises of America as the new Israel, serving as a light and model to all the nations of the world.

Alongside the glowing optimism emerged a fundamentalist movement skeptical of the prospects for bringing the Kingdom of God to earth through preaching and reform movements. Before the second half of the nineteenth century, Protestant Christianity on the whole tended to look upon science as a co-laborer with theology in searching out the great mysteries of God's special revelation (the Bible) and general revelation (nature and history). Then Charles Darwin's bomb changed everything for many earnest believers, leaving them confused and angry. Feeling that in Darwin and his followers science had betrayed both itself and true religion, some of those believers resolved to fight back in defense of their orthodox Christian faith.

Simultaneously, the historical-critical method rose rapidly in the study of Scripture. Tradition had designated Moses as the author of the first five books of the Bible, but the new biblical scholarship began

to view the Pentateuch as a quilt of diverse pieces composed by unknown writers and stitched together over many years by unknown
editors and redactors. Believing they could read the ominous handwriting on the wall, one group of Christians deliberately organized a
resistance movement against Darwinism, the old evangelical optimism about America and the world, and the new method for studying
Scripture. Their resistance movement was early fundamentalism.

THREE CONTEMPORARY STYLES OF CONSERVATIVE CHRISTIANITY

In the United States today, conservative Christianity includes
roughly three groups: evangelicals, fundamentalists, and noncreedal
conservatives. Even though Southern Baptists harbor all three groups,
each can be distinguished from the others. Evangelicals and fundamentalists are alike in insisting on strict theological orthodoxy and
embracing a deductive creedalistic statement of it. It is common to
hear that fundamentalism has narrowed the list of fundamental doctrines down to five: Christ's virgin birth, the infallibility of Scripture,
Christ's death as the substitutionary atonement for sin, Christ's physical resurrection, and Christ's physical return to earth. The list is arbitrarily short, as any such list would be. Nevertheless, fundamentalism in particular tends toward building a creed of articles for the
purpose of marking off true Christianity from imitators.

Evangelicals regard modern fundamentalists as unduly preoccup-
pied with predicting the last days of the world, too exclusivistic, and
in recent decades too anti-intellectual. Evangelicals tend to believe
that throughout the centuries various theologians have made significant contributions to the explication and systematization of Christian
doctrine. By contrast, modern fundamentalists tend to view most of
church history after the first century as the process of corrupting the
clear and explicit teachings of the Bible.

Whereas fundamentalists are inclined to regard as non-Christian
those who do not hold to all the fundamentals, evangelicals are prepared to say that Christians can harbor error or inconsistency in at
least some of their beliefs without ceasing to be Christians. There is an
exclusiveness in fundamentalism that evangelicalism struggles to escape. There is also a clear antidemocratic and anti-intellectual side to
hyperfundamentalism that cannot be attributed to evangelicalism at
its best.

THE NONCREEDAL CONSERVATIVES

No profound understanding of Southern Baptists is possible without an understanding of their noncreedal conservativism, which at first glance might appear to be evangelicalism under another name. That appearance is deceptive, for although noncreedal conservatives hold to most of the five fundamentals (and many other fundamentals), they do so in a distinctive way. Or more accurately, they hold that evangelicals and fundamentalists are often superficially precise in formulating doctrinal statements. To say that Christ rose bodily from the grave is one thing. To specify the precise sense in which the resurrected body was physical is another. The noncreedal conservative scholars tend to be cautious in attributing twentieth-century categories to biblical texts.

Not that they slavishly follow Rudolf Bultmann and those existential scholars who sometimes translate the New Testament events into symbols or social phenomena. As a noncreedal conservative, Russell Dilday makes it clear that there is a point beyond which he cannot go in precision of interpretation and understanding of biblical texts. The numerous noncreedal conservatives among Southern Baptists do not come from a background of mysticism but rather from what they regard as one of common sense and disciplined restraint. To press beyond a certain point of precision is, for them, to venture into the realm of self-contradiction under the flag of piety. Fundamentalist Jimmy Draper, in searching for the smallest list of doctrines possible to serve as a Southern Baptist creed, includes Christ's "literal bodily ascension into heaven." Evangelicals and fundamentalists sometimes like to say that Christ's resurrection was literal and bodily, so that had audiovisual technology been available in the first century, the resurrection of Jesus could have been recorded. Noncreedal conservatives might ask Draper if he means to imply that Jesus could have been filmed as he entered a physical heaven where presumably he now grows a physical beard and fingernails. Or pressing for more precision, one might ask about the fish that Jesus ate after the resurrection. Did it become glorified, since it became a part of Christ's glorified body? Is there a difference between ordinary protein and glorified protein? In what sense are they physically alike? If Jesus was physically on earth forty days after the resurrection, did he urinate? Was the urine glorified, since it too had been a part of Christ's glorified body?

Noncreedal conservatives look upon evangelicals and fundamentalists as somewhat naive in their relentless push for still another degree of precision in creedalism. Noncreedal conservatives speak of the death of Christ rather than dwelling on the spilled blood. Many fundamentalists seem to veer off into an alchemy of blood as the magical essence of sacrifice and atonement. They use the phrase "the blood of Christ" frequently and ritualistically in their sermons and are suspicious of ministers who do not.

Southern Baptist fundamentalists have followed Jerry Falwell's politics and interpretation of Scripture almost blindly, but the noncreedal conservative Southern Baptists tend to regard Falwell as a mediocre student of the Bible. They regard his prooftexts against abortion as superficial reactions hastily advanced without benefit of scholarly debate. While uncomfortable with abortion, they are far from agreeing with the fundamentalists who brand abortion as premediated murder. Falwell is on record as advocating capital punishment in cases of premeditated murder. His premises force the conclusion that women who have abortions and physicians and nurses who perform abortions should be prosecuted and executed by the State. Whether Falwell is consistent in following his premises to their logical conclusion remains to be seen. The careful study of the abortion question done by faculty members of the Southwestern Baptist Theological Seminary reveals just how far removed these noncreedal conservatives are from modern fundamentalists like Jerry Falwell.

Because of their empirical approach to the Bible, noncreedal conservatives are not easily taken in by theological fads or charismatic preachers. Although conservative in theology, they do not share the fundamentalist and evangelical knee-jerk reaction to liberal scholarship. With an air of self-confidence that comes from understanding their Baptist roots and traditions, noncreedal conservatives are able to learn from fundamentalists and liberals alike. They are catholic but not Catholic. Even though they are not fundamentalists, liberals, or charismatics, they are prepared to make room for those groups within the Convention and to interact with them.

J. FRANK NORRIS AND MODERN FUNDAMENTALISM

Evangelicals have done academic battle with the theory of evolution, but it was largely fundamentalists who fought politically to prevent evolution from being studied in American public schools. Unlike either evangelicals or noncreedal conservatives, American fundamentalists tend to associate themselves with the political right wing and to label as liberal anything to the left of themselves. Extreme fundamentalists appear to make few clear distinctions among liberalism, socialism, and communism. Evangelicals, on the other hand, are more sophisticated in classifying views and people. In some respects, modern fundamentalism is an evangelicalism that has pulled away from conservatism to embrace the right wing.

Ordinarily, fundamentalists are led by men with an extraordinary gift of charisma, males who inspire incredible loyalty and often considerable hostility. One of the most exaggerated and bizarre examples of a forceful fundamentalist preacher was J. Frank Norris, who was eventually expelled from the Pastors' Conference at Fort Worth in 1914 because he had constantly attacked the character of some of his fellow Southern Baptist ministers. In 1926 he shot and killed an unarmed man at the church, declaring that he thought the man had come to attack him. For some reason, Norris detested George W. Truett, the First Baptist Church minister who immediately preceded W. A. Criswell. For several Sunday mornings, Norris sent snide telegrams to the popular Truett, making certain that each arrived just before Truett left his study to go to the pulpit. During the McCarthy days, Norris saw red under every liberal bed. (He was buried wearing a red tie in 1952.) In 1927 his church building burned to the ground, but arson was never proved. In the current Convention controversy, no one equals Norris in the capacity to smear opponents and misrepresent what they believe, but in a June 1985 address at the Pastors' Conference, Criswell came close when he denounced Baptist seminary professors as infidels.

In the forties and fifties Norris charged that Southern Baptists were growing too centralized and that the denominational leaders had too much power. At the same time, he was building an empire with himself as undisputed head. As early as 1936 fundamentalist evangelist John R. Rice broke ties with Norris because of his dictatorial policies.[1] While proclaiming that the Holy Spirit was the only true superintendent of the churches, Norris succeeded in convincing his followers that the Holy Spirit was especially prone to work through the local church pastor rather than through denominational bureaucrats. Referred to often as the Texas Cyclone, Norris was not above regarding the misfortune of his enemies as God's wrathful visitation upon them. A district attorney who had pressed charges against Norris died in a violent traffic accident in Fort Worth. With a taste for the sensational and macabre, Norris denounced the attorney from the pulpit and declared the accident to be a divine act of retribution.[2]

As Norris's movement increased in bitterness and factionalism, it only occasionally erupted into violence. In Jonesboro, Arkansas, a factional fight over who controlled the First Baptist Church brought out the national guard. When Joe Jeffers, a member of Norris's fundamentalist cohorts, was taken to the city hall, he asked for permission to pray. Upon receiving permission, he proceeded to call for lightning to strike down the mayor. A fistfight broke out. Two years later fundamentalist preacher Dale Crowley killed a man in a dispute over control of the Jonesboro church. In 1947 another minister wrote Norris and charged wildly that the modernists had "burnt my great church."[3]

The major split in Norris's own denomination (Fundamentalist Baptist Missionary Fellowship) came in 1950, when G. Beauchamp Vick, who had been groomed to receive Norris's mantle, gathered a group of preachers around him to stage a revolt against their leader, who kept postponing his retirement. They attacked Norris on the same grounds that he had attacked Southern Baptists—the centralization of power.[4]

The feud between Norris and Vick sank to a bitter haranguing contest, Norris accusing Vick's daughter of adultery and exposing another affair between one of Vick's men and a cabdriver's wife. In addition he offered evidence that one Vick supporter had committed sodomy with a thirteen-year-old boy. Norris's obvious aim was to discredit his former friend and copastor as well as the new fundamentalist movement by portraying Vick as a man surrounded by moral perverts instead of dedicated Bible-believing leaders.

In 1956 Luther Peak, a fundamentalist pastor and president of Norris's seminary, led his Dallas church out of the Norris camp and returned to the Southern Baptist fold. In the April 7, 1956, issue of *Baptist Standard*, he wrote, "In the Fundamentalist Movement we were usually in a fight of some kind. If we were not fighting Southern Baptists, Northern Baptists, the National Council of Churches, the Catholics, Communism or Modernism, we fought each other." He had earlier charged that it would be impossible to find a more dictatorial machine than fundamentalism itself.[5] In the same year, Norris's fundamentalist colleague A. Reilly Copeland, in a racist article entitled "Black Heart or Red Signal?" charged that the Communists were behind the National Association for the Advancement of Colored People and warned that if the NAACP got its way, there would be no "superior race."[6] When Southwestern Seminary's ethics professor Thomas B. Maston and several prominent Southern Baptists (not including W. A. Criswell) came out in support of integration and political and social equality for Negroes, they became targets of bitter verbal abuse from fundamentalist leaders.[7] As late as the sixties fundamentalist preacher Jerry Falwell had no supportive words for fellow Baptist minister Martin Luther King, Jr. Instead, he attacked Christians for becoming involved in politics. Today Falwell thinks a fertilized human egg is a person as surely as the blacks of South Africa are, and he has devoted great energy to portraying himself as the defender of the zygote's civil rights. He does not believe, however, that this civil rights movement of the eighties is Communist inspired.

Fundamentalism in America has been cursed with the inveterate use of invective. New York fundamentalist preacher John Roach Straton once said that the New York liberal preacher Harry Emmerson Fosdick was too dangerous to be at large and ought to be locked up in jail.[8] Fundamentalist stalwart W. B. Riley, who persuaded young Billy Graham to become president of his Northwestern Bible Schools in 1947, once became so enraged with Norris that he called him "a moral leper and the most inordinate liar living. No crime he has not committed—murder included."[9] Another fundamentalist bulwark and longtime friend of Norris's, T. T. Shields, wrote that "we know of no living man who can talk more nonsense in five minutes on world affairs than Dr. Norris."[10]

After breaking away from Norris, Beauchamp Vick and his supporters organized the Baptist Bible Fellowship in the early fifties and opened the Baptist Bible College in Springfield, Missouri. Norris, in his paper *The Fundamentalist*, venomously accused Vick of being a man who was "boastful and conceited, . . . who believed that he could step in and set aside God's servant and take over a movement that God himself established."[11]

Meanwhile, Vick and the Baptist Bible Fellowship had not given up attacking Southern Baptists. The first editor of the new group's publication, *Baptist Bible Tribune,* was Noel Smith, former editor of *The Fundamentalist.* With unflagging zeal Smith attacked the Convention's Cooperative Program; his covetous glances toward the money going into Southern Baptist colleges and seminaries were not too cleverly disguised. The *Baptist Bible Tribune* also attacked Billy Graham, a Southern Baptist, as "one of the most compromising, irresponsible evangelists this country has ever known."[12]

In the fifties one of the graduates of Vick's Baptist Bible College was a young man destined to reach national fame beyond that of any of his Springfield teachers or classmates. His name was Jerry Falwell.

THE CHARGE OF LIBERALISM

Harold Lindsell asserts, "In almost every case, unorthodoxy has its beginnings in the theological seminaries."[13] Paige Patterson believes that liberalism has taken over every Southern Baptist seminary, with the possible exception of his alma mater, the New Orleans Baptist Theological Seminary. Some of Patterson's critics charge that he represents the new creeping fundamentalism bent on turning all Southern Baptist seminaries into bastions of Criswellian fundamentalism, with *The Criswell Study Bible* becoming the paragon of exegesis and Criswell's book *Why I Preach that the Bible Is Literally True*[14] as the lighthouse to guide all Southern Baptist ministerial students.

With a Doctor of Philosophy degree from Oxford and a master's from the New Orleans Seminary, Richard Land, vice president of academic affairs at the Criswell Center, describes himself as an evangelical. He will identify himself with fundamentalism so long as the word is not spelled with a capital F. President Roy Honeycutt of the seminary in Louisville also sometimes calls himself a small-f fundamentalist. Patterson and Land nevertheless insist that Honeycutt is a liberal, which Honeycutt flatly denies.

In some respects the most heated battle among Southern Baptists is the battle for words. Most Southern Baptists would wish to be called fundamentalist, if by it one means adherence to fundamental values and beliefs. No one in his right mind is going to say that what he believes is not basic and fundamental.

Both Honeycutt and Land hold to the five fundamentals listed earlier, although Honeycutt is a noncreedal conservative and Land is an evangelical. When each man denies being a capital-F Fundamentalist, he is trying to dissociate himself from men like J. Frank Norris, who relentlessly attacked the motives of theological opponents and sought to weed out of the Southern Baptist Convention all who did not follow his version of fundamentalist doctrine. Land and Honeycutt have upon occasion, in moments of ordinary human weakness, attacked the motives of their opponents, but that is not their normal style. Unfortunately, if the holy war among Southern Baptists continues, as it clearly will, such lapses can be expected to increase.

Land has moved in the direction of J. Frank Norris by resolving to weed out of the seminary faculties all who do not subscribe to the tenets of orthodoxy. Unlike Norris, he would not try to weed noninerrantists out of all Southern Baptist churches, since he adheres to the policy of the relative autonomy of the local church.

Dr. Land is also more Fundamentalist than evangelical when he labels people like Honeycutt as liberals. Honeycutt embraces so many doctrines of historic orthodox Christianity that it is misleading to classify him as a liberal. It is one thing to argue that Honeycutt's view of the inspiration of the Bible would lead to liberalism if carried out to its conclusion, but it is another to show that Honeycutt has explicitly embraced theological liberalism. Making that distinction opens the door for people like Land and Honeycutt to debate the charge that a noninerrancy view of Scripture leads to liberal theology. Perhaps Land is correct in his charge. It needs, however, to be demonstrated and not carelessly asserted. Southern Baptist scholars know that the word "liberalism" elicits a knee-jerk response from many laypeople. Scholarly dialogue should rise above such appeals.

It would be misleading to say that Jerry Falwell personally holds that anyone who has an abortion or assists in an abortion ought to be executed. As far as I can determine, Falwell has never drawn the conclusion of his premises and advocated putting to death everyone directly involved in abortion, and therefore it would be inaccurate to attribute the conclusion to him. His arguments must be heard out to discover whether he wishes either to introduce some intervening rules to prevent the conclusion from being drawn or to simply make an exception to his premises without giving any justifying reason. The point here is that Fundamentalism tends to draw conclusions from the premises advanced by others and then to give the impression that those others drew the same conclusions secretly even though they never admitted to doing so.

Every attempt to define Christian fundamentalism must eventually deal with the collection of twelve scholarly works published between 1910 and 1915 under the broad title *The Fundamentals*.[15] Among the works may be found James Orr's forceful defense of the virgin birth of Jesus, the authority of Scripture against modern negations, and supernatural revelation.

After the Scopes trial of 1925, the term "fundamentalism" became synonymous with anti-intellectualism, even though the scholarly writers of *The Fundamentals* were far from anti-intellectual. Unfortunately, their modern heirs have often made it clear that they are hard set against educational institutions in which various schools of thought can be explored. Even the call for equal time between creationism and evolution serves more to thwart the study of evolution than to advance the academic study of creationism. Although fundamentalist creationists may disagree among themselves on the political issue of teaching evolution in the schools, they seem to agree on failing to call for a systematic and careful study of the various doctrines of creationism in the public schools. They want evolution to be studied as a theory (as it should be), but they reject the proposal to study creationism as a theory (as it should be).

Currently, fundamentalists hold to the inerrancy of the Bible. The authors of *The Fundamentals*, however, were not all inerrantists of one camp only. Even though unquestionably orthodox in his theology, James Orr rejected inerrancy and debated with B. B. Warfield, the Princeton scholar, on the issue of inerrancy. In his approach to the Bible, Orr was often closer to the noncreedal conservatives than to contemporary fundamentalists or evangelicals. Some evangelicals claim Orr as one of their own, but other evangelicals are ambivalent about his approach to the Bible. In his works on authority Russell Dilday, president of the Southwestern Baptist Theological Seminary, shows that he has been profoundly influenced by Orr's view of biblical authority. I will return to Orr in a later chapter.

7.

The Crisis of Southern Baptist Education

LINDSELL'S PURGE

Harold Lindsell has been forthright in exposing the fact that the majority of Southern Baptist religion professors do not subscribe to inerrancy. He has been less than forthright in exposing in print what specifically he and his comrades would do about the professors and Southern Baptist educational institutions if the Inerrancy Party should come to dominate the Convention. Would they fire the professors and replace them with Lamar Cooper and others from the Criswell Center and similar strongholds of inerrancy? In a March 1, 1985, interview with me Lindsell finally said plainly that he would like to see most of the Southern Baptist seminary professors fired along with the seminary presidents. He denounced the seminary trustees for lacking "the guts" to dismiss them. Clearly, nothing less than a sweeping purge will satisfy him and those who have joined forces with him. In *The Battle for the Bible*, the final sentence of Lindsell's chapter on Southern Baptists states that the rejection of inerrancy is a "disease now eating at the vitals of the Convention," a disease of which the patient should be "cured." Repeatedly he refers to the spreading "infection" that sooner or later will require a "showdown."[1]

THE HOTHOUSE MODEL

In 1984 Zig Ziglar, as first vice president of the Southern Baptist Convention, made it clear that he thinks the gift of teaching religion courses at a Baptist university entails the gift of classroom evangelism. He writes, "An enthusiastic born-again professor teaching the biblical claims of Christ in his religion classroom should regularly win converts to Christ." Ziglar would like parents to ask religion professors on Baptist campuses, "How many students have you led to Christ in the last twelve months?"[2]

Some Southern Baptists appear to subscribe to the hothouse model for their colleges and seminaries. They view young people as tender plants that must be cultivated and protected from foreign elements that threaten to infect them. In his 1957 tome on American Catholicism and Protestantism, Kenneth W. Underwood points out that for many years a number of Roman Catholic leaders in the United States wanted their own parochial schools for at least three reasons: to isolate Catholic children from Protestants and others, to instill into Catholic children an uncontested, uncritical version of Roman Catholic faith and history, and to provide the children with an unchallenged and slanted version of Protestantism.[3] Some of the Catholic caricatures of Baptists, Jews, and especially Lutherans were as distorted and filled with half-truths as Tim LaHaye's caricatures of humanism, which has become a new scapegoat for such TV preachers as Falwell, Pat Robertson, Oral Roberts, and LaHaye. Catholic scholars eventually began to criticize the hothouse model of their Catholic schools, arguing that Catholic young people were being systematically misinformed about their Protestant and Jewish neighbors.

Whether embraced by Catholics, Baptists, or Mormons, the hothouse model tends to treat education as a dangerous exposure to infectious viruses of the mind. According to the model, teachers should be gardeners of the mind, employed to protect students from direct contact with views that do not adhere to the party line. Some Southern Baptist leaders appear to be like those members of the Mormon hierarchy who remain suspicious of teachers who allow rival ideas to enter the classroom or textbook. When it goes beyond indoctrination, education is viewed as evil, as an aggressive act comparable either to exposing defenseless children to the polio virus or to placing delicate houseplants outside in a hailstorm.

Few Southern Baptists would consciously agree with the American psychologist B. F. Skinner, who not only denies free will but also contends that human beings are largely the product of conditioning through contingencies of reinforcement. In practice, however, some Southern Baptists subscribe to Skinner's behaviorism, despite their talk about the age of accountability or human freedom and dignity. They appear to want to apply the principles of behaviorism to Baptist schools by turning them into little more than centers of party-line conditioning and programming. They want to approximate a total environment, in which no alien ideas will be admitted. In computer terminology, they want strict control of every input into the students' minds, programming them to exemplify a predictable set of beliefs and responses.

Judge Paul Pressler of Houston apparently had something like the hothouse model in mind when he sent out a June 18, 1980, letter in support of removing Professor Jack Flanders from Baylor University's religion department. He stated that if the university's trustees did not remove Flanders (who does not embrace the inerrancy of the Bible), then the issue would be brought before the Baptist General Convention of Texas. The judge is usually more ambivalent about the Southern Baptist professors who do not subscribe to the doctrine of inerrancy; he wants to let them keep their jobs but constrain them severely so that their influence on campus will be choked off. He likens himself to a doctor who has "diagnosed the fact that the patient has a minor cancer that needs to be cut out," but his treatment could quickly become major surgery. One of the tumors in the Southern Baptist institutional body is, for Pressler, none other than Roy Honeycutt, president of the Southern Baptists' oldest seminary. The grounds on which Pressler apparently wants to remove Honeycutt from the seminary are the same grounds that might logically apply to all but a handful at Southern Seminary in Louisville. If Pressler's measuring rod of inerrancy were used, the Southeastern Seminary theology faculty in North Carolina would be practically vacated, and Southwestern Seminary in Fort Worth might be driven into decades of internecine conflict. Golden Gate Seminary would become demoralized, and the seminary faculty members at New Orleans would have to carry out their work under intolerable conditions of intimidation.

Paige Patterson and Jimmy Draper talk at times as if they had no interest in purging Baylor University or any other Southern Baptist school. If they are in reality breaking with Paul Pressler on the issue, they need to make it abundantly clear as soon as possible. With Pressler, there can be no compromise. Like Lindsell and Ziglar, Pressler appears to want no one to have full freedom to teach religion on Southern Baptist campuses unless he or she openly embraces the doctrine of inerrancy.

In a 1985 article titled "Standing Firm," William Powell appears to want Jack Flanders fired from Baylor because he believes in progressive revelation. But that would prevent fundamentalist Jimmy Draper from teaching there, too, since Draper also embraces the principle of progressive revelation. One Southern Baptist Seminary professor thinks all the shifting back and forth on the question of firing or not firing professors is political rhetoric. A consistent tactic of attempting to fire tenured professors could, he believes, involve Southern Baptists in a series of lawsuits, which the Inerrancy Party leaders are eager to avoid. Instead, he charges, the inconsistency within the Inerrancy Party regarding the firing of professors, missionaries, and denominational officers is a tactic of control by intimidation. Paige Patterson answers that he does not want to intimidate anyone but is simply tired of paying money to professors whose teaching undermines what he believes in. The professors reply that far from trying to undermine the Christian faith, they are trying to teach it with understanding while contributing to the students' broader education and training.

THE FREE MARKETPLACE MODEL

All responsible parents wish to protect their children from ideas that might overwhelm them. Somewhere along the way, however, their offspring must graduate to become more or less independent adults.

Paige Patterson and Richard Land make it crystal clear that they want no one on the faculty of the Criswell Bible College and Graduate School of the Bible who does not embrace the epistemology of the Bible's inerrancy. To justify their part in Criswell's indoctrination center in downtown Dallas, Land and Patterson insist that they are doing only what a large percentage of Southern Baptist people want them to do.

Clearly no friend of Baptist higher education, W. A. Criswell resigned from Baylor University's board of trustees in 1961 because the university would not be reduced to a center of indoctrination. In the tradition of J. Frank Norris, he tried to persuade the Baptist General Convention of Texas to pressure Baylor University's administrators to force all faculty members to sign a document rejecting the theory of evolution. After failing to intimidate Baylor's faculty, the relentless Criswell succeeded in getting his document accepted at the Dallas Baptist University, where he was chairman of the board of trustees. The eight faculty members who refused to sign the document were forced to find work elsewhere.

Some Southern Baptists have of late become hostile to the model of the free marketplace of ideas. Even when appealing for a balance of opinion, or equal time, they seem to be paying lip service to the principle only to get their own views admitted to an arena where previously they had been excluded.

Jimmy Draper insists that Baptist schools should be centers of education rather than fortresses of indoctrination. Instead of being a free marketplace of ideas, an indoctrination fortress is like the company store in the old mining towns. The selections in the store were severely restricted, and the signs of a heavy-handed monopoly were evident everywhere. To be sure, where there is a free marketplace of ideas, there is also the risk of going out of business because a rival has enticed customers away with a better deal. In the free marketplace of manifest religious beliefs, Southern Baptists have been remarkably competitive and successful. In the arena of education, however, a number of them have lost their nerve. Terrified of direct competition, they want to turn as many of their schools as possible into fortresses where rival views are colored and filtered by party-line indoctrinators hired to guarantee that Baptist students will be introduced to only a minimum of foreign ideas. If direct challenges to the party line cannot be kept away from the students, then those challenges can at least be slanted and interpreted so that the students will never be tempted to read unapproved authors firsthand. Some Baptists actually want the students to develop severe reactions to education, viewing it as a temptation to be resisted rather than as a goal to pursue for the rest of their lives. In such a framework, the desire for education is treated as sinful lust, as wickedness to be overcome.

BRAINWASHING AND INDOCTRINATION
VERSUS EDUCATION

Not all brainwashing takes place behind literal prison walls. For children, it takes place in the home and at school. Parents and elementary schoolteachers are understandably reluctant to admit that to a degree they brainwash children, but the fact is that almost every culture and subculture attempts to brainwash its very young by indoctrinating them within one dominate framework (with its network of beliefs and values) and by sheltering them from every alien framework that severely rivals the dominant group's.

A truly educational environment must nurture a twofold freedom that allows individuals to learn a variety of viewpoints and to acquire and use the tools of critical evaluation of each viewpoint without exception. The freedom essential to education is political, social, and psychological. To the degree that individuals are denied such freedom, their environment may be labeled as a brainwashing process.

Indoctrination is the goal of the brainwashing environment. By contrast, indoctrination may serve as a means or stage in the educational process even though it cannot be education's highest goal. Usually indoctrination narrows the range of learning to the inculcation of one viewpoint. If other viewpoints are studied at all, it is not for the purpose of seeing what can be learned from them. The indoctrination process tends to distort and misrepresent rival viewpoints, if it represents them at all, because the social and political freedom to challenge those in charge of instruction has not been cultivated. The best way to overcome the limits of indoctrination is to invite the proponents of rival viewpoints to speak directly for themselves. Indoctrination does not willingly give a platform to rival viewpoints. Education must give them a platform and ideally will create an environment where lively and rigorous criticism of every viewpoint flows freely.

THE PARADOX OF INTENSIVE INDOCTRINATION

When carried out with intensity and rigor, indoctrination can have a paradoxical effect. If the teacher wants nothing more than effective indoctrination of the student, then that, rather than education, is the ultimate goal. Often, however, the teacher indoctrinates with the goal of education in mind, indoctrination then serving as a step toward it. Sometimes, the teacher who pursues indoctrination alone as the goal cannot control the consequences, and all his labor in indoctrination becomes a means to the students' education. That point will be spelled out shortly, but first more should be said about the sort of indoctrination that never develops into education.

When the teacher succeeds in making indoctrination an end in itself, the students become so thoroughly entrenched in one framework that they will never be able to step imaginatively inside another to see why its beliefs and values are meaningful to those who subscribe to it. It is as if the students carry a portable prison with them wherever they journey, guaranteeing that they remain incapable of exploring another intellectual terrain even temporarily. They may talk confidently about other frames of reference, but in reality they cannot intellectually step into another and learn to think within it. If the indoctrination process has been effective, the subjects will experience a kind of terror at the thought of even temporarily understanding other beliefs.

Their terror should not be ridiculed. It is genuine, for in the final analysis education is a risky and unpredictable venture. To understand views from within a rival frame of reference is to run the risk of doubting some of the beliefs within the home-base framework. The design of indoctrination as an end in itself is to make it psychologically impossible for the subjects to view beliefs from any perspective or bias other than the favored one.

Education will suffer severely if confused with an evangelism designed to instill indoctrination as an end in itself. Zig Ziglar and Paul Pressler are anti-intellectuals if they fail to grasp fully that elementary point. It is not the function of education to pressure students to surrender their own convictions. Whereas evangelism stresses exchanging one's basic beliefs for another set, education stresses primarily the understanding of each belief within its home framework. What some Baptists want from their educators is nothing other than additional indoctrination in one framework only. The idea of understanding another viewpoint is perceived as betrayal, as opening the way to a disease or infection, to use Harold Lindsell's metaphor.

Paradoxically, intensive indoctrination sometimes leads students over the walls of the portable prison and toward objective inquiry. If individuals happen upon an environment that is intellectually open and stimulating, their indoctrination may turn into a powerful asset, advancing them on their intellectual journey. This twist is nothing mysterious. Far from growing in a vacuum, thinking develops only against a background of beliefs. If individuals have been intensely indoctrinated, they possess a richer-than-ordinary tradition to serve them in their intellectual growth. If and when they do learn to think within a variety of frames of reference, their new understanding will possess depth just because they had once been thoroughly indoctrinated. If they are able to advance beyond the point of indoctrination only, the disadvantage of rigorous indoctrination will become a powerful advantage, for then their comparative study of various points of view will rise above superficial polemics.

FEAR AND DISTRUST

Southern Baptists are at war over their colleges and seminaries for one principle reason: fear of one another. When asked point-blank why no scholars who believe in the Bible's inerrancy have been brought into Baylor University's religion department and given tenure, Bob Patterson answered with some questions of his own: "How can we have collegiality with people who won't abide by the terms of collegiality unless we adopt their epistemology? How can we work in peace with those who are dedicated to eliminating us from our jobs?"

Southern Baptists frequently charge each other with creeping creedalism on the one side and creeping liberalism on the other. Each charge is regularly contested and denied. But one charge remains uncontested: among Southern Baptists the level of mistrust and suspicion is shockingly higher today than it was only one decade ago. And there are clear signs that the trend will accelerate. Missionaries and others have pleaded desperately with Convention leaders, urging them to do something to check the trend before it is too late. It may be too late already.

A psychological analysis of those contributing to the rising mistrust will throw little light on the trend. No one party harbors more egotists than the other. Given the intensity of the battle, it is surprising that the level of megalomania is quite low among these Southern Baptist warriors and strategists. Fundamentally, the opposing parties are made up of individuals guided by their belief systems. It is the belief systems that have come into conflict with one another.

The two Pattersons—Bob and Paige (no blood ties)—are engaging and likable individuals. They are men of character and courage. Each has a sense of humor and an enviable kindness that cannot be denied even in their fierce struggle against one another. The problem is that they adhere to belief systems that at certain points are irreconcilable, as each man clearly recognizes. Paige Patterson said flatly in his office that ideally no one should teach in Baylor's religion department unless he believes in and openly subscribes to inerrancy. That makes Bob Patterson's question quite to the point: "How can we have collegiality with individuals who won't abide by the terms of collegiality unless we adopt their epistemology?"

Philosopher Sidney Hook argued during the McCarthy days that members of the Communist party should not be allowed to join university faculties. His reasoning was not that communist ideas should be excluded from campuses. Hook welcomed communist views in his classroom and spent a good deal of time criticizing and refuting them. Distinguishing the party members from the views that they held, Hook wanted to bar Communists from faculty membership because they had sworn to destroy the freedom that made academic exchange possible.[4] Similarly, some proponents within the Inerrancy Party make two of their goals clear: they do not want anyone on the faculty who does not subscribe to the inerrancy doctrine, and they will do whatever they can to fetter the academic freedom of faculty members who refuse to embrace inerrancy. Fortunately, there are scholarly inerrantists who are committed to upholding the rules and regulations that make possible the free academic exchange of competing ideas and beliefs.

Jimmy Draper says that he does not favor "a wild-eyed witch hunt," but his plan to set up a doctrinal test for the faculties of Baptist schools would effectively usher in a witch hunt no matter how smoothly carried out initially. It would turn Southern Baptist life into a masochistic orgy of conflict and turn colleges, universities, and seminaries into glorified indoctrination camps despite Draper's earnest desire to prevent that.

If the battle is to reach the negotiating table, many of those who do not hold to inerrancy are also going to have to become more forthright in saying what they do and do not mean about the Bible's role in church life. The plain truth is that the overwhelming majority of Southern Baptist religion professors have been using the historical-critical method for years, as Lindsell and David Beale have charged. Except for a few, those who use the method discover sooner or later that they cannot in good faith accept certain parts of the Bible as unqualified, right-off-the-page divine revelation. All their attempts to distinguish infallibility from inerrancy are understandably infuriating to many members of the Inerrancy Party; to them the attempts seem designed to conceal just how far Southern Baptist teachers and many ministers have moved epistemologically and theologically from the throngs of Southern Baptist laypeople who pay the bills.

In an interchange with Fisher Humphrey, Paul Pressler makes his point brilliantly through one question regarding the *Baptist Faith and Message* statement, according to which the Bible has "truth, without any mixture of error, for its matter." Pressler asks, "How can anybody believe that there is error in Scripture and ascribe to a phrase that says that the Bible is truth without any mixture of error? If you have a way you can do that, then I would be interested in hearing it."

Fisher Humphrey ducks Pressler's question.[5] Pressler contends that a lot of "mental gymnastics are exercised in the theological world, where words do not mean to the theologian what they mean to the person in the pew. Therefore, I would like to have a negative of what you cannot believe in the Christian gospel, and what you cannot believe in the Scripture, what part of Scripture you can believe is wrong and still teach our young people."[6]

Pressler goes on to clarify exactly what he means. He does not want people like Jack Flanders of Baylor University and G. Temp Sparkman of Midwestern Baptist Seminary teaching at Southern Baptist schools. Flanders holds that there are errors in the Book of Daniel, and Sparkman holds that the Old Testament ascribes terrible things to God.

On the other side of the fence, the Inerrancy Party leaders, Pressler included, have been no more forthright than their opponents on the question of education. The overwhelming majority of Inerrancy Party leaders do not believe in Southern Baptist institutions of higher education, and they ought to come out in the open and admit it. They want the respectability that comes with genuine education, but they are dedicated enemies of education despite their double-talk and weasel wording. The Baptist Press, far from libeling Pressler, has done its job well by exposing his designs on Baptist institutions of higher learning. Behind all his complaints against President Dilday of Southwestern Seminary stands one steel-hard conclusion: If carried out, the plan of Pressler and some of his followers would effectively eviscerate Baptist higher education, and turning up the wattage on the judge's halo will not obscure that prospect. What many Inerrancy members want are narrow enclaves of indoctrination with a thin veneer of education disguising their real interest. They rightly criticize their opponents for being less than candid in informing the Baptist people about what is going on in the seminaries and college religion departments, but they themselves are wolves in sheep's clothing, disguising from the same Baptist people their goal to obliterate the ideal of education and establish slick indoctrination programs in its place.

If the Southern Baptist Convention sinks still deeper into political infighting, the tragedy will have been brought on largely by those ministers, editors, professors, and hardworking denominational officers who have treated the laypeople as an inferior species incapable of religious education beyond the stage of adolescence. This charge can be spelled out.

According to the 1963 version of the *Baptist Faith and Message*, the Bible has "truth, without any mixture of error, for its matter." In the controversy over the authority of the Bible, Southern Baptists in the Inerrancy Party and in the Moderate Party insist that they embrace that statement without reservation. Nevertheless, the party leaders themselves finally admit that false statements do exist in the original documents of the Bible. According to Matthew 12:24, for example, some Pharisees stated that Jesus performed great deeds by the power of Beelzebub. Southern Baptist leaders regard the Pharisees' statement as false. There are many other statements in the Bible that leaders on both sides of the controversy hold to be false. So how do they resolve those statements with their insistence that the Bible is "without mixture of error"?

The *Baptist Faith and Message* sentence in question ends with the phrase "for its matter," and that innocent-looking qualification will itself be qualified endlessly by apologists on each side of the controversy. Herschel Hobbs, who served as chairman of the committee that wrote the statement, says that he holds to the inerrancy of the Bible, but in the same article he denies the verbal plenary view of the Bible, a view embraced by many proponents of inerrancy among Southern Baptists. Hobbs goes on to point out that Luke differs from Matthew and Mark regarding the kind of needle that a camel could not pass through. Luke uses the word for surgical needle, whereas Matthew and Mark use the word for sewing needle. The point here is twofold: there are degrees of inerrancy, but there is no inerrant rule specifying what degree of inerrancy applies to the Bible. Those who profess to believe in the inerrancy of the Bible argue that the discrepancies between the parallel passages of the Gospels are only apparent. They can argue in that way only by holding to a weak degree of inerrancy, whereas their opponents (who profess to reject inerrancy) hold to a strong degree of inerrancy. The weaker the degree of inerrancy, the easier it is to contend that the Bible is inerrant; the stronger the degree, the more difficult it is. If the word "liberal" can mean "loose," and if "conservative" can mean "strict," then the advocates of inerrancy seem to hold to a liberal meaning of inerrancy, while those who deny that the Bible is inerrant hold to a conservative meaning of inerrancy.

The difference between a surgical needle and an ordinary sewing needle is significant if one is performing surgery or mending clothing. But the difference can be ignored if one has a loose sense of inerrancy and wishes to focus not on the needle but on the moral of the proverb about a camel passing through a needle's eye. If one holds to a strict view of inerrancy, two questions arise: What exactly did Jesus himself say? And why would Luke change the ordinary sewing needle in the Gospel of Mark to a surgical needle?

Luke was a physician and therefore would be more interested in surgical needles, but that tells us only about Luke himself. It does not tell us exactly what Jesus said. In short, those who profess to believe in inerrancy must recognize a limit to the Bible's degree of accuracy. If they step beyond that elusive limit, then inaccuracy actually increases. If Jesus used the ordinary word for "sewing needle" (as Mark and Matthew record), then it is inaccurate to assert (as Luke does) that Jesus used the word for "surgical needle."

The proponents of inerrancy insist that it is the spiritual message of the proverb, not the technology of needles, that is the point of Jesus' words regarding how difficult it is for the rich to enter the kingdom. But a similar argument is made by many who reject inerrancy. For them, the theological message of Genesis is the important point and not its scientific accuracy or inaccuracy. When pushed beyond certain limitations, the first eleven chapters of Genesis contain many scientific inaccuracies, but why push beyond that line? It is only by crossing over it that problems of scientific, technological, or historical inaccuracy emerge.

To be sure, whether one does or does not hold to the Bible's inerrancy of whatever degree, there will always be difficulties. There is even the problem of articulating one's theory of inerrancy and of specifying the necessary degree of inerrancy. In practice, considerable leeway is required to formulate the inerrancy hypothesis coherently. Apparently, a number of Southern Baptists on either side of the controversy are quite nervous about letting laypeople in on just how many problems there are in the Bible and how much leeway there sometimes is in dealing with them.

When Richard Land and Paige Patterson say that the vast majority of Southern Baptists believe the Bible is inerrant, they should keep in mind that the people in the pews have never been supplied the pros and cons of the issue in a systematic and readable form. The Baptist state papers and the Sunday school material have provided mostly a few loosely connected arguments on both sides. When the United States was locked in combat with Germany during World Wars I and II, J. Frank Norris used to smear biblical higher criticism by representing it as an exclusively German phenomenon, the work of a foreign enemy. Even though most of the leaders of the Inerrancy Party profess to having no objection to what is called lower criticism, the people in Southern Baptist pews are still poorly informed of it.

Lower criticism is perhaps better described as textual criticism, the scholarly process by which the specialists examine and evaluate the vast assortment of ancient documents for the purpose of reconstructing the vanished original manuscripts of the Bible. Higher criticism includes source criticism, form criticism, redaction (or editorial) criticism, and other approaches to biblical literature that are used also in the study of extrabiblical documents and traditions around the globe. In the seventies scholars began to scrutinize biblical texts from the perspectives of sociology and anthropology as well.

One of the most authentic collections of ancient biblical manuscripts is without question Codex Sinaiticus, which the remarkable Constantin Tischendorf took from the monastery library in the desert at the foot of Mount Sinai. An orthodox believer who devoted most of his adult life to using lower criticism to counter higher criticism, Tischendorf learned to his dismay that the story in John 8 of the woman taken in adultery was not included in the priceless Sinai collection of the Bible. Also, to his total surprise, two Christian writings—the Epistle of Barnabas and the Shepherd of Hermas—were included in it. Tischendorf had grown up with the assumption that neither epistle was a genuine part of the Bible. The question of how some documents came to be regarded as Scripture and how others were excluded has been largely kept out of Southern Baptist Sunday school literature, even though it belongs to the study known as lower criticism. In a severely misinformed article in an Inerrancy Party publication, William Powell, editor of the publication at the time, denounced two of Christianity's leading nineteenth-century conservative biblical scholars—B. F. Westcott and F.J.A. Hort—branding them as liberals. The point here is that some inerrancy supporters are nervous about the study of even lower criticism.

Cambridge scholars Westcott and Hort—conservative, brilliant, and with an impeccable reputation among scholars—devoted most of their lives to organizing and collecting texts of the Bible into a coherent whole that would reinforce their orthodox Christian beliefs. If Westcott and Hort come under the censure of the Inerrancy Party, then who is to escape suspicion? Like the French Revolution or the paranoia under Stalin, the Inerrancy Party may have created a monster that its most informed and enlightened leaders will be unable to control. Jack Prince of Knoxville, Tennessee, tried to explain that to Paul Pressler at Pressler's 1985 Knoxville meeting, but the point was lost in the discussion.

When I asked Paige Patterson if Westcott and Hort were liberals, he said, "On my scale they are liberals." But then he added that in all honesty, looking at the esteemed scholars on the broader scale of Christendom at large, they may be considered at least as "quasiconservatives but not fundamentalists." Patterson went on to explain that Westcott and Hort had a deep reverence for the biblical text and an a priori judgment that the text was trustworthy. Clearly, Patterson has an a priori resolution to apply the word "conservative" to none but those who hold to the doctrine of inerrancy, no matter how theologically orthodox the person may be. It is interesting, nevertheless, to learn that Patterson can call someone a liberal and at the same time acknowledge that that person harbors a reverence for Scripture and an a priori judgment of its trustworthiness. That might well be a shift in his thinking or at least a point where fruitful discussion is possible among Southern Baptists.

As a believer in inerrancy William Powell is probably justified in his fear of lower or textual criticism, to say nothing of so-called higher criticism. James Bentley, in his recent book *Secrets of Mount Sinai: The Story of the World's Oldest Bible (Codex Sinaiticus)*, writes:

> The evidence of the manuscript from Mount Sinai was proving more and more difficult to digest. In the received text [the less reliable text of sixteenth-century Erasmus and Stephanus], Luke chapter 24, verse 51, tells how Jesus left his disciples after his resurrection. He blessed them, was parted from them, "and was carried up into heaven." Sinaiticus omits the final clause. As the textual critic C.S.C. Williams observed, if this omission is correct, "there is no reference at all to the Ascension in the original text of the Gospels."[7]

Professor T. C. Smith, who taught New Testament and Greek for several years at Southern Seminary and Furman University, is convinced that the single most influential individual in determining what would and would not be called Scripture for Christians was the fourth-century Patriarch Athanasius of Alexandria. Written some years before Athanasius sent his famous epistle to the bishops of

Egypt, Codex Sinaiticus includes two Christian writings not on the patriarch's list. As late as the sixth century, the Codex Claromontanus gives a list of the books of the Old and New Testaments omitting the Epistle to the Hebrews but placing the Epistle of Barnabas between Jude and the Book of Revelation.

It is possible that under the right circumstances Patterson and Land could persuade the majority of Southern Baptists to change their minds regarding John 8 or Mark 16. By the same token, other professors under favorable circumstances might be able to persuade millions of Southern Baptists to change their minds about still more passages, for there are texts other than the long ending of Mark that some Southern Baptist professors regard as less than authentic. Their reasons may be different from Paige Patterson's reasons for rejecting the ending of Mark, but those reasons have not been presented to the vast majority of Baptists. No one can say what those millions of Baptists would believe if they knew at least five percent of what the Baptist professors know about everything that comes under the heading of scholarly biblical studies.

It is easy to make it appear that any gap between what Baptist laypeople are said to believe and what the Baptist professors teach is a betrayal on the part of the professors. It would be surprising, however, if the gap did not exist. In the field of physics, the gap between a trained physicist and the average layperson is as wide as the Grand Canyon. Why would parents spend their hard-earned dollars to send their offspring to college if the professors were not miles beyond the students and the parents in their knowledge of their particular discipline? As might be expected, a highly technical seminar in which students and professors explore various avenues and alternatives, with each participant possessing a reasonable command of large quantities of literature, is far removed from Ziglar's Sunday school class or inspirational talks.

8.

Toward a Model for Southern Baptist Colleges and Seminaries

he Mormons are one of the fastest-growing religious denominations in North America. Yet none of their bishops attended their seminaries, for there are no Mormon seminaries. The numbers of charismatics and neo-Pentecostals have been growing by leaps and bounds in the eighties with little benefit of ministers trained in seminaries. Billy Graham did not attend a seminary. Neither did D. L. Moody, Charles Finney, W. V. Grant, Lee Roberson, John R. Rice, Oral Roberts, J. Harold Smith, George Truett, Kathryn Kuhlman, A. A. Allen, G. Campbell Morgan, Leroy Jenkins, James Robison, R. G. Lee, Jim Bakker, Charles Spurgeon, John A. Broadus, Jimmy Swaggart, William Freeman, and scores of other evangelists and preachers who have attracted huge crowds. Demos Shakarian, founder of the Full Businessmen's Fellowship International, was a dairy farmer before he launched his successful ministry.

The question that Southern Baptists face is this: Why is it so important that their evangelists, pastors, and denominational officers graduate from a seminary? With the millions of dollars poured into the Southern Baptist seminaries each year and with all the controversy perpetually generated by the seminaries, why not sell the buildings and fire the faculties en masse? There is every reason to think that seminaries contribute little to the evangelistic fervor of Southern Baptists. In fact, the fervor of hundreds of would-be flaming evangelists is cooled severely at the seminaries. Seminaries have a way of raising questions that create ambivalence and doubt. Evangelists function better if those questions are never raised. There is ample evidence that most pastors, too, do not need seminary training to carry on elementary church work, for thousands of churches exist without seminary-trained pastors. Many Southern Baptist pastors and certainly most evangelists will use only a portion of the theology and biblical studies that they encounter at the seminary, no matter what kind of seminary it is. There is not even a compelling reason for pastors and evangelists to learn Greek or Hebrew. Billy Graham's sermons are classic examples of what can be done by an industrious individual whose formal biblical training is quite meager. The simple gospel and the old, old story do not require biblical scholarship or any great depth of historical understanding. Mormon leaders do not inform their people of difficult passages in the Book of Mormon. They severely limit academic freedom at Brigham Young University to keep questions from being raised excessively. Most members of the Church of Jesus Christ of Latter-day Saints are kept in ignorance about much of their faith. Should the same apply to Southern Baptists? The fewer troublesome questions that are raised about the Bible, the easier it is to carry out the mission of evangelism.

Admittedly, graduating from a Southern Baptist seminary bestows prestige on a minister, allowing him (infrequently her) to compete socially and intellectually with ministers of the mainline churches. But as Criswell and Pressler have noted, most of the mainline denominations are losing members. For some Southern Baptists, it is as clear as day that a seminary education often tempers the go-get-'em spark of evangelism in young ministerial students. They charge that the seminaries bestow prestige and respectability at the price of bridling the spirit-filled enthusiasm that is necessary for a minister to be a perpetual recruiter of converts. According to many fundamentalists, Jonah led the entire people of Ninevah to the Lord, and he did it without the prestige of a degree from any seminary, orthodox or whatever. Most of the early Christian preachers were apprentices to specific individuals on earth—to Christ or a disciple or an apostle. In the secular world, lawyers go to a professional school to learn to be lawyers. The seminaries represent a secular movement away from biblical apprenticeship and toward the professionalism of formal schools. In that connection, evangelist E. J. Daniels and William Powell call attention to the case of Max F. Morris, a story worth exploring.

Converted at the age of twelve in a Baptist church in Alabama, Max began conducting evangelistic crusades as a teenage boy. Dr. Daniels believes that God was using Max to save hundreds of people wherever he preached. After graduating from college, Max organized a team of

singers and advance men to conduct evangelistic crusades at home
and abroad. "And the Lord was using my ministry," Max added. He
was also enrolled at Southern Seminary in Louisville. Men like his
classmate Harper Shannon studied diligently and graduated from
Southern with their faith strengthened, but Max failed to apply himself to his studies and eventually forsook his calling to become something of a drifter. "I wasted my substance in riotous living."[1] Later he
recovered his faith and is now sole owner and chairman of the board
of a multimillion-dollar cosmetics empire. Why he failed to return to
preaching after his recovery remains unclear. Does the divine call have
a time limit? Fundamentalist preachers who stand to receive money
from his cosmetics organization do not appear eager to insist that Max
return to full-time preaching.

Max's example shows that while a lot of preachers in the Inerrancy
Party are spending time and energy trying to turn the seminaries into
professional schools of their own liking, they are fighting the wrong
battle. They openly admit that Max Morris was doing the Lord's work
before going to seminary. He was carrying out his call faithfully. What
these Inerrancy Party people do not face is that there is no unequivocal biblical calling for anyone to attend a seminary. Perhaps the sin of
pride infects all but a small portion of the party. Most want the prestige of the world. They want to be like lawyers, doctors, engineers,
and dentists. They lust for that professional degree. But Billy Sunday
moved straight from the baseball diamond to the pulpit without getting a seminary degree. Why did Max Morris feel the need to go after
one? Was it the Holy Spirit or his pride that sent him to the seminary?
"By their fruits ye shall know them." Before going to seminary Max
Morris was producing fruit, winning converts around the world. So
who told him that God wanted him to go to the seminary?

As a young evangelist, Billy Graham spent hours praying and discussing the Bible with Charles Templeton, a close friend and gifted
evangelist. They knew there were serious problems in the Bible that
they could not resolve. Templeton pleaded with Graham to go with
him to study at an American seminary, but Graham steadfastly refused. Templeton then went to Princeton Theological Seminary and
eventually left the Christian faith. Graham stayed out of every seminary, including the Dallas Theological Seminary, and soon became
America's leading evangelist. How many potential Billy Grahams have
been turned into smooth professionals by the seminary finishing
schools—including the fundamentalist and evangelical seminaries?

The only biblical option for the Inerrancy Party is to bale out of the seminary business. Of course, Paige Patterson and Richard Land would have to find work elsewhere. But a lot of evangelical churches would be more than eager to call them as pastors.

Sociologists note that many Southern Baptist churches have grown so secular that they require a minister with a professional seminary degree. Instead of fighting back heroically, the leaders of the Inerrancy Party are yielding to secular pressure, and to assuage their sense of betrayal they are trying to create seminaries that are not seminaries. They want educational centers that do not educate. They want the worldly respectability found in the educational institution, but they want to smother education with an intensified indoctrination program. What they will end up with, if they get their way, is a hybrid that is neither an educational center nor a biblical fulfillment of the call to the ministry.

In contrast to Dallas Theological Seminary, at least five of the Southern Baptist seminaries can boast of being significantly more than centers of party-line indoctrination. And not one of the six falls behind the Dallas seminary in emphasizing evangelism. The presidents of three of the Southern Baptist seminaries have recently demonstrated considerable courage in facing the outspoken enemies of education among Southern Baptists. Before the Inerrancy Party leaders step up their campaign to transform the seminaries, they need to ask why they are interested at all in keeping the seminaries alive. There is little evidence that evangelism and church growth require seminary-trained ministers. Such preachers are plainly not always the most successful recruiters of converts. Even the argument that these expensive institutions are needed to give ministers a defense against heretical views is weak for the conspicuous reason that no Southern Baptist minister needs a seminary degree to counter Moonies, Muslims, Mormons, Roman Catholics, or whatever supposed heresy happens to be stirring up the neighborhood.

Hence, there is no crying need for seminaries of the kind designed solely to indoctrinate for a period of three years. Southern Baptists would do well to take a long, realistic, and forthright look at the methods employed so successfully by the aggressive charismatics and Mormons. They need to understand how such churches thrive without benefit of seminaries.

If creating more Southern Baptists is the overriding goal of Southern Baptists, they should forget about their seminaries and focus attention on recruitment techniques. They might even establish an agency in Nashville to encourage Southern Baptist couples to procreate more frequently, the way Latin American Catholics and old-line Mormons are doing. There are many ways to expand the church rolls, but subsidizing seminary education is not one of them.

If, on the other hand, Southern Baptists have a strong commitment to the ancient and perpetual search for truth to accompany the dissemination of the truths that they believe they have, and if they are committed to an in-depth church ministry of quality not measured solely by the quick expansion of church rolls, then they may have to continue to support their seminaries and colleges. To be sure, education is not going to perish from the land if Southern Baptists close their schools. But they do have the tradition and capacity to contribute something special to American education.

Paige Patterson raised a poignant but fruitful question about Baylor University's religion department. "If all they do is present various viewpoints, why do we need Baylor? By definition a Baptist school advocates a certain viewpoint."[2] How indeed is Baylor's religion department to be distinguished from the religion department that, say, North Texas State University envisions for itself? The philosophy department and the administrative leaders at North Texas have in mind to develop a religion studies program that will include a wide spectrum of biblical studies as well as studies in Islam and other religions, and the university already offers several religion courses. Paige Patterson's question is, therefore, quite relevant. Why should Texas Baptists raise large sums of money year after year for Baylor if Baptist students can obtain the same education at North Texas State at considerably less expense?

The answer is easy to find. North Texas will never be able to duplicate Baylor's program, just as Baylor will never be able to duplicate North Texas'. Objective inquiry does not require a uniform curriculum or syllabus for all major universities. On the contrary, each university will make its own special contribution. In the first place, at Baylor University stands a library in religion studies that is the envy of Texas' state universities. North Texas State, the University of Texas, Texas A&M, and the others will never be able to compete with Baylor's magnificent collection of books in religion. In the second place, just because Baylor University is a Baptist school, it will invariably deal with religious issues that are traditionally of interest to Baptists, such as the First Amendment issues considered at the Center for Church-

State Studies near the Baylor campus. And Baylor will have wide interests, too, since Baptists themselves have wide interests. The main difference is that because state universities have a broad public to serve, they cannot become the servants of any one group exclusively. Within three months Baylor University will feature on its campus more conferences and studies peculiar to Southern Baptists than North Texas State University will feature within three years.

Baylor University is Baptist. It is also a university. Its responsibility is therefore twofold. As a university it must maintain its long tradition of objective inquiry. As a university it cannot be an extension of the pulpit or the Sunday school class. No academic department can be reduced to a tool of evangelism. As a Baptist school, on the other hand, Baylor must have on campus the best scholarly representation of Baptist beliefs, history, and life that can be found. Because it is committed both to its multifaceted Baptist heritage and to objective inquiry even in religion, the school has no alternative but to have a superlative and multifaceted department of religion studies. Anything short of that would be a retreat from its twofold commitment.

It is inevitable that those two commitments will at times come into conflict. One way to overcome the conflict is to extinguish one of the commitments. If that is not what Texas Baptists want, what can they do when the tension between the two poles increases? The answer is clear. Any Baptist college can turn the tension into something creative by renewing its commitment to both its masters. If biblical inerrancy needs to be better represented in Baylor's religion department, the improvement can and ought to be made as quickly as possible. And in making it, the cause of objective inquiry will be advanced, for the commitment to represent one tradition strongly does not entail that the representation of every rival tradition in the department be weakened.

Paul Pressler is perfectly correct to demand that the doctrine of inerrancy and related doctrines be not presented at Baptist schools but be presented well. Unfortunately, he shows no sustained commitment to theological or religious education when he seems to demand that alternative doctrines be prevented from being presented well. Paige Patterson and Adrian Rogers show that they do not grasp what education is about at a Baptist school when they complain that they do not want their hard-earned money to pay professors to present views they do not believe in. What they seem honestly to overlook is that it is impossible to have an education center unless people are willing to pay to be presented with ideas and views that they do not embrace as well as with views that they do embrace.

The religion department at Baylor would do well to invite a well-known inerrancy proponent to join its religion faculty, someone of the caliber of Clark Pinnock (Paige Patterson's former seminary professor), Carl Henry, or perhaps the polemicist Norman Geisler. If Richard Land were to join the faculty of Baylor's religion department, it would enrich the intellectual stock of both the department and Dr. Land. The spirit of collegiality would be tested and find greater depth.

When I presented the above proposal to several Southern Baptist professors, one of them (who happens not to teach at Baylor) made a comment that bears repeating because it represents what many Southern Baptist educators feel. "This is all very nice in theory, Joe. But somewhere you seem to have forgotten that fundamentalism is built on true believers who are not about to accept the collegiality you talk about. A real Inerrancy Party member on the Baylor faculty would create all kinds of tension and fragmentation. The spirit of objective inquiry is foreign to the framework of fundamentalism."

Perhaps present-day fundamentalism, carried to its logical conclusion, does prohibit its adherents from participating wholeheartedly in a truly academic environment. But individuals do not always follow with perfect consistency the direction of their worldview. Colleagues who accept collegiality and also challenge each other with strong rival views create an intellectually enriching atmosphere. Richard Land has at various times challenged my viewpoint, and I have always found the challenges enlightening even when we continue to differ sharply. If Land cannot accept the right of proponents of rival views to enjoy academic freedom on the Baptist college campus, then he should not seek to become a member of the college faculty. Having found his criticisms always insightful, I would hope that he can accept collegiality. And I am not at all convinced that he has in principle rejected it. Or accepted it.

OBJECTIVITY AS A SOCIOPOLITICAL ACHIEVEMENT

It is imperative to think of objective inquiry more as an achievement of sociopolitical structure than as a psychological state of mind, for objectivity is rarely found originating inside the individual's private mental recesses. It emerges as an enormous social and institutional accomplishment, thriving within the university or seminary as a social whole. It is not an achievement that even dedicated faculty members can maintain through their efforts alone. Powerful forces inside and outside the university work relentlessly against the freedom to develop a multiplicity of biases on campus and against the freedom to subject those biases to rigorous criticism. The school's trustees and administrators are essential in helping the faculty maintain the social and political conditions that keep inquiry open and flowing with informative dialogue, severe and incisive critique, and imaginative leaps. At rock bottom, thinking travels by trial and error, and academia is a protected environment in which new trials and the process of learning from error are intensified and accelerated.[3]

Ideally, university professors ought to represent every major view fairly and in depth. But it is naive to suppose that will ever come about. In fact, rare professors like Bob Patterson, with his extraordinary ability to understand several worldviews in depth, are not essential to the development and maintenance of a dynamic university. What is required is an open social and political structure that guarantees each professor the freedom to present his biases with maximum articulation and depth. Furthermore, each teacher must be guaranteed complete freedom to criticize in detail the rival biases presented. That is what the model of the free marketplace of ideas and biases means, a point that needs to be explicated further.

Consider Jimmy Draper. His book *Authority* offers an excellent expression and defense of the inerrancy position. His commentary on the Book of Hebrews is admirably articulate. Such ingredients make for good teaching. Draper would make an excellent faculty member. His understanding of other frames of reference, such as humanism, liberalism, and neo-orthodoxy, appears to be superficial, but that is irrelevant. So long as he presents his own position with profundity and assigns readings in articulate books whose views compete with his own, Draper would make an interesting and contributing professor of religion. In time, his critique of rival views would improve significantly. On a dynamic campus and at professional meetings where professors are challenged to refine their biases in the fire of debate and dialogue, he would eventually improve his criticisms to the point that they would become not only valuable but also essential to the free, competitive marketplace of ideas. In short, in a vital marketplace like a seminary campus, views are criticized and the criticisms themselves are criticized. The process produces a more rigorous and informed intellectual community. Unfortunately, after having stated the importance of distinguishing education from indoctrination,

Draper seems at times to backslide. Having eaten at the table of educators, he sometimes draws back and separates himself, fearing perhaps the reputed pillars of indoctrination within the Inerrancy Party.

ADMINISTRATORS AND ACADEMIC FREEDOM

Baylor University was strengthened academically when it lost W. A. Criswell from its board of trustees. It is clear that Criswell has no conception of what a university is. For him, academic freedom exists primarily for those who teach what he regards as truth. In *The Criswell Study Bible* (page 1460) he implies that a Baptist university should have no more openness of inquiry than a fundamentalist church that simply gets rid of false teachers. Compare Criswell with Baylor University's president, Herbert Reynolds, who has demonstrated again and again that he grasps what a university is and what must be done to defend it against its enemies. Instead of calling Professor Bob E. Patterson into his office to pressure him, President Reynolds actively encouraged Patterson to publish his book on the Gospel of Matthew. That kind of administration is more eloquent than a hundred speeches on academic freedom.

At the same time that Reynolds was courageously fulfilling his responsibility as a university president, another administrator at another denominational institution of higher learning showed that he did not understand the importance of his role on campus. Instead of encouraging his faculty to use their training to address the theological issues before the denomination, this other administrator called a faculty member into his office and told him to resign because of an academic paper he had presented before a group of colleagues. The administrator was understood to have offered the faculty member a full year's salary for leave of absence if he would agree not to return to the campus. The faculty member interpreted the offer as an attempt to use the denomination's money to protect the administrator's position.

Universities sometimes do find themselves saddled with self-serving administrators. The off-campus enemies of education quickly learn that they can count on such people to do their work for them. A little pressure goes a long way. Southern Baptists seem to have been cursed by a fair share of administrative incompetents over the decades, largely because they can easily be removed from office at those schools where other administrators and trustees seem never to have considered that a church-related college should be more than an indoctrination center. On an October 1985 television program Jerry Falwell spoke of his dream of a campus that a child could enter at the age of four and attend through the completion of his Ph.D. without ever sitting in the classroom of an instructor who does not subscribe to the inerrancy of the Bible. Falwell made it clear as well that only his brand of political conservatism would be required of the political science faculty. Falwell cannot persistently think of education as anything beyond indoctrination.

Once a college seeks accreditation, it finds itself in conflict with its commitment to indoctrination. External pressures force the institution to open its curriculum. Internally, pressures come also from faculty members who understand the difference between education and indoctrination. Falwell has sometimes spoken of faculty members as if they were hired to speak only what he approves of. In some cases he may be able to pull that off, but eventually that kind of high-handed control will wane. After talking with one of Liberty University's deans, Dr. Robison James of the University of Virginia is convinced that Liberty's biology department has gained a relative degree of independence from the creationist enthusiasts, who, it seems, have been more or less isolated in an institute apart from the biology department. That was done so that Liberty graduates could be accredited to teach biology in the public schools. The noted English atheist Antony Flew told me in early 1985 that he was scheduled to debate with theists at Liberty University. That too is the sort of step that eventually carries a school away from indoctrination and toward education. Even though the founder of a college may wish to keep it as an indoctrination center, there are forces within the institution that pull away from the founder's intention to have a college that is a college in appearance only.

OPENNESS TO CRITICISM

Criticism is one of the two essential ingredients of objective inquiry and education, for without it biases and views will lack the pressure essential to stimulate revision and improvement. Draper's critique of one of the textbooks used at Baylor University cannot but strengthen the academic climate of that university, provided the free marketplace of ideas is not cut off and turned over to Pressler's vision of monopolistic control issuing into a socialism of thought.

Thought control is rarely achieved by psychological techniques. Its primary means are economic manipulation and political repression. Strange as it may sound, an open academic environment can profit from the writings of individuals who happen to be fiercely dogmatic. "Dogmatism" may be defined for some purposes as the process of tenaciously clinging to a view that most rational individuals would have abandoned. An informed dogmatist on a faculty can serve as a whetstone on which colleagues sharpen and refine their criticisms. As the philosopher Karl Popper notes, sometimes a view has possibilities that will go unactualized unless a dogmatist works with it for many years in the face of criticism. Individual dogmatists can contribute to the educational process provided the social and political structure of free academic exchange is maintained. Often dogmatism is not so much a property of views as a style of behavior. Even when an individual holds to liberal views he may be dogmatic in the way he holds them, and a conservative may be open to a multiplicity of views and a criticism of his own view. Or the converse may hold.

THE IMPORTANCE OF INDOCTRINATION

Indoctrination, oddly enough, can make a positive contribution to education and objective inquiry. "Indoctrination" may be defined as the presentation of one view or framework with little or no severe criticism of it. Most high school and undergraduate math courses are taught by indoctrination. The high school biology class seldom raises any serious criticisms of the principles of evolution or natural selection. A course in biblical Greek or Hebrew tolerates almost no questioning of the foundations of the subject matter. In many courses, indoctrination is quite appropriate as a means of preparing students. But preparing them for what? For many things, one of which is an education. Education depends upon a thorough indoctrination in various areas of learning. But unless the school advances far beyond indoctrination, it will never become an educational institution. Falwell's Liberty Baptist University is an example of an environment in which the efforts of education are too often stillborn.[4]

THE LOSS OF BAPTIST SCHOOLS

At an evangelism conference in Dayton, Ohio, in early 1985 Zig Ziglar lamented the number of Southern Baptist colleges and univer-

sities that have either cut their ties with sponsoring state Baptists or
are seeking to cut them. He mentioned Wake Forest University (North
Carolina), the University of Richmond (Virginia), Stetson University
(Florida), Furman University (South Carolina), Baylor University
(Texas), and William Jewell College (Missouri). But Ziglar seemed not
to understand that it is because of individuals like himself and Pressler that the universities have found it necessary to gain independence.
No university can survive as a responsible center of learning if it must
perpetually endure the political undermining of academia. Instead of
seeking either to purge or repress the Baptist faculties, the responsible members of the Inerrancy Party should be negotiating to have
their position ably represented in the classroom and on reading lists.

THE PATTERSON-LAND PROPOSAL

Sitting in the presence of Richard Land and myself, Paige Patterson
outlined a plan for turning three of the six Southern Baptist seminaries into inerrancy schools. According to the plan, three of the six
Southern Baptist seminaries will have only those faculty members,
administrators, and trustees who publicly subscribe to the Bible's inerrancy. (Land at one time spoke of bringing about this drastic change
without firings; as the seminary personnel died, retired, or resigned,
they would be replaced by individuals embracing inerrancy. He esti-
mated that the desired goal would be reached within one generation.)
   According to Paige Patterson's plan, the other three seminaries
would then be free to go their own way without interference from the
proponents of inerrancy. On the surface the plan appears to contain a
healthy policy of live-and-let-live mingled with a measure of inter-
seminary competition. In reality, there is a price to be paid. Paige Patterson doesn't seem to have the slightest interest in supporting even
in principle a seminary where various views of inspiration can thrive
in a free academic environment. His plan is fundamentally a tactic for
dividing and demolishing, and to that end he wants to institute something called negative designation. Under his plan, when a local church
sends money to the Southern Baptist Cooperative Program, the church
may specify that none of it is to go to any of the seminaries where the
inerrancy premise is not in control. Patterson would also stipulate that
no money within the Cooperative Program will be shifted to compen-
sate for negative designation. He confidently assumes that if churches
are given a choice, the patrons of inerrancy will win hands down. He

is convinced that only a few churches in the Convention would voluntarily send money to seminaries where inerrancy does not reign exclusively.

Apparently Patterson has not seriously considered the genuine possibility that his plan would split thousands of Southern Baptist churches into factions embroiled in bitter fights over where the church's money should go. The flame of infighting would likely grow more intense as representatives from each seminary went into the churches to sell themselves and to denigrate their competitors. Baptist fellowship could be turned into a soap-opera intrigue that would make news editors jump with glee. The carnival of bickering, slandering, and backstabbing in the name of Jesus would give a new public meaning to the word "Baptist." Many people have suspected all along that the Southern Baptist Convention was a tribe of J. Frank Norrises waiting for the day when they could do what they are best at—slugging it out in a good old-fashioned haranguing contest that will last for years to come.

Draper thinks the Patterson plan is unworkable. His alternative, though, looks even more destructive of Southern Baptist fellowship. Insisting that he would not fight over the word "inerrancy," he nevertheless proposes using his list of eight beliefs as "the irreducible minimum theology that a person must subscribe to in order to be acceptable as a professor in one of our schools, or as a worker, writer, or policymaker in one of our agencies."[5] He apparently thinks his list will eliminate a number of Baptist faculty members who cannot subscribe without qualification to every point on it.

Pressler contends that the controversy is not about interpretation but about the nature of biblical inspiration, whereas Draper is prepared to be flexible on the word "inerrancy" only to become inflexible on certain interpretations of the Bible. Lindsell stands, meantime, with his favorite twenty questions to fire at faculty and trustees.

Draper offers eight doctrines that he thinks an individual must accept in order to fill a key Southern Baptist position. A conservative guess would place roughly fifty to sixty percent of the seminary professors within the theological boundaries that Draper has set down. If a compromise could be made to allow seven of the eight doctrines to count as the minimum, then perhaps ten to twenty percent more could pass muster after a decade or so of haggling over the theological fine points. But then, Draper is only one individual with his pet list of doctrines (which incidentally does not include belief in the virgin birth or love your neighbor as yourself, although Draper personally believes in both and strives to practice the latter). By the time the Convention finished revising the Draper list, it would have a long train of amendments trailing after it, each item drenched in Southern Baptist enmity, strife, venom, and acrimony. Many items would eventually perish by a death of a thousand qualifications. Pressler stated in 1985 that although he held to the inerrancy of Scripture, he did not use the phrase "plenary inspiration" because it focused on the process of inspiration rather than on the product. Others insist that since God controlled both product and process, neither should be stressed at the neglect of the other.

In the end, Draper's plan would be no more practical than Patterson's. Instead of using it as a creed for the purpose of purging people from positions of leadership in the Convention, however, Draper's list might well be used as an agenda to help guide Southern Baptists over several years in the study of Christian doctrines. Southern Baptist life suffers far more from biblical and theological illiteracy and ignorance of Baptist history than from whatever heresy is supposed to exist at the seminaries or inside the agencies in Nashville, Atlanta, and Richmond.

9.

Relativism
Among Southern Baptists

ome readers of this book are old enough to remember Charles E. Fuller's "Old Fashioned Revival Hour," a radio experience of thrilling music, gentle but stirring preaching, and personal, fireside warmth perhaps never equaled in the history of electronic evangelism. Unlike some current TV preachers, Fuller remained a thoroughly honest individual whose style of living became neither sumptuous nor vainglorious. Content with the gift of evangelism, he steadfastly resisted the temptation to become a Bible-waving news commentator or a flag-waving, self-appointed campaign manager for his favorite politician. With the help of a few faculty members and trustees, he established the Fuller Theological Seminary in 1947 in Pasadena, California. Even though dedicated to training ministers and church workers in the conservative Christian tradition, the faculty and trustees did not until years later adopt the following creed regarding the Bible: "The books which form the canon of the Old and New Testament as originally given are plenarily inspired and free from all error in the whole and in the part. These books constitute the written Word of God, the only infallible rule of faith and practice."

Sometime between 1947 and 1960, Fuller Seminary took a sharp turn. Dissatisfaction with the creed developed as some of the faculty members began using the historical method to study the Bible. The change was not an entirely conscious decision. Usually the most far-reaching changes in thinking cannot be carried on at the fully conscious level. Historian and philosopher of science Thomas S. Kuhn explains that sometimes scientists discover to their surprise that a change has taken place in the way they go about solving scientific problems. They look back and find that somewhere in their past they began viewing things in a new way, as if shifting from thinking in one language to thinking in another. At no point along the way did they know for certain that they were in the process of making one of the most crucial decisions of their careers. Despite the gradualness of the change, it can become so sweeping and radical that Kuhn uses the word "conversion" to describe it. [1]

For many conservative Christian scholars the line dividing the historical method from the traditional method is so blurred that they can never be sure they have not crossed into new territory. They even disagree among themselves over the appropriateness of using the historical method. Whereas some contend that it will serve no purpose but to undermine Scripture, others hold that it confirms their faith in the Bible's trustworthiness. One of the most relentless polemicists against it is Harold Lindsell, a former professor at Fuller Seminary and currently one of the most strident voices within the Inerrancy Party. He left Fuller while bitterly protesting the use of the historical method on campus.

To use the historical method (sometimes called the critical historical method or even historical-critical reconstruction) is to approach the Bible as one would approach any other ancient document. Scholars who use the method think they have no genuine alternative but to put the Bible through the tests that other bodies of literature are put through. An increasing number of conservative Christians believe that although they as scholars must continue to use the historical method, they cannot conclude that the results have been either entirely favorable or entirely unfavorable to every aspect of their faith. Research always carries its risks. On the surface the historical method appears innocent enough, with its patient quest for sources and historical settings that lie behind the reconstructed biblical text. After all, do not some books of the Bible readily admit to having drawn from prior sources?

Daniel Fuller, son of the esteemed evangelist Fuller, is a well-trained biblical scholar, noted author, and professor at the seminary. With unnerving honesty, he has written several important articles that confront the historical-critical method. Instead of following Harold Lindsell in dismissing it, he insists that it is an essential tool of biblical scholarship. Since Fuller has devoted years of his life to exploring the subtle implications of the historical method, I will not attempt to summarize his position in a few words. The spring 1983 issue of *Journal of the Evangelical Theological Society* (volume 16) provides perhaps his own best summary. Daniel Fuller exemplifies the oft-forgotten truth that uncompromising scholarship requires as much courage as brains. Harold Lindsell left Fuller Seminary in part because he could not accept his role as a teacher working with colleagues who did not fully share his particular theory of inspiration. A few years after leaving the seminary, Lindsell became a trustee of Gordon-Conwell Seminary in Massachusetts, where as chairman of the trustees he has apparently succeeded in turning the school into a fundamentalist enclave.

Many of the students who come to college and seminary to take religion courses are naive about the process and development of biblical literature and the formation of the Canon. Some are deeply upset when confronted with the simplest notions—for instance, learning that biblical writers had earlier documents and sources at their elbows or in mind as they wrote down their words on parchment, papyrus, or whatever. When certain ministers lash out against religion professors for despoiling the students' innocence, they are perhaps covering up their own sense of guilt for having neglected their responsibility to these young people. Such ministers may be compared to parents who do not want the schools to provide sex education and yet fail to educate their offspring at home. Most religion professors believe their responsibility as educators is to provide their students with some knowledge of the Bible's background, content, and development. They wonder why some ministers have treated them as if they were introducing virgins to the world of prostitution. Where, the professors ask, did most of these students get the idea that the writers of the Bible simply rolled their eyes while the Holy Spirit "told" them what to write? The answer is not clear.

What is clear is that a number of evangelical ministers are edgy about the quest for sources behind the Bible. When questions invariably emerge about the reliability of the sources, more hypotheses have to be invented to handle the questions, creating an air of uncertainty. It is the nature of scholarship, like the detective searching for clues, to probe constantly. In time, surprises turn up. Conservative Mormons become nervous when they are told that some of Joseph Smith's inspired writings apparently existed in earlier sources, just as conservative Muslim writers resent the suggestion that the inspired Qur'an drew material from earlier sources.[2] Christian students sometimes become upset upon learning that, say, the Book of Revelation had numerous literary ancestors or that II Peter and Jude drew material from the spurious Book of Enoch. Jude 9 states that the archangel Michael contended with the devil in a dispute over the body of Moses. Historical research discovered decades ago that the scenario came from the Book of Enoch, although no reputable scholar today holds that the book was written by Enoch. Jude apparently believed that the man Enoch was the recipient of a divinely inspired prophecy, which raises the question of whether Jude believed (erroneously) that the entire Book of Enoch was divinely inspired and penned by Enoch.

From their pulpits Christian ministers do not usually ask the following question, but it is the sort of question that New Testament scholars must ask themselves all the time: If Jude could have been in error about the human authorship of a prophecy, could Jesus have been in error about or at least ignorant of the authorship of Isaiah or the Pentateuch? E. J. Young and similar inerrancy defenders insist that if Jesus attached a name to any passage of Scripture, then the matter is closed. For them, there can be no doubt that the name refers to the true author of that passage. Another evangelical, James Orr, who seems to have strongly influenced Dr. Russell Dilday, takes a different stance: "It may readily be admitted that when Jesus used popular language about 'Moses' or 'Isaiah' He did nothing more than designate certain books, and need not be understood as giving ex cathedra judgments on the intricate critical questions which the contents of these books raise. Had such questions been proposed to Him for decision, He would probably have dealt with them as He did with the appeal about inheritance: 'Man, who made me a judge or divider over you?'" [3]

Strictly speaking, the problem is not that Jesus used popular language. No advocate of inerrancy denies that. James Orr's real point is that Jesus often embraced popular opinion. Hard-core inerrancy advocates might balk at the idea of Jesus' accommodating himself to certain popular thoughts. If Jesus could accommodate himself to fallible human opinions in even one case, how could readers of the Bible know that he had not accommodated himself to fallible popular opinion on matters of salvation, immortality, God, demons, angels, and so on? Once again the slippery slope argument comes to the fore.

Yet hard-liner Harold Lindsell appears to think that upon at least one occasion Jesus did accommodate himself to a popular and false opinion of his time. In Matthew 13:32 Jesus says that the mustard seed is the smallest of all seeds, and Mark 4:31 calls it the smallest of all seeds on earth. When faced with the botanical fact that the mustard seed is not the smallest seed, Lindsell tries to make Jesus adapt to modern botany by holding that Jesus merely went along with the popular opinion of the day. In Lindsell's own words, "If Jesus was talking about the seeds commonly known to the people of that day, the effects of His words was different from what they would have been if He was speaking of all seeds on the earth."[4]

Many people will ask with a shrug, "What difference does it make, so long as Jesus got his point across?" But Lindsell cannot adopt such an easygoing attitude. He cannot consistently believe that the problem of the mustard seed is in the category of the medieval monks' problem of how many angels can sit on a pinhead. The mustard seed may indeed be tiny, but Lindsell's problem is not. One of his close friends, Gleason Archer, explains why when he writes about the results of admitting so much as one error in Scripture: "Ultimately the small crack in the dike leads to the washing away of the dike as a whole."[5]

It is understandable that Lindsell or anyone embracing the theory of inerrancy would find it painful to state openly that because Jesus was fully human he was inevitably ignorant and misinformed in a number of areas. But that is what being human entails. Anything short of that is Docetism, the view that Jesus only appeared to be human. There is an ancient assumption that ignorance is always a symptom of sin; accordingly, to admit that Jesus was ignorant in any area is to hint that he was sinful. But most people who believe that Adam and Eve were actual human beings do not think they were omniscient and free of error in all their opinions even before they ate the forbidden fruit. Among scientists, the tendency to regard ignorance and error as a moral flaw has yet to be fully overcome. Even though Sir Isaac Newton's sweeping theory was superseded decades ago by a more powerful theory, many scientists still become indignant at the suggestion that Newton's theory has been refuted. They erroneously think that to admit that his great intellectual achievement was refuted after more than two centuries of acceptance and replaced by Einstein's superior unifying theory is to imply that Newton was somehow not as respectable a scientist as they had thought. It is perhaps one of the tragedies of the human species that ignorance and error came to be classified in the minds of many as sinful. Those who have a vested interest in universal sinfulness will naturally wish to continue classifying ignorance as sin, since there will always be human ignorance.

James Orr argued that since Jesus was fully human, he could not have been an inerrant expert in every field of learning, including the fields of biology and botany. "No one who thinks seriously on the subject will maintain that during His earthly life Jesus carried in His consciousness a knowledge of all events of history, past, present and future, of all arts and sciences, including the results of our modern astronomies, geologies, biologies, mathematics, of all languages, etc. To suppose this would be to annul the reality of His human consciousness entirely."[6]

So, the question remains—Is it possible that when speaking to his disciples or to a wider audience Jesus made statements that were innocently inaccurate? Does Lindsell want to assert that throughout his entire adult life Jesus never uttered one word in ignorance or made sincere statements that turned out to be false? Does Lindsell wish to make Jesus not human?

Most of the proponents of inerrancy have been less than forthright in dealing with the question of Jesus' finitude. They do admit that Jesus was ignorant of the precise time of his return to earth, but Lindsell has ducked the more fundamental question: Were there any areas of knowledge in which Jesus thought he was well informed but in which it appears he was misinformed? Was the relative size of the mustard seed one of those cases? Could Jesus have been honestly in error about what was the smallest seed on earth? And could he have innocently passed that piece of misinformation on to others in his preaching?

It is perhaps unclear as to whether the questions in the above paragraph are examples of the historical-critical method. They are certainly questions that might have been asked by persistent theologians in the Middle Ages, when presumably the historical-critical method was not a part of the Christian thinker's repertoire. Lindsell says that the real father of the method was Johann Semler of the eighteenth century.[7] The historical method leads students of the Qur'an or of any other putative Scripture to look behind the scenes, that is, to go far beyond the arbitrarily drawn context that tradition assigns to any given body of Scripture. Contexts and sources beyond the traditional boundaries cast their light on problematic texts and refract that light in surprisingly insightful and sometimes disturbing ways.

Even though relentlessly critical of other scholars who reach outside the Bible to make judgments about its meaning and truth, Lindsell reaches out to modern botany. Or, to be more accurate, modern botany has forced on him the problem of the mustard seed. Had he known nothing of modern botany, he would probably have taken the statements in Mark and Matthew at face value. It would never have occurred to him to call into question the prima facie interpretation that the mustard seed was the smallest of all the seeds.

Although Lindsell rejects the theory of evolution because it runs counter to his view of Genesis, he cannot bring himself to believe that modern common sense and science are wrong in affirming that there are seeds smaller than the mustard seed. Had the mustard seed been the smallest seed in the first century, then Jesus' statement would not have been false even if in subsequent centuries smaller seeds had been developed by botanists. Lindsell realizes that he cannot take that route, for he believes that seeds smaller than the mustard seed did exist in the first century. So, he is forced back to the original question: Why did Jesus say plainly that the mustard seed was the smallest on earth if he knew full well that what he was saying was false?

Lindsell's answer may one day be known as the Lindsell Shuffle. He tries to shift the problem to make it appear that it is merely a matter of identifying Jesus' immediate audience. But the issue is not what the audience believed but what Jesus himself said. Lindsell creates a smoke screen by attacking Daniel Fuller's way of handling the problem, and he almost succeeds in diverting attention from his own brazen attempt to put words into the mouth of Jesus: "I regret Dr. Fuller's notion that I affirmed that Jesus said that the mustard seed is the smallest of all seeds. I did nothing of the kind."[8]

Let's look at Matthew and Mark to see exactly what it is that Lindsell wishes to deny.

> Another parable he put before them, saying, "The kingdom of heaven is like a grain of mustard seed which a man took and sowed in his field; it is the smallest of all seeds, but when it is grown it is the greatest of shrubs."
>
> Matthew 13:31f
>
> "It is like a grain of mustard seed, which, when sown upon the ground, is the smallest of all the seeds on earth."
>
> Mark 4:31

Immediately after denying "that Jesus said the mustard seed is the smallest of all seeds," Lindsell goes on to become an embellishing redactor by concocting words not in the Gospel accounts and then placing them in the mouth of Jesus: "All Jesus said was that this was the smallest of seeds cultivated by his learners in their gardens or fields."[9]

Instead of admitting that the qualifying words were cultivated and fabricated inside his own head, Lindsell asserts that the context provided them.

Instead of following Lindsell in mangling these two passages and inventing phrases out of thin air, Daniel Fuller accepts the prima facie meaning, namely, that Jesus was repeating the popular belief of his day. The belief about the size of the mustard seed happens to be in error, but the revelatory point that Jesus made suffers nothing. Only Lindsell's peculiar theory of inerrancy suffers. (By the way, *The Criswell Study Bible* glides over this passage as if it posed no problem for the inerrancy hypothesis at all.)

Lindsell patches up his awkward interpretation, but the repairs have long-term consequences. Quite naturally he worries about admitting that Jesus and the biblical writers sometimes made concessions to customary views not wholly true or to practices not wholly up to standard. (In the latter case, Paul accommodated a group in the town of Lystra by having his coworker Timothy circumcised; earlier Paul had inveighed against the so-called circumcision party.) Missionaries then and later had to decide how much to concede to local customs and beliefs. Once the interpreter of the Bible admits that Jesus and the biblical writers sometimes adapted their message to communicate effectively, the interpreter must decide where to draw the line. Are references in the Bible about blood sacrifice simply adaptations to the religious thought forms of antiquity?

Is it a step on the slippery slope to admit that biblical writers sometimes accommodated their message to their audience? Lindsell thinks it might well be, which doubtless accounts for his almost desperate attempt to avoid leaving the impression that he has taken the step. When pressed to the edge, some inerrantists seem willing to say that God did not really want the infants of the Canaanites slaughtered by Joshua's army. Rather, they say, God had to accommodate his revelation to the limited understanding of the human race at that early period in human history. After all, they say, according to Jesus, the Mosaic ruling on divorce in the Hebrew Bible represents not what God intended but what the people could receive under their sinful and limited conditions. Unfortunately, the slippery slope of accommodation in revelation poses an unwelcome dilemma for the inerrantists. Either the slippery slope of accommodation exists without anyone's employing the historical method, or Jesus himself used the historical method when he stated that Moses received a revelation that was historically conditioned and relative. Many inerrantists are forced to call on the tactic of progressive revelation to try to escape the charge of relativism, but the whole idea of progressive revelation might be an irrevocable concession to the historical method. Fundamentalist editor William Powell identifies progressive revelation with none other than liberalism.

The numerous repairs and shifts needed to keep the hypothesis of biblical inerrancy afloat can quickly add up to a costly sum. To avoid concluding either that Jesus did not know what the smallest seed on earth was or that Jesus did know but simply went along with popular misinformed opinion, Lindsell is forced to insert his own words into the text. It is a strange way to defend biblical inerrancy and to attack Robert Gundry's theory of editorial embellishments of material.

Most biblical scholars admit that they cannot harmonize the four Gospel accounts of the cock's crowing upon Peter's denial of Christ. Lindsell claims to have effected a harmony, which has proven embarrassing to fellow inerrantist James I. Packer. In his February 1985 guest lecture at the Southwestern Baptist Theological Seminary, Packer demonstrated how Lindsell's tactic of simply adding up the several accounts leads to self-contradiction. Cautioning against making absurd harmonies, Packer says it is wiser to admit that a harmony of apparently discrepant passages cannot yet be made. Even though Packer is a noted proponent of biblical inerrancy, some Southern Baptist inerrantists flinch when he speaks critically of the "crudities" of interpretation at "the popular piety level." After criticizing "the prosaic predictions of the future" by the pious who fail to grasp the poetic aspects of the Book of Revelation, he cautions those who profess to find in the Bible "technical scientific, as distinct from naive observational, statements about the natural order."

Among the biblical scholars at Fuller Theological Seminary and at the six Southern Baptist seminaries, the great majority have given up the conjecture of total inerrancy. They have gradually found that the cost to them personally in clinging to it created too severe a strain intellectually and morally.

JOSHUA'S KILLING FIELDS

A prime example of that strain is the story of Joshua's slaughter of the Canaanite children. One crucial point of convergence between the defenders of inerrancy and those Baptists who reject inerrancy is their agreement that if God had given a commandment against murder, he could not have given Joshua an order that would violate his original commandment. Standing now at the fork of the road, the defenders of inerrancy take one route and their opponents take the other. The strict inerrancy defenders insist that since Joshua was ordered by God to kill children, the killings cannot be characterized as murder. The opponents of inerrancy insist that since Joshua's killing of innocent children was clearly murder, it could not have been ordered by God.

There is a second theological point on which almost every Southern Baptist will agree. In the words of the strict inerrancy defender Norman Geisler, "God cannot decide to be unloving, nor can he desire that cruelty and injustice be performed." In other words, "his nature demands that he be absolutely good." [10]

Sitting in his study, Draper said plainly that killing innocent children today would be cruel and immoral. He agreed further that God would not command anyone to kill innocent children today and that anyone who killed them would be guilty of murder.

Now the question is, if in God's mind killing innocent children is cruel and murderous today, has it not always been cruel and murderous? Anyone who would answer no is obligated to state when it was that God changed his mind. Draper denies that God has ever changed his mind on the moral absolutes. Such a denial ought to lead straight to the conclusion that Joshua's killing of those innocent children was a cruel and murderous act, but Draper instead asserts that God ordered Joshua to commit the act.

Struggling to justify his macabre conclusion, Draper calls on his own version of accommodation, which he calls progressive revelation. In so doing, he turns God into a bizarre model of situation ethics at its perverse extreme. The astronomical price that Draper and his colleagues seem forced to pay to keep their inerrancy epistemology is nothing less than moral relativism projected into heaven itself. Some of Draper's fellow Southern Baptists shake their heads and ask, "How can such rationalization of wickedness serve as the unshakable moral foundation of human civilization?"

Far from subscribing to the moral relativism that the Inerrancy Party charges them with, many of the opponents of inerrancy say that the obscenity that Draper, Paige Patterson, Pressler, and the other inerrancy advocates wish to spread throughout the Convention is absolutely immoral. The word "obscenity," meaning that which is morally offensive and repulsive, is too weak to describe Joshua's chilling act of perversity performed in the name of God, thus adding blasphemy to perversity. All the excuses offered to justify the Joshua atrocity are riddled with more irrationality and dancing paradoxes than fill the combined tomes of neo-orthodoxy and existentialism. Each new attempt to rationalize Joshua's savagery serves only to cut away one more nerve of moral sensitivity. The assertion that God commanded Joshua to carry out a Nazi-style program of tribal extermination stands in no danger of the slippery slope only because it starts at the bottom of the slope and never succeeds in rising an inch above it. It may be the first example of a human holocaust in history.

Readers unfamiliar with the lengths to which inerrancy defenders are prepared to go will likely be morally shaken by Lindsell's defense of Joshua's extermination program. To many, he might sound like the apologists of the Nazi liquidation of Jews when he explains that none of the children that Joshua slaughtered were innocent. Since the account in Joshua predictably does not describe them as innocent, Lindsell presumes that the infants and children must have all been too wicked to be worthy of life. Apparently fearful of being taken as an outright tribal bigot, Lindsell tries to explain how he can defend the extermination of children. But he succeeds only in compounding the obscenity by asking, "Indeed, who is there of whom it can be said that he or she is truly innocent?" [11] Such reasoning has allowed some early Protestant theologians to conclude that when unbaptized infants die, they deservedly go to hell forever. Who is truly innocent? One wonders what other atrocities can be perpetrated upon children and adults who apparently do not measure up to Lindsell's arbitrary requirement of innocence to the tenth power.

There is certainly little innocence in Lindsell's attempted justification of wholesale slaughter to protect his doctrine of biblical inerrancy. His doctrine levies a heavy tax on the most elementary sense of moral decency. It is interesting but morally disconcerting to learn that human beings can often commit hideous acts of brutality as long as they believe there is some powerful authority legitimating the atrocity.[12] Despite Stalin's slaughter of millions inside the Soviet Union, some Soviet citizens looked up to him and called him the Dear Father of the Soviet People.[13] Most disconcerting is the realization that many of the same fundamentalists who take seriously the golden rule and practice deeply moving acts of kindness toward their own children and their neighbor's can at the same time weave intricate webs of nightmarish rationalizations to justify Joshua's atrocities, thereby subverting their true decency and manifest humaneness.

Many opponents of Lindsell's doctrine of inerrancy would rather give up the doctrine and its epistemological security than believe that God joined a gang of cutthroats in quest of real estate.

> There was not a city that made peace with the people of Israel, except the Hivites, the inhabitants of Gibeon; they took all in battle. For it was the Lord's doing to harden their hearts that they should come up against Israel in battle, in order that they should be utterly destroyed, and should receive no mercy but be exterminated, as the Lord commanded Moses.
>
> Joshua 11:19–20

10.

Worlds Apart

At least one segment of Southern Baptists is convinced that little will come of the current battle within their Convention. James M. Palmer, minister of the First Baptist Church in Center, Texas, and formerly a professor of sociology, believes that the organizational complexity and sheer bigness of the Convention can absorb the shock of any internal movement. Conceding that the Inerrancy Party will achieve its goal of placing still more of its people on the powerful trustee boards of Convention agencies and seminaries, Dr. Palmer offers three reasons for concluding that the efforts of the Inerrancy Party will have only a minimal impact. First, when the new trustees assume their responsibilities, they will come under the influence of those already in office. A moderating process will in effect rob the Inerrancy Party of its momentum as the new trustees come to understand the complexity of the Convention and the awesomeness of their responsibilities. In short, despite their convictions about biblical inerrancy, they will make compromises.

Second, the Convention's current swing to the right reflects a national trend to the right. As the national trend reaches its point of diminishing returns, a swing back toward the center will take place, carrying Southern Baptists along with it.

The final point that Palmer makes is connected closely with the second. He believes that like most social movements, the present one within the Convention has generated promises it can fulfill only in part. The symbolic victories will give way to apathy. Because only a few individuals can in reality benefit vocationally or gain a genuinely better position within the Convention by supporting the movement, the fervor will eventually wane and the leaders of the Inerrancy Party will be weakened as disillusionment creeps into the entire movement.

THE LUTHERAN COUP D'ETAT

Palmer's prediction strongly appeals to some of the Convention's most astute moderates and seasoned leaders. They are a dwindling minority, however, as memories of the Lutheran Church-Missouri Synod stubbornly resist Palmer's prediction. On January 2, 1974, the Missouri Synod's Board of Control fired the president of Concordia Theological Seminary in St. Louis. The seminary's moderates tried a squeeze play to force the Missouri Synod to come to their aid in the fight against staunch inerrancy advocates, but the moderates ended up outside in the cold with no home. After all but five of the faculty members had left the seminary, the Lutheran Church-Missouri Synod continued without them. A sociologist could have told them that institutions and roles tend to survive much longer than the most dedicated of human individuals who serve them.

In previous decades it was the inerrancy defenders who lost when other Protestant denominations in the United States suffered internal eruption and fragmentation. The Lutheran Church-Missouri Synod reversed that trend. Encouraged by the 1974 triumph of the Lutheran inerrancy party, some Southern Baptist inerrantists have reaffirmed their long-term strategy to remove from Baptist schools and positions of influence all who do not publicly espouse the inerrancy doctrine. The parity that Paige Patterson and others frequently speak of appears to be no more than a temporary tactic in service of the tougher, long-range strategy.

The Battle of the Baptists is far more complex and is fought on a much wider scale than the Lutherans' bitter ordeal. But the Lutheran experience has provided Baptist professors with a laboratory experiment, so to speak, allowing them to predict that if they should walk out of their classrooms en masse, the effect would be mostly symbolic. If every professor resigned this week, the Convention, after a few years of confusion, bitterness, and inconvenience, would replace them and go on about its business. Psychologists would view the situation in terms of stress and extreme frustration for individuals, but sociologists would view it as a couple of decades of social disequilibrium of minor consequence. The Convention's structure and institutions would continue intact. Furthermore, if all the super, jumbo-size churches should pull out of the Convention, taking their money and numbers with them, the Convention would survive that temporary trauma, too.

The jumbo-size churches have become a powerful force within the Convention, a force that has grown into a denominational subculture. Two Southern Baptists who are also sociologists and members of the Association for the Scientific Study of Religion—Dr. Frank Forwood and James M. Palmer—have advanced the tentative thesis that a new coalition has developed within the Convention, a coalition that will have to be reckoned with in the immediate years to come. It is a wedding of the jumbo-size fundamentalist churches, mostly in large metropolitan areas in the South, with the smaller rural churches whose ministers have little formal theological education. With some significant exceptions, the coalition's ministers feel little kinship with the seminaries. The near future of the Southern Baptist Convention will likely be shaped considerably by the coalition of bigness and smallness.

THE GREAT GAP

If anthropologists were to study the Southern Baptist Convention the way they study the behavior and belief-systems of various tribes, they would likely designate its most serious division as not a social but a cultural division of competing worldviews. The Convention is suffering from more than a contest over raw power or a clash of egos; Southern Baptists are split into two worldviews that are drifting farther and farther apart. While each side acknowledges most of the benefits of modern technology, the inerrancy doctrine is firmly set against modern science. Since the late sixties the American (and much of the world's) population has suffered disillusionment with science, encouraging the most outspoken advocates of the inerrancy doctrine to rejoice and to capitalize on it. When modern science in its youth was struggling for survival in the sixteenth and seventeenth centuries, jealous and powerful forces within the Roman Catholic hierarchy treated it as an evil consequence of the Protestant heresy. As it fought back, the insecure scientific community quickly became a victim of its own propaganda, brashly promising to increase the certainty of knowledge through science. Only with the Einsteinian revolution centuries later did the scientific community begin to grasp the disturbing thought that the growth of scientific knowledge precluded cognitive certainty. The current global phenomenon of entrenchment in past religious certainties may be in part a delayed reaction to the news that science cannot provide from generation to generation the dogmatic corpus once delivered to the saints (especially Saint Newton, who was to science what Muhammad was to Islam). With zeal, the high priests of inerrancy around the globe have leaped out onstage to announce that even though science cannot satisfy the craving for absolute certainty, the Scriptures (or whatever) can and will! The disillusionment with science has created a vacuum, and the old illusions of certainty are rushing in to fill it.

Neither the inerrancy advocates nor their opponents regard current scientific theories as the final word of truth. Leaders of each camp point out that science is in perpetual evolution if not revolution.[1] What, then, separates the two Southern Baptist camps regarding science? The Inerrancy Party has decreed that if any scientific theory comes into conflict with its interpretation of Scripture, then that scientific theory must be branded as an impostor, not as true science. From it the Christian must learn next to nothing. Indeed, the Inerrancy Party wants the masses in the churches to think of any threatening theory as a temptation that could seduce the innocent to indulge in evil thoughts and doubts. Any minister or professor who teaches such a theory to the innocent in the schools or the pews is seen as being no better than an agent of pornography who exposes nude bodies publicly. Only a few highly trained members of the faithful are permitted to view the theory that conflicts with the established interpretation of Scripture. And even those few must consider it only with the goal of refuting and destroying it.

The Southern Baptists who reject the inerrancy doctrine look upon the Inerrancy Party as an heir to those inquisitors who tried to suppress Galileo's astronomy. The anti-inerrancy Southern Baptists agree that the crown of absolute certainty and infallibility should be removed from science, but not so that it can be snatched up and placed on the inflated head of fundamentalism. They find it scandalous that the defenders of inerrancy presume to inform the world's geologists, biologists, zoologists, and botanists that one of their basic theories— evolution—not only is false but was never a scientific theory in the first place. Some inerrantists go so far as to announce that their doctrine of creationism is scientific and the theory of evolution is a false religion.

W. A. Criswell is so certain that his sketchy interpretation of the origin and development of the universe and the species is correct that he stands prepared to use political muscle and economic clout to prevent biologists and other scientists from seriously presenting the theory of evolution at the seminaries or any other Southern Baptist school. Joined by his comrades in inerrancy, Criswell now thinks that teachers at any of the Southern Baptist schools who do not agree with him on what he thinks is basic should be fired and replaced by those who do agree. "There are plenty of other places where the infidels can teach," Criswell stated, presuming that those who do not agree with him about creationism and evolution are infidels or unbelievers. Until recently, Criswellian fundamentalism had dominated the Texas public school textbook committee sufficiently to guarantee that an entire generation of Texas students has now graduated without being able to write a two-page paper on the simple notion of natural selection within the evolutionary framework. Dr. Richard Land of the Criswell Center has recently come to see that such scientific illiteracy is inexcusable, even though he is personally an antievolutionist.

Many moderate Southern Baptists have reservations about the theory of evolution, as do scientists themselves. As the noted philosopher of science Karl Popper points out, the life of science as a community depends on the internal generation of criticisms and reservations about its leading theories. A number of moderates hold to the theory of evolution and cast it within a theistic framework, as does Popper's longtime friend, the brain physiologist John Eccles. Theologian Dale Moody has taken up the challenge to try to find ways that Christian Scripture and science may throw light on each other regarding the development of the human species. One of his most fruitful attempts is his exegesis of "Adam" in Genesis.[2] Dr. Eric Rust, for years professor at Southern Seminary in Louisville, Bob Patterson of Baylor University, and scores of other Baptist professors are working diligently to increase the interaction between science and Scripture. In 1979 one of the Convention presses published *Science, Faith and Revelation: An Approach to Christian Philosophy,*[3] in honor of Eric Rust. The book shows what can be done when Southern Baptist scholars are invited to share their views on the interface of theology and science. But on the Inerrancy Party side, some individuals seem to want to follow the papal example of setting up a Forbidden Index, resorting to political and economic tactics in an attempt to restrain Convention presses from publishing similar books and from making such books available in Convention bookstores. It is anti-intellectuals such as these inerrancy zealots whose strategy is to gain control of all Southern Baptist schools and publishing centers. A Baptist minister in East Tennessee recently commented, "They won't be content to run our schools and presses; they want to deny the rest of us access to them." By the same token, the Sunday School Board acted paternalistically in preventing James Hefley's *The Truth in Crisis* from being sold at the SBC bookstore at the Atlanta convention. Fortunately, it can be purchased at other SBC bookstores.

A growing group of Southern Baptist scholars (including professors and ministers) holds that neither Scripture nor science is inerrant. They reject both the demand that science yield to Scripture on every point and the demand that every assertion be scientifically corroborated before acting upon it. For these scholars, faith is not only the reception of unearned grace but also the exercise of courage to go on in a world without inerrancy and absolute certainty.

The relationship between science and religion has not been firmly settled for most enlightened people. The new developments within science itself will in the future thoroughly shake those able to journey with it on its breathtaking vistas. Along with the fact of death, the new twists and turns in science guarantee that the human species will remain incurably religious. The blow that science delivers to every established belief-system will perpetually remind human beings of their inescapable finitude, which is the rock-bottom religious problem. The forms that religion will take in dealing with this finitude-shock can scarcely be predicted, but the longing for inerrancy and certainty is not likely to subside over the generations to come.

As long as the human species survives, it will sense—suffer—its finitude. And if science does not perish from society, it will necessarily intensify that dreadful sense of finitude and the powerful sense of wonder that causes religion to make room for philosophy and art.

MUSLIMS AND MORMONS

Today, the hundreds of millions of Muslims who hold to the infallibility and inerrancy of the Qur'an contend that if and when a scientific theory falls in discord with the Qur'an, the theory must be classified as false science. The same tension between science and Scripture exists among Utah Mormons, bred in the faith that Joseph Smith, though a man of humble origins, received Heaven's inerrant revelation. In the words of one Mormon Apostle, "The Book of Mor-

mon . . . must be either true or false. If true, it is one of the most important messages ever sent from God. . . . If false, it is one of the
most cunning, wicked, bold, deep-laid impositions ever palmed upon
the world, calculated to deceive and ruin millions."[4]

Fearful of what unbridled research in science, history, and philosophy and other fruit of wonder might do to the faith, the Mormon hierarchy maintains a subtle but steady pressure on Brigham Young University professors to say nothing that will indicate that the Book of
Mormon fails to be in perfect accord with modern anthropology, historical inquiry, biology, and geology. Leonard Arrington, official historian for the Latter-day Saints for a number of years, was appointed
by the church hierarchy to employ a crew of professionally trained researchers to work on the original foundational documents of the
church. When eventually the hierarchy learned that the results of the
project seemed to reflect unfavorably on Mormon orthodoxy, it took
three steps to interfere with the project: it moved the historical department away from the main source of manuscripts at church headquarters in Salt Lake City, it unceremoniously relieved Arrington of
his responsibilities, and it blatantly suppressed the sixteen-volume
sesquicentennial history. Today, the historical department sits on the
second floor of the Latter-day Saints Church Office Building. On one
wall of that second floor hang portraits of church historians, beginning with the first and ending with the current, G. Homer Durham.
Dr. Arrington's portrait is conspicuously absent.[5]

SCIENCE, BIBLE, AND QUR'AN

If asked "Do you believe the Qur'an is free of all error?" hundreds
of millions of Muslims would answer yes. Leading advocates of the
Qur'an's inerrancy insist that science cannot contradict Islamic Scripture, which is faithfully memorized and studied in every Islamic university in the world. Roman Catholics who believed in the infallibility
of the Church once took it as axiomatic that true science could never
contradict the established teachings of the Church. The trial of Galileo
stands as a notorious reminder of the Church's past willingness to
erase any belief-system that seriously rivaled it. Efforts of certain Protestant inerrantists to erase the theory of evolution from the public
school curriculum reflect the same kind of anti-intellectualism.

Recently, the Roman Catholic Church, with the belated blessings of
John Paul II, withdrew its condemnation of Galileo. Many Protestants

have dissociated themselves from those who fought to prevent Darwinism from being studied forthrightly in the public schools in the twenties and the early eighties. In the sixteenth century, both Luther and his fellow reformer Melanchthon openly condemned the astronomer Copernicus, of whom Martin Luther wrote, "People gave ear to an upstart astrologer who strove to show that the earth revolves, not the heavens or the firmament, the sun and the moon. . . . The fool wishes to reverse the entire science of astronomy, but the sacred Scripture tells us that Joshua commanded the sun to stand still, and not the earth."[6] Melanchthon cared even less for Copernicus and his astronomy: "Now, it is want of honesty and decency to assert such notions publicly, and the example is pernicious. It is the part of a good mind to accept the truth as revealed by God and to acquiesce in it."[7] To escape the prima facie reading of the biblical text of Genesis 19:23, Norman Geisler says that "what they [the biblical writers] affirmed in the text is that the sun is observed to rise and set." Of course, the words "is observed to" are Geisler's; they are not in the Bible. The distinction between what is and what is observed to be is a distinction that Geisler injects into the Genesis text. One may conjecture that his purpose was to save the text from direct conflict with modern astronomy, but to be perfectly consistent Geisler should have rejected modern astronomy, as he had rejected modern biology's theory of evolution. By doing so, he could have at least remained consistent with the reformers Luther and Melanchthon. Unlike Geisler, the reformers did not draw a line between what the biblical text states and the conjecture as to what the writer intended. For them, there existed only the text, not the Genesis writer's intention. Luther correctly understood the text and did not even attempt to make it harmonize with the new astronomy of his day.[8]

The defenders of the Qur'an's inerrancy may be compared with the defenders of the Bible's inerrancy. Each group strives heroically to demonstrate that its Scripture stands in complete harmony with true science. Where there is conflict between a scientific theory and any passage of Scripture (Qur'an or Bible), the inerrancy advocate will label the scientific theory as false or pseudo science.

W. A. CRISWELL AND HIS ISLAMIC COUNTERPART

For the French surgeon Maurice Bucaille, the only body of literature on earth that is free of all error is the Qur'an. For Criswell, the Bible alone is the Word of God without mixture of error. For these two men, their respective Scripture is not a textbook in science, and they are eager to make that clear. But whenever Scripture touches on any question of science, Criswell and Bucaille insist that Scripture cannot be in error. Indeed, each asserts that some passages of Scripture are so up-to-date in scientific information that they could not be fully appreciated until the twentieth century.

In an address titled "The Infallible Word of God," Criswell comments on the harmony of his Scripture with modern true science:

> The latest scientific theories are confirmed by the Word of God. To take just one other example, turn to Hebrews 11:3: "Through faith we understand that the worlds were framed by the word of God, so that things which are seen were not made of things which do appear." Let me paraphrase that: "So that the things that are visible are made out of entities that are invisible." Did you ever hear a finer statement of the molecular, atomic, nature of this universe in substance and reality than that?[9]

With confidence to equal Criswell's, Bucaille affirms that the Qur'an predicts the human conquest of space and contains an account of the human embryo's development fully in harmony with modern embryology.[10] After studying the Qur'an at length in its original language, Arabic, Bucaille concluded:

> I could not find a single error in the Qur'an. I had to stop and ask myself: if a man was the author of the Qur'an, how could he have written facts in the Seventh century A.D. that today are shown to be in keeping with modern scientific knowledge? There was absolutely no doubt about it: the text of the Qur'an we have today is most definitely a text of the period. . . . What human explanation can there be for this observation? In my opinion there is no explanation; there is no special reason why an inhabitant of the Arabian Peninsula should . . . have had scientific knowledge on certain subjects that was ten centuries ahead of our own.[11]

Like some fundamentalist Christian opponents of the historical-critical method of studying the Bible, the Muslim proponents of Qur'anic inerrancy resent any talk of material taken from human sources.[12] Over and over Bucaille tries to show that the Qur'an harmonizes with modern astronomy and cosmology while incorporating none of the out-dated cosmology popular at the time of its writing.[13] The explanation, he believes, is that the Qur'an is a supernatural revelation. Granting that thinkers in the past were able to arrive at various truths, Bucaille insists that their truths were mingled with error. Only the Qur'an is truth without mixture of error.

> In the Sixth century B.C., they [the Pythagoreans] defended the theory of the rotation of the Earth on its own axis and the movement of the planet around the Sun. This theory was to be confirmed by modern science. . . . However, people quite simply forget to mention the other aspect of what these geniuses of philosophical reasoning produced, i.e., the colossal blunders that litter their work. . . . The brilliance of these human works comes from the advanced ideas they contain, but they should not make us overlook the mistaken concepts which have also been left us. From a strictly scientific point of view, this is what distinguishes them from the Qur'an. In the latter, many subjects are referred to that have a bearing on modern knowledge without one of them containing a statement that contradicts what has been established by present-day science.[14]

After discussing in detail the 1961 human spaceflight around the globe and then comparing the Qur'an with the data of modern science, Bucaille concludes that there are scientifically advanced materials in the Qur'an that cannot be explained as simply the thoughts of a man who lived fourteen centuries ago.[15] Contrasting the flaws that he finds in the Bible with the perfection that he thinks characterizes the Qur'an, Dr. Bucaille writes, "Whether it [the Qur'an] deals therefore with the origins of life in general, or the elements that give birth to plants in the soil, or the seed of animals, all the statements contained in the Qur'an on the origin of life are strictly in accordance with modern scientific data. None of the myths on the origin of life that abounded at the time the Qur'an appeared are mentioned in the text."[16]

Muslim apologists often ask the question, How could an illiterate like Muhammad bring into being the most important document in the whole of Arabic literature? Or as Bucaille asks, "How could he then pronounce truths of a scientific nature that no other human being could possibly have developed at the time, and all this without once making the slightest error in his pronouncements on the subject?"[17] For Bucaille, there can be no human explanation. That is why he eventually converted to Islam. "In the beginning, I had no faith whatsoever in Islam," he writes. He had studied the Bible for years, and in great detail, but he finally concluded that only the Qur'an was truly free of all error.[18]

Returning to Criswell's attempt to harmonize the Bible with modern science, a point needs to be made about Hebrews 11:3, which Criswell believes is about the atomic structure of the universe. Criswell breaks out in unguarded affirmation, but his friend Herschel Hobbs speaks more cautiously of "a hint of the findings of modern science wherein visible matter is understood to be composed of invisible atoms."[19] Assuming that Hebrews 11:3 does refer to invisible entities, there is no reason to pass hastily over the possibility that the epistle's author was aware of one of several ancient philosophical theories of entities not visible to the naked eye.

Five hundred years before the Epistle to the Hebrews was written, the philosopher Anaxagoras advanced the view that observable things were composed of a mixture of an infinite number of invisible "seeds." Ancient Greek philosophy had several modifications of the atomic theory. Leucippus (circa 450 B.C.E.) and Democritus (circa 460–360 B.C.E.) developed an entire ontology of invisible atomic entities. Plato (427–347 B.C.E.) revised the atomic theory to fit with his own metaphysical view. Epicurus (341–270 B.C.E.) and the Latin poet Lucretius (96–55 B.C.E.) adopted Democritus' atomic theory. Some students of the Epistle to the Hebrews believe that its author was versed in Platonic thought, at least in the version reflected by the Jewish writer Philo of Alexandria, an older contemporary of the Apostle Paul. If that is true, it is altogether plausible that the author of Hebrews was acquainted with a Platonic version of atomism. Hence, instead of predicting a modern version of physics, Hebrews 11:3 reflects a view known to most intellectuals of the first century.

Some within the Southern Baptist Inerrancy Party resent even a hint of the historical method in studying the Bible, although their resentment disappears when the same method is applied to the Scripture of Islam.

RIVAL WORLDVIEWS

According to Genesis 9, Noah after the flood planted a vineyard, drank wine, and became drunk. When Ham saw Noah naked, he left Noah's tent and informed his two older brothers about their father. Shem and Japheth took a garment and, walking backward, entered Noah's tent to cover his nakedness without looking at him. Upon waking from his drunken stupor and realizing "what his youngest son had done to him," Noah pronounced what has come to be known as Noah's curse:

> "Cursed be Canaan; a slave of slaves shall he be to his brothers."
> He also said, "Blessed by the Lord my God be Shem; and let Ca-
> naan be his slave. God enlarge Japheth, and let him dwell in the
> tents of Shem; and let Canaan be his slave."
>
> Genesis 9:25–27

Later, the narrator reveals that Canaan is the son of Ham, the one who saw Noah's nakedness. When the Southern Baptist Convention was formed in 1845, most of its leaders and preachers had already been offering Genesis 9 as evidence that God sanctioned enslavement of Africans, who were presumed to be the blood heirs of Canaan. John L. Dagg, whom Jimmy Draper calls "the first truly 'Southern Baptist' theologian," was convinced that the Bible stood free of error and discrepancy.[20] For Dagg, God put every verse into the Bible for a purpose, and one purpose of Genesis 9 was to show how God after the flood wanted the peoples of the world distributed and ranked. A racial bigot of the first magnitude, Dagg devoted years of his life to justifying the capture of Africans for the purpose of auctioning them off as slaves in America.

After the Civil War, the Southern Baptists who owned slaves released them, but they did not give up their belief that God had cursed Canaan and his heirs. Segregation became the heir of slavery among Southern Baptists, and Genesis 9 remained one of their prized texts in defense of unadulterated racism. Criswell helped continue the tradition of biblical segregation until the sixties, when Martin Luther King, Jr., and other political liberals and moderates convinced a large portion of American institutional leaders that racial segregation was heinous and wicked. On February 22, 1956, Criswell stood before the South Carolina Legislature and viciously denounced racial integration, having on the day before delivered the same address before an evangelistic conference. In the vituperative message he made a racist joke before the legislators, a joke comparing the words "Negro" and "chiggero." During the same decade he used condescending racist humor in the chapel of Southern Baptist Seminary. It fell flat before a large audience that had come to hear one of the Southern Baptists' most prominent ministers. A decade later Southern Baptists had already elected Congressman Brooks Hays, an outspoken integrationist, to be their president. By 1968 Criswell had become a serious prospect for the highest position of honor among Southern Baptists. Just one week before the 1968 annual session of the Convention, he persuaded his deacons to back him in announcing that their church had no color barrier to membership. After his election as president, Criswell told his congregation that segregation was unbiblical, citing three passages from the Bible, one of which was Revelation 22:17. As Dick J. Reavis pointed out in an October 1984 *Texas Monthly* article, Criswell had written ten pages of commentary on that one verse in 1965, but he had not seen its antiracism implications until he became a candidate for the Convention presidency.

Doubting that Criswell's political shucking of racism had any profound theological foundation, Reavis noted that *The Criswell Study Bible* still embraces the racist interpretation of Genesis 9 that for centuries had sanctioned slavery as a divine institution. Old John Dagg's influence still lives.

In some ways Criswell and all those committed to biblical inerrancy are stuck with Genesis 9 and many other passages that touch on moral degradation. One evangelical attempted to liberalize his racism by saying that there was no clear biblical proof that Africans were the heirs of the cursed Canaan. He seemed unable to see that the issue was not the identity of Canaan's heirs, as if enslavement of a non-African people were somehow acceptable. Rather the issue had to do with whether any portion of the human race should be turned into slaves.

In the fifties a student at the Southern Baptist Theological Seminary in Louisville offered this view of the Genesis 9 passage: "Where does it say that God himself either cursed Canaan or turned his offspring into slaves? This passage doesn't say that the Spirit of God entered Noah to inspire him to pronounce words of prophecy or to curse anyone. It seems to me that old Noah was filled more with the spirits of the vineyard than with the Spirit of God."

This seminary student had recently given up the inerrancy doctrine, and he was convinced that by moving beyond it he gained enough freedom of mind to read Genesis 9 in an entirely new light. Indeed, Southern Baptists are divided as much over the moral implications of parts of the Bible as over the epistemological implications. One group steadfastly refuses to believe that God is behind the identifiable streams of brutality, bigotry, and vicious chauvinism that course their way through the Bible. Southern Baptists who think this way embrace a worldview that is in uncompromising rivalry with the advocates of biblical inerrancy. The entire Southern Baptist Convention is being stretched to the limit by two competing worldviews that cannot be synthesized even in a superficial way.

A simple example of the last point can be found in William Powell's reaction to Joseph F. Green's statement that "no woman has a moral right to bear more than two children." [21] An employee of the SBC Sunday School Board since 1954, Green has for years been concerned with the alarming rise in starvation around the globe and the rise in population. Infuriated by Green's remark, William Powell of Buchanan, Georgia, asked, "Does this mean that every woman is immoral if they have more than two children?" As editor of *The Southern Baptist Journal* until after the Dallas convention in 1985, Powell seems in his writings to be so obsessed with portraying as traitors those Convention leaders who reject inerrancy that he cannot learn anything from them. It is as if Powell's brain had become over the years a scanning device for spotting statements that conflict with his position on inerrancy. Learning something constructive from the enemy seemed so unlikely that he was genuinely unable to detect any moral concern behind Green's statement. The question that Powell raised—"Does this mean that every woman is immoral if they have more than two children?"—is a good question that surely ought to be asked. And it was perfectly fair to ask it.

Unfortunately, Powell has never dealt forthrightly and systematically with the tougher question of the personal responsibility of Southern Baptist couples in helping to stop the tragic and bewildering rise in population. As a premillennialist, did Powell think that only the Second Coming of Christ would alleviate the problem? Or did he think that there is not now and never has been an overpopulation problem? His attack on Green might have been more convincing had he first tried to offer a realistic alternative or shown some humane feeling for the population problem.

The two dominant worldviews among Southern Baptists are moving apart at a breakneck speed, and no one senses this more keenly than the Inerrancy Party leaders. They steadfastly, sometimes fiercely, oppose any attempt to link the two worldviews. Theologian Paul Tillich has become a special object of their criticism because they believe he serves only to blur the vast difference between the two worldviews. "Tillich is a bridge, all right," said one proponent of inerrancy with bitter sarcasm. "He's a bridge that leads the innocent out of the clear air of orthodoxy and into the acid rain of heresy."

While sharing much of the same biblical vocabulary and singing many of the same hymns, the Inerrancy Party members do not see and hear the same world as many Southern Baptists who reject inerrancy. It is as if two film directors had been given the means to create separate films, each using the same characters and even the same vignettes and episodes. Yet while one director weaves the vignettes and characters into a very special plot, another weaves them into an altogether different plot. The result is two radically distinct stories and messages. To complicate matters, each director is allowed to see the other's film and review it. When they exchange reviews and read them, each insists that the reviewer has not only failed to grasp the central meaning of the story but has also distorted it almost to the point of slander. What is more, the stories are so radically different from one another that it is impossible for anyone to combine their stories into one or combine their talents to rewrite a third story in common. Each is convinced that there is only one way to bring about a reconciliation. One of them must forsake his story and convert to the other's view.

In truth, the two worldviews are irreconcilable. But is there a way the bearers of the conflicting views can agree to work together as one denomination despite their profound moral and theological differences? The question remains unanswered, but not for long.

11.

The Golden Calf

In the old and popular *A Commentary on the Old and New Testaments*, by Jamieson, Fausset, and Brown, the following comment on Noah's curse of Canaan in Genesis 9:25 appears: "This doom has been fulfilled in the destruction of the Canaanites— in the degradation of Egypt, and the slavery of the Africans, the descendants of Ham."[1] Such blatant racist exegesis was common among inerrancy scholars for many years, especially during the nineteenth century. Orthodoxy seemed incapable of entertaining the possibility that Noah's curse might be not an outline of divinely revealed anthropology but the rationalization of an ancient vendetta of the kind made infamous in the Middle East. Commenting on Genesis 9, the Scofield Reference Bible says, "A prophetic declaration is made that from Ham will descend an inferior and servile posterity."

As recently as 1951, the *Biblical Commentary on the Old Testament* by the evangelical authors C. F. Keil and F. Delitzsch asserted without moral qualification that "the curse which Noah pronounced upon this sin still rests upon the race."[2] Fully convinced that they were exegeting nothing less than God-breathed sacred script, Keil and Delitzsch explained that Ham's

> whole family was included by implication in the curse, even if it was to fall chiefly upon Canaan. And history confirms the supposition. The Canaanites were partly exterminated, and partly subjected to the lowest form of slavery by the Israelites, who belonged to the family of Shem; and those who still remained were reduced by Solomon to the same condition (I Kings ix.

20,21). . . . The remainder of the Hamitic tribes either shared the same fate or still sigh, like the negroes . . . and other African tribes, beneath the yoke of the most crushing slavery.

In another part of the same commentary, where a case is made for the possibility of individual salvation for Ham's presumed descendants, the authors seem to suffer no reservations in speaking of "the accursed race."[3]

The evangelical *New Bible Commentary*, first edition, makes no attempt to counter the assumption that a curse leading to mass slavery of generations of human beings was a just and fitting punishment for Ham's sin. In the fifties the question of racism and segregation was strongly debated in the United States. In the middle of that debate, in 1957, Dr. Russell Bradley Jones devoted several pages defending biblical inerrancy and attacking evolution in his book *A Survey of the Old and New Testaments*. To the issue of racism he devoted one token sentence: "There are no Scriptural grounds for racial pride or prejudice" (page 52). He made no pretense of arguing that the curse of Genesis 9 was not God's curse on an entire race. In self-contradiction, he characterized it as the curse of God (page 51), which is cruelly ironic in light of the book's subtitle, *The Bible Story of Redeeming Love*.

In the early sixties fundamentalists raised a cry of indignation against Dr. Ralph Elliott's book *The Message of Genesis*.[4] In it, this Southern Baptist professor introduced his readers to the documentary hypothesis of the formation of Genesis. In addition, he tried hard to expunge the ninth chapter of Genesis of its racism. He did not succeed, since Genesis 9 reeks conspicuously of racial bigotry. Eventually, on a technicality Elliott was fired from Midwestern Baptist Theological Seminary. Most Baptists who know about the details of Elliott's case know that he was in reality fired because his book paid no homage to the inerrancy doctrine. Within the Inerrancy Party, racism is clearly less sinful and threatening than the denial of inerrancy. No Southern Baptist professor has ever been fired for racism. That is not to say that such professors should be fired, even though racism is a blatant contradiction of every strand of decency within the Bible, including the Golden Rule.

THE NEW PURITANS WITHIN THE MODERATE PARTY

A number of the Inerrancy Party leaders keep repeating the charge that those Southern Baptist ministers and seminary professors who reject the inerrancy position do so because they reject the principle of supernatural revelation. Although expressed with neither malice nor a strong desire to misrepresent, the charge is wildly inaccurate. Because of their preoccupation with uncovering evidence to show that their opponents truly do reject inerrancy, the Inerrancy Party leaders have not been able to see what is before their eyes. A new and unofficial movement has quietly emerged among some of the moderates. Even though it stirred to life almost a generation before the holy war erupted, it is not an organized group that is fully conscious of itself. Scarcely a sweeping tide, its slow and inconspicuous spread among Southern Baptists has proceeded with neither deliberation nor forethought. It is nonetheless real, and some of the Inerrancy Party leaders have sensed it. Its influence is so subtle and steady that many of those most involved in it have been unable to understand it in historical perspective.

This movement is a new Christian revisionism or new Puritanism. Whereas the old Puritans of the seventeenth century set out to purify the churches, the new Puritans, now among Southern Baptist moderates, have set out to purify the tradition itself. They reject the inerrancy doctrine just because they are undaunted Puritans. They have chosen to remain a part of the Southern Baptist Convention because they belong to the nonseparating branch of Puritanism.[5] Far from being schismatics, they cannot even think like schismatics. They are Puritan reformers or revisionists, not restorationists.[6]

Within the Inerrancy Party there are genuine restorationists who, like one wing of the Church of Christ, believe that it is possible to restore first-century Christian churches in the twentieth century. By contrast, the new Puritan revisionists among the moderates are so truly conservative and suspicious of utopian ventures that they look upon restorationists as strange enthusiasts entangled in a self-spun mythology about first-century Christianity.

Unimpressed with the restorationists within the Inerrancy Party, the new Puritans believe that being a Southern Baptist means being the heir of a many-splendored tradition that came by grace before them and will continue by grace after them. They see themselves as passing on their heritage to the next generation, not by rote or by passive indulgence but by personal conviction and heart-felt experience. Their Baptist heritage is not to them a dead hand from the past reaching up out of a closed grave but rather a flowing river fed by many springs, a river in which Providence has allowed them to be baptized. Furthermore, as Baptists with a fierce sense of individuality, they are obsessed with the commission to help make their world and their tradition more Christian if possible. Their new Puritanism is itself the revival of the Puritan spirit of gradualistic reform that they received by the devotion and sacrifice of those who traveled before them. As a part of the Puritan tradition, they could not imagine transmitting to their successors what they have received without attempting to purify and enrich it. With a daring equal to their forebears', these new Puritans throughout the Southern Baptist domain make bold to purify, when necessary, the polluted currents that might have found their way into the biblical Canon itself. For them, Scripture interprets Scripture, and Scripture *corrects* Scripture.

Not that the new Puritans wish to rip pages from the Bible. To the contrary, they demand the freedom to study the Bible forthrightly and to dissociate themselves without apology from manifest wickedness and perversity even within the Bible. They seek to have this freedom without losing their sustained identification with those deeper currents and streams of the Bible, which, they believe, are more revelatory of God.

The new Puritans are not naive about the epistemological problems involved in the critical reading of the Bible, but they refuse to purchase epistemological certainty at the price of moral perversity. Their underlying moral absolute is simple. Any passage, within or without the Bible, that severely retards human community and social justice cannot be divine in origin. No passage can reveal the divine Creator if it degrades that being who is created in the divine image. While freely acknowledging that no mortal can fully grasp the concept of supreme goodness, these new Puritans condemn the old Puritan propensity for subordinating supreme goodness to raw omnipotence. For the new Puritans, God cannot be reduced to omnipotence.

Even though, or rather just because they have roots in the old Puritanism of the seventeenth century, the new Puritans judge their forebears sternly. The Puritans of the Massachusetts Bay colony took Genesis 9 as their text and labeled the Indians as Canaanites for the purpose of murdering them in the name of God, the way Joshua had murdered Canaanites in the name of God. The seventeenth-century preacher Roger Williams serves today as a heroic forebear of faith and moral courage to the new Puritans, for he spoke swiftly and unequivocally against the atrocities committed by his fellow Puritans and also rang a clear and certain bell in favor of political liberty for all religions whose members were willing to keep the civil peace. Whereas the old Puritans often appropriated the ancient curse of Noah as a text and pretext "to follow a multitude to do evil" against their fellow human beings, the new Puritans do not flinch to purify texts of obscenity within the Bible itself. They will yield not one inch to those who bow their knees to the golden calf of inerrancy!

12.

The Status of Southern Baptist Women

A fundamentalist theologian once told me that his wife and he had a biblical marriage. He meant that as husband he was the head of his wife. When asked how he exercised his headship in financial matters, he explained, "My wife keeps the bills and makes out the checks for them. Near the end of the month, I sit down with her and look over all the checks and bills. If she has written the checks properly and everything looks in order, I sign the checks and then she mails them." Whether or not their arrangement captures the heart of biblical teachings on wifely submission, it at least made the fundamentalist theologian feel that he was maintaining his headship and obeying a scriptural requirement. An ordained minister as well as a theologian, he also had in mind a scriptural passage regarding the elder, or overseer: "He must manage his own household well, keeping his children submissive and respectful in every way; for if a man does not know how to manage his own household, how can he care for God's church?" (I Tim. 3:4, 5).

Criswell is sure that the writer of that passage did not entertain the thought that a woman might become an elder or spiritual leader. And if I Timothy 3:11–13 refers to women deacons (which Criswell doubts), the word "deacon" must be understood "in its first-century sense of 'servant.'"[1] In short, when it comes to church affairs, women may serve, but they cannot have a position of authority. Such a position is reserved for men only.

Among Mormons, women are permitted to have their own organizations, but all the officers are elected by the male hierarchy. Most Southern Baptist women would not make good Mormons for many reasons, one being that they understand too well how essential they are to their denomination's life and would not tolerate the arrogance of the Mormon hierarchy. Still, Southern Baptist women have been relegated to subordinate roles within the Convention. The exception is the Women's Missionary Union, which was denied a place at the annual Convention meeting for many years.

In 1954 Paul K. Jewett, noted evangelical scholar at Fuller Theological Seminary, wrote a detailed defense of the inerrancy of the Bible.[2] Twenty-one years later, he gave up the inerrancy doctrine and passed judgment on the Apostle Paul for his inconsistency regarding the status of women,[3] much as Paul, according to Galatians 2:11–14, passed judgment on Cephas for his inconsistency regarding the status of Gentiles in the churches. Today, Harold Lindsell passes judgment on Jewett for giving up his earlier commitment to inerrancy and forsaking "the clear teaching of the apostle Paul about female subordination."[4] Professor Jack Weir of Texas Baptists' Hardin-Simmons University states in unequivocal language that the Bible cannot be inerrant if it advocates the subordination of women to men.[5] Baptists are sharply divided over the status of women. There is also no question that several passages in the Bible insist on female subordination to men. Some advocates of biblical inerrancy may secretly wish that those passages (and the passages on slavery) were not included in Scripture, but they are there. According to I Peter, "Sarah obeyed Abraham, calling him lord" (3:5), and husbands are enjoined to honor "the woman as the weaker sex" (3:7). But in what sense are women weaker than men? The most charitable interpretation is that on average women have smaller shoulders and lungs than men and are normally unable to lift as many pounds as men can. How those statistics qualify men to be the spiritual leaders over women is unclear. The London Baptist preacher Charles H. Spurgeon thought that God would not call a man to be a preacher if he lacked a large chest with large lungs. But that was before the invention of the P.A. system. Perhaps Spurgeon, if he were alive today, would revise his comment, saying that God would not call into the TV ministry any man who was not handsome and wavy haired.

There are indications that parts of the Bible presume females to be mentally and morally weaker than males. That presumption may lie behind the Southern Baptists who stand absolutely opposed to ordaining women for the ministry. The New Bible Commentary (page 1137), commenting on "the weaker vessel," insists that although the moral and intellectual inferiority of women was assumed in biblical times, the biblical authors meant only that women were physically weaker. "The man is held to be the stronger vessel in the sense of being more muscular and of carrying heavier responsibilities in the home as breadwinner and support of the family." The commentary does not raise the question of whether women are denied ordination because the work of the minister is too heavy or physically taxing for them.

Some Southern Baptist preachers wish to deny ordination to women not only for the pastoral ministry but for the office of deacon too. Their logic entails that women be prevented from teaching in Christian schools of higher education.

In I Corinthians 14:33–35 Paul instructs women to "keep silence in the churches. . . . And if they will learn anything, let them ask their husbands at home: for it is shameful for women to speak in the church." Some biblical scholars conjecture that the passage was not in Paul's original epistle (which has been lost), because it conflicts with his statement that in Christ "there is neither slave nor free, there is neither male nor female" (Gal. 3:28). Inerrantists one and all believe nevertheless that Paul, inspired of God, told women to keep quiet in the churches. Because Southern Baptist churches would close down if the inerrantists insisted on enforcing the passage, concessions have been made to modern Western custom by moving away from the ancient Eastern custom of female silence. Today in Saudi Arabia, where some women are still treated like children, a number of women would not think of going out unveiled or entering a restaurant unescorted by a husband or a close male relative. In I Timothy 2:9 women are admonished not to adorn themselves with "braided hair, or gold, or pearls, or costly array" (KJV). It is amusing to see how W. A. Criswell elects to rewrite that biblical injunction so that female members of his affluent First Baptist Church in Dallas may braid their hair and adorn themselves in gold, pearls, and costly diamonds—as long as they are "tasteful accessories" (Criswell's subjective embellishment, not the biblical author's). In his commentary on I Timothy 2:11–12, which forbids the woman to teach or usurp authority over a man and tells her to "learn in silence with all subjection," Criswell writes, "When a woman chooses to marry, she accepts the responsibility of voluntarily 'lining up under' (hupotasso-, Gk.) her respective husband."[6]

The concept of female subordination pervades the Middle East, that part of the world in which the Qur'an and most of the Bible were written. Women did not receive the vote in Syria until 1949, in Lebanon in 1952, in Egypt in 1956, and in Iraq in 1967. According to one study of the Middle East, *The Arab Mind*, by Raphael Patai:

> The Arabic language has no literal equivalent to the English word "child." Every noun in Arabic is either masculine or feminine. Therefore, while there are words for "boy," "son," "girl," "daughter," there are no words for "child," "baby," "infant," "toddler," and so on, which in English refer to human beings at various stages of their early development without specifying their sex. When asking a man (e.g., in connection with a census) how many children he has, the word used will be "awlad" (the plural of walad, meaning male child), and, accordingly, the answer will specify the number of sons. Then the experienced census taker will have to ask again: And how many daughters (banat)? Only thus can he arrive at the total of the man's progeny.[7]

In the Arab world the overwhelming desire of the majority of married couples is to have sons. On the wedding week, friends and relatives wish the young couple many sons. In many remote sections of the Arab world female infanticide was common for many generations into the late nineteenth century despite Muhammad's denunciation of it in the Qur'an. Men like Charles Stanley and Paul Pressler's pastor, John Bisagno, are unwitting heirs to the Arab way of thinking. Their roots are deep in the culture of the ancient Middle East because their sacred book has roots in it. In the conflict of cultures, compromises must be made, so although the female's life is not cut off, her authority is.

Donald W. Dayton, author of *Discovering an Evangelical Heritage*,[8] is probably correct to say that by reexamining the role of women in the Christian tradition, many evangelical scholars have gained a new understanding of the historically conditioned character of Scripture and the thorny problem of applying it across thousands of years of social change. The Apostle Paul's statement in Galatians 3:28 that in Christ "there is neither male nor female" cannot be fully appreciated for its radical moral advance until it is viewed against the background of the Middle East's attitude toward women. Musa Alami, a descendant of one of Jerusalem's leading Muslim families, writes that after the midwife cries out joyfully "It's a boy!" the baby is hastily washed and dressed so that it can be proudly passed around. The father then receives widespread adulation and congratulation for having sired a boy. But if the firstborn is a girl, she is tolerated, not celebrated. The tolerance diminishes as each new girl is born without a son to brighten the picture, until eventually the father and mother are greeted with silence.[9]

The widespread folk custom of dressing boys like girls until the age of five grew out of the belief that the omnipresent evil manifest in evil persons can be tricked into thinking that the highly prized Arab boy is really a girl and therefore not worth snatching away or making the object of malediction.[10]

A few years ago I received a letter from a man—he said he was a professor in India—asking for money to help him out of his calamity. It seems that the man had suffered the misfortune of having many daughters. Not being a wealthy man, he was unable to afford a dowry for them; that is, he could not pay potential suitors to take his daughters off his hands by marrying them. The Indian father saw himself as trapped financially for the rest of his days because his daughters were a serious economic liability and of little value in themselves. Traditionally, the women of India had only one vocation open to them— giving birth to and raising children.

Criswell assures his readers, "Particularly does God affix great value to the womanly attitude of a meek and tranquil spirit." Most definitely, God has not called women to exercise strong leadership in the churches, Criswell warns, and if they teach, they should try to instruct primarily younger women and children lest they assume authority over males.[11] The Pastoral Epistles of the New Testament seem to say that the mature woman may teach younger women but not teach men (Titus 2:4). Nevertheless, Criswell concludes that the woman is not denied every aspect of the teaching ministry as long as she comes under her husband's direction.[12]

Carolyn DeArmond Blevins of Carson-Newman College points out, "As late as 1929 when Mrs. W. J. Cox rose to be the first woman to give the Woman's Missionary Union (WMU) report before the Southern Baptist Convention, one prominent man got up and walked out. On more than one occasion the convention adjourned to a nearby room for the WMU report so they could avoid the unscriptural practice of a woman speaking from the pulpit."[13] In the early part of the twentieth century, Southern Baptist Theological Seminary in Louisville allowed women to enroll in classes but denied them the right to speak or earn a degree.[14]

The question arises as to why such precautions are taken regarding women. Are women suspect for some undisclosed reason? Can they not be trusted? At first W. A. Criswell implies only that wives need to communicate with their husbands to reduce family confusion—"as a means of avoiding confusion and maintaining orderliness."[15] His advice makes sense, although what does not make sense is his singling out of women to receive the advice. Why are husbands not advised to consult with their wives to avoid confusion?

The cat soon crawls out of the bag. The woman is to be "placed under" (Criswell's translation) the man and is "to learn quietly and submissively" because it was Eve and not Adam who was deceived and lured into transgression in the Garden of Eden. The implication is that women lack the intellectual acumen and the moral firmness of males. "I permit no woman to teach or to have authority over men; she is to keep silent. For Adam was formed first, then Eve; and Adam was not deceived, but the woman was deceived and became a transgressor. Yet woman will be saved through bearing children, if she continues in faith and love and holiness with modesty" (I Tim. 2:12–15).

Assuming that the Adam and Eve story is literal history, Adam does not appear to be overly sharp intellectually in this instance in the Garden of Eden. Eve transgresses because she is deceived. Adam, knowing that his wife has fallen, transgresses with his eyes wide open. Instead of learning from her error, he follows in her steps, as if unable to learn from another's experience. That scarcely makes him brighter than his wife and may leave him dimmer. It also reflects poorly on his moral leadership and trustworthiness.

In a 1949 lecture in Knoxville, Tennessee, evangelical scholar H. A. Ironside of Moody Bible Institute suggested a way to rescue Adam's image. Ironside turned Adam into an Old Testament version of Christ. Instead of leaving Eve alone in her sin, bighearted Adam elected to join her in sin, voluntarily taking sin upon himself for her sake. Ironside's interpretation transforms Adam's deliberate transgression into a deed of gallantry, saving the benighted weaker sex by his grandiose act of self-sacrifice and foreshadowing the sacrifice of the Messiah. Unfortunately, Sir Adam proves to be less than gallant in Genesis 1:12; caught flat-footed with the forbidden fruit and the new consciousness of his nakedness, he blames his wife.

To deflect the charge that fundamentalism portrays woman as intellectually inferior to man, Criswell insists that "woman's susceptibility to deception" (which he blandly takes for granted) can be explained in an acceptable way. The explanation goes as follows. God had not directly forbidden Eve to eat the fruit but had, instead, allowed Adam to pass the warning on to her secondhand.[16] Because the warning wasn't directly from God, she was somehow more easily deceived, and all women thereafter remain for some reason more easily deceived. Criswell's convoluted explanation suggests that Adam was incompetent as a communicator or he deliberately deceived Eve, with God's full foreknowledge of the consequences. In either case, Adam does not stand as a towering leader who inspires confidence.

In his book entitled *Bobbed Hair, Bossy Wives and Women Preachers,* Baptist evangelist John R. Rice used to include pictures of his many daughters, each of whom had flowing, uncut hair. It was important to Rice that his wife and daughters have uncut hair, for it signified their subjection to him. According to Rice, I Corinthians 11:3–10 warns women to keep their heads covered when praying and prophesying because the cover signifies that the husband is the woman's head.

In 1958 at a faculty meeting of Carson-Newman College in Jefferson City, Tennessee, President Harley Fite insisted that the faculty vote to recommend that college coeds wear hats to church. The debate was as heated as it was trivial. A potential compromise emerged when someone recommended that the proposal be revised to recommend hats for Sunday morning only. Despite his stern lecture to the faculty, Fite watched his proposal sink in defeat as the school's treasurer and others at the meeting raised the question of what counted as a hat. It so happened that in the year 1958 an attractive felt band two to four inches wide was popular among women and had come to be defined as a hat. After the vote, President Fite scolded the faculty for shirking their responsibility to Christian womanhood.

The passage in I Corinthians is unclear as to whether the head covering is long hair or a cloth for the entire head. Some evangelicals appear to agree that this passage is infallibly ambiguous. A few interpreters believe that Paul is referring to a veil. In any case, one point is not ambiguous in this epistle: a man should not have his head covered. Why? Because he reflects directly the image and glory of God, whereas "woman is the glory of man." And as if that were insufficient to keep woman in her derivative place, Paul reminds her that man was not created for woman, rather she was made for him (I Cor. 11:7–9). Needless to say, not all interpret Paul to mean that woman was created subordinate to man.

Bill Bruster, minister of the First Baptist Church of Abilene, Texas, and Dillard Mynatt, minister of the First Baptist Church of Oak Ridge,

Tennessee, are typical of those Southern Baptists who choose to break with the current inerrancy doctrine rather than violate what they regard as an elementary principle of moral decency. "I've always thought women were people, too," Mynatt says plainly. "God doesn't label anyone a second-class person." Unwilling to compromise on the question of women's status, Bruster is one of the new Puritan revisionists among Southern Baptists who will not back down before Paul the Apostle himself if they think he has sold out a moral principle. They insist that the Golden Rule is not an incidental piece of advice that is optional for Christians. In his East Tennessee way, Mynatt says, "Brother, either the Golden Rule is the word of God or it isn't. If it is, then it's time we Southern Baptists got serious about it." By contrast, the evangelical *New Bible Commentary* states, "The tragedy of the fall establishes the general truth that a woman is more easily deceived than a man; so it is out of place for her to take the lead in settling either doctrine or practice for the Christian community. (Note that it is, however, a woman's privilege to teach children and younger women.)"

Without denying that it is a privilege for anyone to teach children and the young, the Southern Baptist revisionists are likely to say that it is a male prejudice, not a general truth, that women are more easily deceived than men. The revisionists also think that women are neither saved nor lost by bearing children. In short, they have resolved to try to ameliorate their tradition when it is bigoted toward women, just as they have openly opposed racial bigotry even when it pervaded Southern Baptist churches. With no delusions about the difficulty of self-reform, they have resolved never to look back despite intense opposition from some of their fellow Baptists.[17]

In June 1984 the annual meeting of the Southern Baptist Convention in Kansas City voted against ordination of women. Thirty years earlier the fundamentalist Baptist Lee Roberson (never a Southern Baptist) proclaimed in Chattanooga, Tennessee, that although all races were equal before God, God had ordained segregation on earth. In a similar vein some of the Southern Baptist fundamentalists today speak of the "equal dignity of men and women" out of one side of their mouths, while denying women ordination out of the other side. The following resolution carried with 58 percent of the vote at the Kansas City meeting in 1984: "While Paul commends women and men alike in other roles of ministry and service, he excludes women from pastoral leadership to preserve a submission God requires because man was first in creation and the woman was first in the Edenic fall.

Scriptures teach that women are not to assume a role of authority over men in public worship lest confusion reign in the local church.

It is difficult to avoid the conclusion that a number of men in the Inerrancy Party play up sexist passages and tone down other passages because they dread the entrance of women into what has been an exclusive men's club among Southern Baptists. Correctly, they sense that there is more to ordaining women than appears on the surface. It is a threat to their worldview. To yield on this point would be like receiving a tiny chip in the windshield. It may seem harmless initially, but it will eventually spread.

Fundamentalists and evangelicals have a talent for adapting to moral, social, and cultural changes and finding biblical grounds for doing so. Thanks to legal suits in seventeenth-century Massachusetts and to important social developments, accusations of witchcraft have been mostly phased out of Western Christianity. Belief in witches and involvement with them exacted so high a price socially and psychologically that the practical advantages of that belief disappeared. The Saxon jurist Benedict Carpsov (1595–1666) prided himself on having read the Bible 23 times and on having signed the death sentences of twenty thousand witches.[18] Needless to say, labeling women as witches and murdering them had a brutalizing effect on communities. It terrorized especially the vulnerable who had no supportive family to defend them. In Europe and colonial America it was usually women who were labeled as witches, a tendency that may be traced to the belief among medieval writers that since women were limited in reason, they, like Eve, were more vulnerable than men to demonic influences.[19]

A society cannot survive in any humane way unless it develops an internal social thermostat to control the rise of witchcraft accusations and persecution of the victims. Among European and American Christians, the witchcraft fever began to decline sharply at the end of the seventeenth century. Even though the Old Testament commanded the execution of witches, the executions were suspended, and by the mid-twentieth century, evangelical scholar E. J. Carnell could conveniently and arbitrarily proclaim that "the Mosaic laws against witchcraft perished with the old economy."[20] Carnell does not reveal what he thinks happened to witches. Were there no more witches to be tormented and executed after the first century? Was the Reverend Cotton Mather of Boston and Salem simply deluded? Carnell offers no sound exegetical reason for elbowing the crude text on witches out of the Bible.

Already, blatant bigotry toward women is phasing out in the United States, slowly but effectively. Dr. Paul Brewer, professor of philosophy at a Baptist college in Tennessee, observes that the battle over ordination of women has in principle ended. Some local Baptist churches have begun electing women, including Imogene Brewer, to the board of deacons. With the current emphasis on the autonomy of local churches, little can be done to prevent individual churches from going their own way regarding the ordaining of women. Even those who still defend the subordination of women do not define it precisely as it was defined by their forebears. Strong secular trends have helped force the change. First, inflation and the inability of the male breadwinner to earn enough money to maintain the family's position in the middle class have pushed wife and daughter into the work force. Second, women in the United States are attending institutions of higher education in unprecedented numbers. Far from opposing this revolutionary trend, Southern Baptists have opened their seminaries, colleges, and universities to women.[21]

Third, birth control, delayed marriage, and a variety of career options for women have made pointless the ambiguous biblical proclamation that "women will be saved through bearing children" (I Tim. 2:15). Historical and external conditions, not sound exegetical principle alone, have made the text irrelevant. The attempt to deny women ordination may be seen as one of the last and most pathetic efforts of the ecclesiastical men's club to retain its traditional meaning as it falls back in retreat. In 1925 the Reverend John Roach Straton, a famous fundamentalist Baptist preacher in New York City, denounced the Birth Control League of his city as "a chamber of horrors." Shocked at the decline in the birth rate, Straton joined a leading Roman Catholic prelate in opposing a bill to legalize the right of married people to obtain information about birth control. Another noted fundamentalist Baptist preacher, J. C. Massee, at about the same time denounced birth control as legalized concubinage.[22] The contemporary Southern Baptist preachers who oppose women in the ministry may within less than a generation be looked upon as peevish cranks who used religion to veil their own bigotry just as John L. Dagg used Scripture to rationalize slavery.

The Convention's immediate past president, Charles Stanley, has already begun to qualify his bigotry. Again, historical conditions, not exegetical principle alone, have dictated his policy. Fundamentalists practice situational ethics in their own way while simultaneously denouncing it. Despite the unequivocal New Testament command that women remain silent in the churches and despite his own opposition to the ordination of women, Stanley has no problem with letting women speak from the pulpit.

So what is the problem?

Stanley answers that it is the problem of authority.

ORDINATION AND AUTHORITY

Because of their understanding of the New Testament, some seventeenth-century and early eighteenth-century Baptists gave little weight to ordination, if they bothered to ordain ministers at all. In a recent article entitled "Ordination: The Issue Turns on Authority," a former associate director of the Home Mission Board's Interfaith Witness Department warns that Southern Baptist ministers are in danger of slipping into a pattern from which some Roman Catholic priests are currently struggling to free themselves.[23] He fears that authority in ordination may lead to authoritarianism. Remembering the arrogant authoritarianism that had bred religious persecution in Europe, seventeenth-century Baptists stressed belief in the priesthood of all believers. Women as well as men were priests. Early in that century, Roger Williams, a Baptist for a while, named his daughter "Freeborn" to signify the break with authoritarianism. Because it is a standard belief among Southern Baptists that every believer, male or female, is a minister, the following question naturally arises: What special authority does ordination bestow upon men but never upon women?

According to W. A. Criswell, men alone are called to rule, at home and in the church. Having already conceded that the male cannot claim intellectual, physical, or spiritual superiority to the female, Criswell insists that God has assigned leadership and headship to the former but not to the latter.

But on what grounds? As noted earlier, Criswell, turning to the Adam and Eve transgression story, leaps to a theoalchemical Lamarckian conclusion that women are susceptible to being taken in by fast talkers and deceivers. Apparently, Criswell has not been talking fast enough, for a growing number of Southern Baptist women have not been taken in by his or Bisagno's arguments. Susan Lockwood Wright, an ordained Southern Baptist minister, is only one of many who think Criswell's logic, or lack of it, is unworthy of females and males alike.

Pressed to the wall, Criswell and his brothers in inerrancy can produce no good reason to deny women ordination except that God does not want them ordained. Often in their preaching, these ministers attempt to show that God is not an irrational force but the quintessence of reason. He is not a Cosmic Existentialist who chooses on the grounds that he simply chooses. So what do Criswell and his comrades offer as the divine ground for denying women ordination? A careful search through their writings and sermons reveals that they have nothing to bring out of the closet for intelligent men and women to examine in the daylight of reason and common sense. Many of these preachers will denounce reason itself whenever it serves their purpose, undermining Calvin's contention that compared with men, women were especially lacking in the ability to abide by the canons of reason.

God does not want women to rule men. That is the rock-bottom rule by which Criswell and his comrades stand.[24] What it has to do with the ordination of women is unclear. When Criswell and T. A. Patterson were ordained, the words of the ceremony made no connection between ordination and any gift of rulership. Indeed, the New Testament contains considerable ambivalence on the question of rulership. After years of working together, two of the most respected first-century missionaries, Paul and Barnabas, parted company in a dispute over the latter's kinsman, John Mark. Earlier in his ministry, Paul had rebuked Peter to his face (Gal. 2:11), despite Peter's authority. The reason Paul gave for his outburst was that Peter's behavior was inconsistent with the principles he had preached and with the Christian behavior he had earlier shown toward Gentiles. Regarding the principle of rulership itself, Jesus is reputed to have severely criticized it. When the disciples argued about who among them was the greatest, Jesus said that the one who desired to be first would be "last of all, and servant of all" (Mark 9:35). When James and John asked to sit one on Jesus' right hand and the other on his left hand in his glory, Jesus saw that they had raised the indignation of the other ten. "And Jesus called them to him and said to them, 'You know that those who are supposed to rule over the Gentiles lord it over them, and their great men exercise authority over them. But it shall not be so among you, but whoever would be great among you must be your servant, and whoever would be first among you must be slave of all'" (Mark 10:42–45).

If God does not want Susan Lockwood Wright to rule the people in the Southern Baptist church that she serves as ordained minister, does He want a male like Criswell to rule the people in the Dallas church? If so, how does a pastor go about ruling over fellow Baptists? Criswell's ambivalence at this point becomes eloquent. Just as Peter's behavior toward the Gentiles was inconsistent with the principles he had preached, so Criswell's behavior toward women is today inconsistent with the principles that he preaches regularly from his Dallas pulpit.

There is a passage in the Epistle of Hebrews that admonishes the readers to obey and submit to their leaders (13:17). Certain that the leaders were pastors in the early churches, Criswell suggests that the chief emphasis is upon "the administrative responsibilities of the chief officer of the church." [25] That would seem to settle the question of the chain of command, except that when the Apostle Paul writes of the diversity of gifts and operations, he ranks the gift of administration quite low—second from the bottom. Lest readers think that the New Testament provides anything like a uniform organizational chart, they should recall that Jesus allegedly forbade that his disciples be called rabbi, that is, teacher (Matt. 23:8; John 1:38). Nevertheless, Criswell regards the pastor as a teacher possessing the authority that somehow cannot be received or acquired by women. [26]

SUBMISSION AND SUBORDINATION

In Mississippi a Southern Baptist pastor once asked a woman (not his wife) to submit to his sexual advances. Would Criswell have urged the woman to submit to her minister's advances on the grounds that the biblical call for obedience requires modern church members to submit to their pastors? Clearly not, because the leader was not abiding by the standard his congregation and he had agreed was binding on them all. Strictly speaking, the common standard rather than the pastor became the woman's authority. And it led her to resist her minister's overtures. If a female minister made sexual advances to a deacon who was not her husband, the deacon would be in perfect order to remind her of that standard. In this case, there is no difference between male and female. It is the objective standard that governs, not the individual minister.

There is a biblical passage (Ephesians 5:22) urging women to submit to their husbands. There is also a biblical passage (Ephesians 5:21) urging all members of the church to submit to one another. Is the for-

mer injunction binding but not the second? There are passages en-
joining husbands to respect and love their wives. Does Criswell wish
to suggest that those bonds are not reciprocal between husband and
wife?

According to Ephesians 5:24, wives are to be subject to their husbands in everything. The followers of John R. Rice and popular male
supremacist Bill Gothard profess to take the injunction literally. Rice
argued in the forties that if a woman were uncompromisingly obe-
dient to her husband in every way, the husband would be so grateful
and moved by her faithfulness that his heart would melt and he would
never again instruct her to do anything that brought harm to her.
Most Southern Baptist women ignore Rice and the enigmatic biblical
passage, preferring to remain thinking persons rather than sheep.
They leave Rice and Gothard to live in their self-constructed air castles
of male vainglory.

THE GREAT CHAIN OF BEING

It is misleading to conclude that the ambivalence and sometimes
hostility that inerrancy proponents show toward women is the result
of their conscious resolve to follow a biblical injunction. In many ways
these men are also the victims of an ancient cultural prejudice that has
for centuries denigrated women. The bigotry in the New Testament
cannot be explained away by contemporary interpreters eager to
whitewash the texts. The New Testament reflects its setting in antiquity. It is the recipient and bearer of a tradition that portrayed women
as naturally inferior to men. For Aristotle, the universe is a great chain
of being, with everything in its proper place and fulfilling its natural
end. Seeing women as subordinate to men in this chain of being, Aristotle argues that it is natural and expedient that the man should rule
the wife and children. Aristotle is confident that "the male is by nature fitter for command than the female, just as the elder and full-
grown is superior to the younger and the more immature" (*Politics I*,
12). Conceding that woman, unlike the natural slave, has a native de-
liberative faculty, Aristotle still concludes that she lacks the natural authority to rule. Quoting Socrates, he insists that "the courage of a man
is shown in commanding, of a woman in obeying." Quoting Sophocles, Aristotle writes, "All classes must be deemed to have their special attributes; as the poet says of women, 'Silence is a woman's glory,'
but this is not equally the glory of man'" (*Politics I*, 13).

Aristotle's great chain of being rooted bigotry in nature rather than in a male-dominated society, and it has spawned immeasurable harm and cruelty over the centuries. The Apostle Paul's prejudice toward women came not by divine revelation but by his indoctrination as a child into a culture that had little or no means to correct itself for centuries. Of all the religions that competed with Christianity in the second and third centuries, none had wider appeal in the Roman Empire than Mithraism, even though it was the only major mystery religion to exclude women from membership. Orthodox Christianity excluded women only from offices and roles of significance and influence. In the Galatian epistle the Apostle Paul made a remarkable and revolutionary breakthrough, declaring that the traditional wall of demarcation between male and female did not hold in Christ. Despite his breakthrough, the wall remained firmly intact in the Catholic Church for centuries; men could become cardinals and popes, while women could bring them breakfast on trays, change their bed linen, and as nuns serve the Lord in subservient ways.

The new Puritans, both men and women, among Southern Baptists do not attempt to rationalize the bigotry that their Christian tradition has inherited and continued. But they are convinced that a redemption of their religion, despite its ancient corruption, is possible. In the name of Christian love and elementary justice they have begun to challenge the great chain of being, vowing to disconnect systematically those heavy links and specific connections that have for centuries perpetuated the demeaning of women.

MINISTERING TO THE DIVORCED

In the late forties an unofficial, self-appointed group within a Southern Baptist church in Tennessee asked a member to leave the church. Because he and his wife had ended their marriage in divorce, he was a walking scandal in the church. The pastor of the church did not minister to him.

Today many Southern Baptist churches have learned the hard way that they cannot be so choosy about whom they will minister to. Divorce has stricken the families of deacons, church school teachers, and ministers, forcing ministers to ask new and disturbing questions about the implications of their calling. One experienced and insightful minister in the South who supported Charles Stanley told me that for years he had declined to perform the wedding ceremony for anyone who had been divorced. "But then after a while I began to see that I was inconsistent. If a divorced couple wanted to join the church, my people and I would accept them into our church family. We didn't turn them away. So, I saw that I was inconsistent. Today, if a divorced person comes to me and asks me to perform a marriage ceremony, I counsel with the couple. I'm a minister of Christ. I'm to help people when they need me."

That pastor was typical of what is happening in Southern Baptist churches today. As another Baptist pastor noted, "We've come to understand that we have to serve in an imperfect world—imperfect preachers trying to help imperfect people. Divorce isn't the unpardonable sin. A church is sometimes a hospital where people can get their shattered emotions cared for and their broken hearts mended." Britton Wood of Fort Worth, Texas, became a pioneer among Southern Baptists by ministering to singles: the widowed, the divorced, and the never married. For nearly nine years he served as the single-adult minister at Park Cities Baptist Church in Dallas. In 1972 he began the Texas Single Adult Conferences and served as president of the Texas Council on Family Relations in 1982–83. The Christian Life Commission of the Baptist General Convention of Texas honored him for his commitment to and ministry with single adults. He holds a position at Southwestern Baptist Theological Seminary that did not even exist until a few years ago: adjunct professor in the adult education section called "The Church's Ministry to Single Adults." In 1977 Broadman Press published his book *Single Adults Want to Be the Church, Too.* In addition to the compassion and insight of the hardworking ministers in the trenches, there are economic and structural reasons for the relatively recent change in attitude toward the divorced. In the first place, the divorced have become a sizable minority in Southern Baptist churches. To cast them out would be to lose both their financial contribution and their volunteer labor. Given their obsession with—or perhaps even worship of—the growth of church membership rolls, Southern Baptists have been compelled to modify their behavior toward the divorced. In the second place, the divorced also have relatives and important friends in the churches. In past decades, when there were few divorces, the risks of offending relatives and friends were insignificant. Today, they carry considerable weight. If a church member personally requests that a divorced relative be ministered to, the sensitive pastor will find it almost impossible to turn down the request.

For years the Southern Baptist tradition tended to brand divorce and remarriage as adultery except when obtained on the grounds of adultery or fornication. Today, divorce has touched numerous Southern Baptist families. When Criswell's divorced daughter wanted to marry another man, one of Criswell's compassionate ministerial friends offered to perform the marriage ceremony and take Criswell off the hook. There are many divorced people in Criswell's sprawling church who contribute money, time, and talent. Dallas County has one of the highest divorce rates in the world, and Criswell is not about to alienate all those people from his church. Regardless of what the Bible says about the grounds for divorce, few Southern Baptist ministers today will insist that a person remain married to someone who is physically abusive or makes life a misery because of drinking, gambling, or mental abuse to the family. The notion that the husband is autocrat in his home no longer receives unqualified support from most churches. In many communities it is the minister and spouse who provide the model of mutual respect between husband and wife.

MARRIAGE OF MUTUAL RESPECT

A case in point is Bob and Willodene Peek of Mars Hill Baptist Church in Knoxville, Tennessee. If any couple is solid Southern Baptist stock, it is these hardworking people who met at a Baptist college and then married upon graduation. Bob, a graduate of Southwestern Baptist Theological Seminary, has one of those powerful pulpit voices that could probably, if called upon to do so, make a lion stop and shudder in its tracks. And yet, his family correctly sees him as a gentle man and an incurable sentimentalist with a buoyant sense of humor. His youngest brother, Joe, is a respected Southern Baptist minister in South Carolina. In addition, the three Peek children are graduates of a Baptist college. Steve has since pioneered as a minister of childhood education, Janice is married to a ministerial student at Southeastern Baptist Theological Seminary in North Carolina, and Philip works in his church's youth and recreational programs.

Willodene holds the distinction of being the only woman second vice president of the Tennessee Baptist Convention. She served as one of the presiding officers of the state convention in November 1975, four years before the Inerrancy Party began to prevail in the Southern Baptist Convention. From 1971 to 1975 she was president of Tennessee's Woman's Missionary Union, perhaps the most influential position that a woman has ever held in the Tennessee Baptist Convention. For four years she served as president of the union's executive board and in 1975 officially represented the union at the Baptist World Alliance in Stockholm, Sweden. Today she teaches school five days a week and carries out her diverse roles in the family and community. Bob and Willodene are models of solid Southern Baptist life in its contemporary mainstream, but they also embody the profound change that has taken place even in the pastor's home. No one who knows the Peeks could imagine that they achieved their remarkable marriage of mutual respect without enormous struggle. Bob's hobby is gardening; he grows some of the most beautiful roses in Knox County, Tennessee. But more impressive is the way he and Willodene have cultivated their marriage in times of despair and triumph for more than three decades.

Willodene is justly disturbed about the distrust that some Southern Baptists have of women. She wonders why Tennessee Baptists have failed to elect more women to positions of influence. Her concern must not be seen as a product of what the electronic media call women's lib; it has deeper historical roots and is the flowering of her Baptist tradition. In the early seventeenth century, that tradition dared to speak of the priesthood of all believers, including women, and insisted on the distinctive Baptist contribution of "individual soul competency." Willodene, having demonstrated her competency as a member of the board of directors for the Tennessee League and in numerous other ways, now expects her Baptist tradition to manifest overtly what for centuries it has professed regarding individual soul competency.

Without doubt, the Peeks represent the future of Southern Baptist family life at its best. In her recent book *The Second Stage*, Betty Friedan explores how husband and wife can learn to work in separate careers while working together to meet family needs.[27] It is clear that Friedan in the past few years has been studying marriages like the Peeks'. She apparently likes what she sees, and she finds hope in that kind of relationship of mutual respect and reinforcement. If one were to look at the Peeks and ask who was the authority in that family, the question would seem quaint. To Bob and Willodene, it is no longer relevant.

IN THE LOINS OF ABRAHAM

The Southern Baptists categorically deny reincarnation even though several biblical passages say or clearly imply that God knew all individuals before they were conceived. (See Eph. 1:4 and 2 Thess. 2:13.) "Before I formed thee in the belly I knew thee" (Jer. 1:5 KJV). "The Lord said to me, 'I knew you before you were formed within your mother's womb'" (The Living Bible). If the emphasis is on the individual who is foreknown, then the above text suggests reincarnation. If the emphasis is on the Lord's foreknowledge (as I believe it is), then it need not imply reincarnation. If passages can be quoted to show that the Lord knew prophets before they were born, it need not follow that they were persons in the womb before birth. Rather the emphasis is upon divine foreknowledge and providence, not upon the metaphysical status of the fetus.

Antiabortionists like Falwell and Criswell have used texts from Christian Scripture to try to prove their metaphysical view that a human person comes into being the moment the sperm cell fertilizes the ovum, or egg. Criswell has not always held abortion to be murder. In the February 16, 1973, issue of *Christianity Today* he wrote of the fetus, "I have always felt that it was only after a child was born and had life separate from its mother that it became an individual person, and it has always, therefore, seemed to me that what is best for the mother and the future should be allowed." Sometime after writing those words, Criswell must have read the Bible in a different light and reversed his thinking, agreeing with Falwell. He and Falwell have failed, however, to consider seriously Hebrews 7:9-10, which, if one uses Falwell's questionable style of exegesis, implies that the sperm cell alone, before it unites with the egg, is a 100-percent person. The author of Hebrews says plainly that Levi was within the loins of his ancestor Abraham. It will be recalled that Abraham was Levi's great-grandfather.

Partisans have twisted biblical texts to push the view that the fetus is a person, but no plausible case has been made or borrowed by Southern Baptist fundamentalists to date. In Luke 1:44 Luke does not affirm that it was "for joy" that the babe inside Elizabeth's womb leaped. He merely records Elizabeth's claim that it was. Her claim is not inerrant, and even if it were, it would not make her fetus a person. A pup can leap for joy, which does not render it a person. Paige Patterson appears to think Joshua was justified in killing pregnant Edomite women and thereby sending their unborn to heaven, even though it is wrong to send the unborn to heaven by way of abortion. Adrian Rogers gave an impassioned speech at the Convention on behalf of the unborn, but he has made no case for thinking that the fertilized egg is a person. On this topic Southern Baptists have no respectable forum for engaging one another directly in a manner worthy of intelligent human beings, so those who oppose abortion and those who favor the woman's right to make her own choice have been talking past one another. The question "If the fetus is not a person, then when does it become a person?" has not been discussed widely in Southern Baptist literature or forums. Southern Baptists are apparently going to allow the abortion issue to polarize them, and they are doing it with minimal intelligent in-house interchange on the issue.[28]

Social scientist Nancy T. Ammerman, after carefully studying the Southern Baptist Convention on the abortion conflict, concluded that it is one of the most, if not the most, divisive issues among Southern Baptists. I see the conflict as symptomatic of something more far-reaching than the abortion problem, as does Ammerman.[29] What continually impresses itself upon me is the shockingly small amount of time and energy that the Southern Baptist opponents of abortion have exerted in preventing it. If I truly thought my American neighbors were murdering one and a half million innocent persons annually, I would certainly feel compelled to do more than Jimmy Draper and his group have done about it. Recently, an unofficial organization—Southern Baptists for Life—elected Draper as its head. This organization outside the regular structures of the denomination will be interesting to observe in its political effect on the Convention. But little can be expected in terms of a rational defense of its view on abortion beyond that of, say, Richard Land's comments on fetal heartbeats and brain waves (which scarcely exceed those of a laboratory hamster). To suggest that brain waves are a necessary condition of the presence of a soul is one thing. To say that they are the sufficient condition is another. Not one plausible argument has been offered to establish the heartbeat's or brain wave's link with the human soul's presence in the body.

For many years, a number of preachers like Jerry Falwell and W. A. Criswell raised no prophetic voice against the known brutalities of racism or the unjust treatment of women. Now suddenly they have turned into bleeding hearts over almost microscopic zygotes. With little sustained concern for the civil rights movement when it had to do with conspicuous persons of minority status, some of the antiabortion preachers have recently begun to deliver impassioned and eloquent speeches about the civil rights of the fertilized egg. Many women believe that the crocodile tears for the fetus serve mostly to distract from the guilt that these preachers bear because of their past racial bigotry and their present male chauvinism. Whatever the preachers' real motives may be, the by-product of their antiabortion stand will likely be to reaffirm the old hard line of male dominance over females. Shedding tears for the zygote might allow some of them to feel that they have not totally rejected the civil rights movement that they once spurned and denounced, but a lot of men and women will, rightly or wrongly, continue to see their display of piety as a cynical smoke screen covering an unrepentant drive to keep women in their place— under male domination.

The efforts on behalf of the zygote will probably not last more than a decade and a half, waning as improved morning-after pills and other contraception control methods appear on the market. The new methods will gain wide acceptance just as the condom and the current pill have come to be accepted despite papal pronouncements and the preachments of such fundamentalists as Clarence E. Macartney, John R. Rice, Walter A. Maier, J. C. Massee, and John Roach Straton.

13.

The Great Beast Liberalism

nce upon a time there were Christians who dreamed of the day when the whole population of planet Earth would convert to their faith. Their wild and naive vision took flame in England in 1792 when a young Baptist missionary named William Carey ignited the modern missionary movement. Throughout the entire nineteenth century, the hope spread, and in 1845 a new denomination called the Southern Baptist Convention started its remarkable career as the most successful missionary-minded Protestant denomination in the world.

"Postmillennialism" was the term employed eventually to describe this quixotic fantasy, which had reached the status of being labeled prophecy. According to postmillennialism, as the nations and peoples of the world voluntarily turned their backs on their ancient customs and embraced the Christian faith, the Kingdom of God would descend to earth, where Christ would reign in peace, with Jerusalem as his headquarters. To hasten the day of Christ's return, missionaries were sent to evangelize the benighted peoples of such exotic places as Africa, China, Japan, and South America. The missionary movement became for the churches a series of adventure stories filled with larger-than-life heroes and heroines who often returned to the home churches to relate their triumphs for the Kingdom. Romanticized legends began to build around missionaries. Local church members shared emotionally in the missionary adventure. Individual missionaries were seen as courageous explorers forging into the far corners of the world, and the church people traveled vicariously with their missionaries, thrilling at the thought of facing the unknown and teeming with the expectation of claiming the lost globe for Christ.

But the myth finally came face to face with reality. Paul Stevens, former president of the Convention's Radio and Television Commission, said, "When we came home from the Second World War, we were premillennialists. Criswell, who hadn't served in the war, stayed home to write a dispensational, premillennial view of the world for a lot of Southern Baptists." Stated in another way, the postmillennial dream had faded. The Southern Baptist myth of converting the world to Christ and bringing his Kingdom to earth had receded to the lower caverns of their minds. In its place emerged the apocalyptic vision of a planet deteriorating so rapidly that God could barely tolerate it. As in the days of Noah, God would soon punish the world for its unbelief. And just as Noah's family had been spared divine wrath in times past, so now Christian believers would be spared the Great Tribulation soon to befall the planet. With dramatic suddenness, Christ would appear in the air for one purpose only, to snatch away all believers from this corrupt planet, leaving those who remained behind to suffer the most horrifying outpouring of wrath since the dawn of creation.

Today, Southern Baptists are more than fourteen million strong, the largest Protestant denomination in the United States. But as one Southern Baptist minister, T. T. Crabtree, has pointed out with devastating frankness, there are "three billion unsaved persons in the world; and unless there is a radical change in the mindset of Southern Baptists toward giving [to missionary enterprises], we are just whistling in the dark."[1] Paul Pressler says there are four billion unsaved. The evidence is clear: Christianity is losing in the world. Even before the Communists forced themselves upon China, Christian missionaries had made scarcely a dent in China. Compared with the Chinese population, the Southern Baptist population is scarcely a drop in the ocean.

The postmillennial dream of winning the world to Christ has managed, even among hard-bitten premillennialists, to stay alive. Among mission-minded Christians the dream is a tiny pilot light ready to burst into a roaring flame again. For some Christians, the myth cannot die because, to let it perish forever, to give up permanently the hope of converting at least most of the world, is to admit in their heart of hearts that Providence has suffered a blow from which there can be no full recovery. To admit that the flame of postmillennial optimism has been snuffed out would create unbearable despair in some Christians. Not even a staunch premillennial pessimist like Criswell can face reality without releasing angry, bitter cries of protest. The optimism inspired by postmillennialism dies hard because to lose it is to lose a childlike innocence that can never be fully recovered.

It is not surprising that the wild and fanciful postmillennial vision should ignite again in modern disguise. When a group of inerrancy advocates among Southern Baptists met at the First Baptist Church of Atlanta to form a self-conscious movement called the Baptist Faith and Message Fellowship, Inc., they pumped one another with buoyant boasts of "winning our generation to Christ."

Jerry Falwell's Moral Majority, Inc., and the Religious Roundtable that once were so dear to evangelist James Robison are only the postmillennial fantasy welling up again in premillennial hearts. If the world cannot be converted, then at least dedicated efforts on the part of fundamentalists can "bring America back to God." Even though the world cannot be saved, perhaps America can become a righteous nation, a Christian Israel on earth, where perverts can be put in their place and the Great Beast Liberalism mortally wounded.

As the president of the Home Mission Board solemnly pointed out, well-tested statistics demonstrate that "we are not winning our nation to Christ." Writing a candid article entitled "What Has Happened to Our Global Vision?" in the January 17, 1986, issue of *Christianity Today* (North America's most popular evangelical journal), a professor of missions at Trinity Evangelical Divinity School charges, "We are bankrolling an evangelical boom at home and sending nickels and dimes overseas." He adds that while Islam and Hinduism are growing at the same rate as world population, Christianity has begun to slip behind. By 1994 thirty thousand missionaries will retire, with only five thousand stepping into their shoes.

In the same issue of *Christianity Today*, one of the senior editors, James I. Packer, apparently thought it necessary to refute the view that people who have not heard the gospel will be exempted from eternal hell. Southern Baptists represent a major stream of Christianity that exempted children and the very young from suffering the eternal torments of the damned. Packer seems concerned to deny any further exemptions of the vast unevangelized population of humanity. Evangelicals fear that if Christians come to believe that non-Christians overseas will escape eternal damnation, then the whole motive for sending missionaries around the globe will dry up.

In trying to understand the current battle among Southern Baptists, it is important to keep in mind that Criswell's predecessor at the First Baptist Church of Dallas was George Truett, a noted postmillennial optimist. It has fallen to Criswell and to dispensational fundamentalists like him to explain why Truett's great vision of converting the world has remained unfulfilled. Despite the size of Criswell's church (one of the largest in the world), his personal influence in Dallas and Texas has declined in recent years. In the spring of 1986 Dallas was crowned the divorce capital of the *world*. Despite all the revival meetings throughout the state of Texas, the Baptist and Protestant influence is receding while the number of Catholics and the unchurched is on the rise. Half the population of Texas adheres to no church. The Home Mission Board publishes a research paper, *RD Digest*, ten times a year. According to the June 1985 issue, 156 million adults in the United States alone are judged to be lost (without salvation). Where has the postmillennial dream gone?

Rather than admit that the dream of converting the world or the United States was a wild delusion from its conception, Criswell has a scapegoat to blame. The name of the scapegoat is "liberalism." With reckless abandon he has spun and embellished a tale that his disciples, along with Pressler, have received uncritically and repeated as a ritual. The tale goes as follows; England ceased to be a powerful empire and a Christian nation because Baptists and others in England turned against their fundamentalist preachers like Charles Spurgeon. In the United States, so the tale goes, liberalism has destroyed mainstream churches and consequently weakened the nation. Liberalism now threatens to undermine Southern Baptist growth unless liberal professors can be prevented from spreading their poison at Baptist seminaries and colleges.

The hope is that Southern Baptist schools can be made into fundamentalist centers of instruction and evangelism, stemming the tide of secularism and unbelief in America and opening the way for a great revival to sweep across the nation. Visions of a postmillennial victory over the world still dance in premillennial heads. Even though the dispensational scheme of things predicts a falling away from the fundamentalist faith, preachers like Criswell remain angry about it and seem unable to yield to the inevitable consequence outlined in their own premillennial preaching. Their attempts to root out liberalism and establish their handpicked fundamentalist professors in the seminaries testify to their inability to swallow completely the premillennial timetable. While Criswell warns that the rapture lies just around the corner, the Criswell Bible College's vice president for academic affairs, Richard Land, is busy outlining a strategy for staffing the seminaries with advocates of inerrancy by the beginning of the next generation.

The so-called holy war among Southern Baptists can be better understood if seen as postmillennial militancy striving to gain at least a token victory in an increasingly alien world. It is as if the drive to capture the seminaries for the fundamentalist and inerrancy cause has gathered strength just when the premillennialists like Criswell have begun to admit that the dream is over, that the expectations of a worldwide revival are delusions. The drive to purge the seminaries springs from a desperate need for a local victory in the face of conspicuous global defeat. Liberalism becomes the convenient scapegoat for the ruin of a dream that was doomed from the start.

In an exceptionally candid article in the *Fundamentalist Journal*, evangelical Christian Nelson Keener says that fundamentalists and evangelicals are only kidding themselves when they blame secular humanists or any other group for the failure of the worldwide revival: "All the things we blame on America's decadence (abortion, drug abuse, pornography, etc.) are superficial reasons that keep us from looking at the real reasons for our spiritual anemia. We need to look at ourselves."[2] Laying the blame squarely on his fellow evangelicals and fundamentalists, Keener goes on to say that they have slipped into a state of moral paralysis, have lost their sense of Christian self-sacrifice, and have forsaken biblical moral principles by yielding to what he calls Christian situation ethics. Furthermore, he reasons, "Fundamentalists seldom, if ever, regard the criticism or evaluation of non-Fundamentalist Christians as worthy of consideration because these critics are not 'of us.' We are seldom self-critical."

Such candor is rare, whether from fundamentalists, liberals, or others. Keener is convinced that if America's born-again Christians were to begin practicing the principles they profess, "we would see a revival that could well surpass anything we might ever imagine or pray for."

That grandiose vision has captivated American Christians for more than two hundred years. For many believers, it seems utterly impossible to question the validity of the vision itself, for the vision gives their lives meaning. They cannot imagine how life would be worthwhile without it. And so they go on dreaming—and blaming.

Ironically, the recent resurgence of fundamentalism, evangelism, and charismatic Christianity in the United States has been accompanied by a resurgence of Muslim orthodoxy and other forms of entrenchment around the globe. That trend only reminds the fundamentalists in the United States that they are losing the battle for the world. In 1984 in the Hindu kingdom of Nepal 55 missionaries were arrested for spreading the Christian faith. Another 24 Christians were arrested in March 1985 on the same charge in the same country. In June 1985, during the same week that the 46,000 Southern Baptist "messengers" were electing their next president (fundamentalist Charles Stanley won with 53 percent of the vote) and strengthening the hold of fundamentalism on the Convention, thousands of Egyptians marched in Cairo to demand a return to Muslim fundamentalism. Not surprisingly, contemporary Muslim fundamentalists use words like "disease" and "infection" to describe the influence of the United States and other Western countries on the East. They have singled out education from the West as the infection to eradicate so that the world may be claimed for the God of Muhammad. *Occidentosis: A Plague From the West*, by Jalal Al-i Ahmad,[3] is born of the grandiose dream that one religion, Islam, will eventually triumph over all others on earth.

LIBERALISM AMONG SOUTHERN BAPTISTS

Pressler, Criswell, and Paige Patterson are prepared to label as liberal any Baptist who believes that the original documents of the Bible contain errors. When pressed in March 1985, Patterson admitted that most theologians and biblical scholars in the world do not regard the denial of inerrancy as sufficient reason to classify someone as a liberal. It appears that Criswell, Pressler, and Patterson have invented their private meaning of liberalism to support their charge that liberalism has made deep inroads into Southern Baptist institutions of higher learning. Most scholars, however, correctly recognize that the real problem is infighting among theological conservatives. There are profound and far-reaching differences among conservatives, just as there are among liberals. Without doubt there do exist many Southern Baptist professors, laypeople, pastors, and denominational officers who do not subscribe to the theory of the Bible's inerrancy or infallibility. By labeling them as liberals, the leaders of the Inerrancy Party have created an internal scapegoat for the conspicuous failure of Southern Baptists to fulfill the grandiose and preposterous dream of conquering the world or at least the United States for their faith.

Internal fighting could tear apart the Southern Baptist Convention, but to the Inerrancy Party that would be preferable to an acceptance of the cold, harsh truth: even if all Southern Baptist schools were staffed by inerrantists like Harold Lindsell and Paige Patterson, the Southern Baptist impact on the world would not change significantly. Southern Baptist schools would, to be sure, decline academically, but other universities and seminaries would fill in the gap.

One Southern Baptist who has been in contact with members of the Fuller Theological Seminary faculty predicts that the following would happen if Southern Baptist seminaries were staffed by inerrancy advocates only: First, a large number of Southern Baptist churches would cease sending money to the seminaries; second, the churches would send their young men and women to such seminaries as Fuller in California, Vanderbilt in Nashville, Duke in Durham, and Union in Virginia. Those and other seminaries would not only be receptive to Southern Baptist students but would also offer courses in Baptist history and employ Southern Baptist professors. T. C. Smith points out that if the seminaries were to fall to the Inerrancy Party, the moderates could work with several private universities to set up new graduate programs for training Southern Baptists in biblical studies and in church-related professions.

Southern Baptists boast of sending out more than 3500 foreign missionaries. If all their missionaries were fired and replaced by advocates of inerrancy, the effect on the world would be slight at best. Many years ago, when Paul Stevens was president of the Convention's Radio and Television Commission, he came to see that it was self-deluding to think there were enough missionaries to evangelize the world. Today, there are not enough to evangelize China even if China removed all barriers to missionaries.

In recent years many Southern Baptists have recognized that liberalism (by any definition) is not to blame for the failure to win the world to Christ. One factor that makes the postmillennial dream utterly unrealizable is the disturbing population increase. According to the February 1986 issue of *RD Digest*, published by the Research Division of the SBC Home Mission Board, "If American Christianity continues sluggish growth there will be between 170 and 175 million lost persons in the U.S. by 1990. This represents a gain of 16 million more compared to 1980 estimates of 155 to 160 million made by the Research Division." The population explosion, not so-called liberalism, is the major reason the grandiose dream is unrealizable. According to the same issue of *RD Digest*, "Since the U.S. Census was taken in 1980, the world's population has increased by about 470 million persons. The increase in the world population since 1980 equals the total residents of the USA and USSR in 1980." World population in 1986 is over 5 billion.

"The population increase is frightening," Billy Graham writes. "Statistics overwhelm us when we take into account the rapidity with which births are exceeding deaths. . . . By the end of this century in 2000 A.D. the world's population will have exceeded six and a half billion. From the year 2000 on, the statistics go berserk."[4] One Southern Baptist missionary points out that in Latin America the population will double in the last quarter of this century. Other Protestant missionaries say they are losing the battle in Africa because of the population increase. Paul Stevens had the foresight to recognize that only by radio could the Protestant Christian message reach the masses around the world. His successor seems to have given up the vision of preaching via radio to every pocket of the world and instead is concentrating on supplementing the work of the local churches primarily in the USA.

CONVERTING THE JEWS

Perhaps the most bizarre expression of the postmillennial fantasy can be found in the prophecy of the last-minute conversion of the Jews. According to some premillennialists, in the rapture Jesus the Messiah will extract all true Christians from the earth and escort them away to be with him for either three and a half years or seven years. Back on earth, the Jews and all other non-Christians will suffer unimaginable agony in the Great Tribulation. Toward the end of the terror, a large number of Jews will as individuals and as a collective people convert to Christianity. The land of Israel will thereafter become the scene of the Battle of Armageddon, wherein Israel's enemies in the Middle East will be vanquished. Jerry Falwell, in whom the postmillennial flame still burns hot, holds that God has raised up the United States for two purposes only: to protect Israel from all enemies and to serve as a base for evangelizing the entire world. Except for those two purposes, Falwell adds, America has no "right or reason for existence."[5]

Christianity in general suffers a built-in ambivalence toward Jews that tends to generate guilt and confusion in the Christian conscience. It would appear that in the premillennial and postmillennial scheme of things God raised up the Jews to be his chosen people and then lost the overwhelming majority of them to eternal damnation, a climax that hardly speaks well of divine omniscience and providence. In the fullness of time God is revealed as incompetent, unable to save his most beloved people. To keep the myth of triumph and victory alive, some premillennialists refuse to swallow the bitter pill of pessimism and defeat prescribed by standard premillennialism. They combine a strong pro-Israeli stand in politics with the prediction of a mass conversion of Jews to Jesus during the Great Tribulation. In that way they hope to ease their Christian conscience regarding the Jews. Instead of facing the clear implication of their orthodox view (namely, that the overwhelming majority of Jews will suffer forever in the Cosmic Concentration Camp called Hell), these Christians fantasize that the Jews will convert en masse, thus relieving Christians of guilt about the damnation of God's chosen people.

For still other premillennialists, the delusion becomes not merely a vague and ethereal vision but a blueprint for radical political and military action. According to many premillennialists, the rebuilding of the Third Temple in Jerusalem is a precondition of Christ's return to earth to set up his reign. To help the Israelis build their Third Temple, a group of premillennial Christians has donated money for artifacts and materials.

The plot to this strange story thickens, for on the spot where the Third Temple is to be erected stands already an Islamic shrine that almost a billion Muslims regard as one of the holiest sanctuaries in the world. One group of Zionists is convinced that God will destroy the mosque through an earthquake or some other miracle to make room for the Jewish temple.

Gush Emunim settlers are not content to wait for a miracle of destruction. Grace Halsell, a journalist and keen observer of the political aspects of Zionism, wrote in 1984, "They plan to take the Haram al-Sharif the same way they took 80 percent of the West Bank—by force."[6] The Calvary Baptist Chapel in Costa Mesa, California, led by its pastor the Reverend Chuck Smith, recently donated $25,000 toward the rebuilding of the temple, where animal sacrifice will be restored presumably in fulfillment of biblical prophecy. James DeLoach, minister of Houston's Second Baptist church, has joined Oklahoma oilman Terry Reisenhoover, Rabbi Doug Krieger, and other dispensationalists in their recent attempts to raise $100 million in one year toward building the temple and aiding the Zionist terrorists determined to replace the mosque with the temple and animal sacrifice. Apparently, these dispensationalists have ignored the Epistle to the Hebrews, which renders immaterial the place of worship. John 4:21 also suggests that there is no one geographical spot on earth that is special to Christians.

Needless to say, the premillennial vision could be volatile in locations that are military powder kegs. Grace Halsell notes that some fundamentalists and evangelicals think they are

> hastening the Second Coming of the Messiah by funding Jewish fanatics who, armed with dynamite, have stormed Haram al-Sharif with intent to demolish the shrines. In May 1984, Israeli terrorists, led by high ranking [orthodox] rabbis and army officers, told investigators they planned to bomb the mosque from the air, using a helicopter piloted by a former air force officer. They said they conducted experiments on models of the Dome of the Rock and Al-Aqsa Mosque to determine the amount of explosives needed to destroy them without damaging the nearby Western or Wailing Wall, Judaism's holiest shrine. They canceled their plans only after it became clear the wall would be hit.
>
> It was in 1979 that I first heard Jewish settlers illegally encamped on Palestinian lands quite openly discuss plans to destroy the mosque. (Usually one refers to both the Dome of the Rock and Al-Aqsa as one entity—the mosque.)[7]

THE BATTLE FOR A WORLDVIEW

Southern Baptist moderates often charge that their opponents within the Convention are really after power. There is some truth in the charge, but the question of what the power is for needs to be given more careful consideration. To say that the leaders of the Inerrancy Party are trying to grab power for its own sake is to misunderstand them entirely. What they truly want is the power to maintain their worldview against the threat of erosion and collapse. They have been criticized for declaring war on their fellow Southern Baptists just when Bold Mission Thrust and other mission-minded projects are in need of every ounce of Baptist effort. "Why?" the critics ask. "Why fight this battle now?"

The answer usually given by Criswell and his followers is that the missionary spirit will die if liberalism is allowed to thrive in the seminaries and other Convention agencies. But others on both sides of the battle have pointed out in one way or another that it is the battle itself that threatens to undermine Southern Baptist mission projects.

An altogether different explanation of the Inerrancy Party's declaration of war can be offered. The battle serves as a diversion from what really strikes fear in the hearts of the Inerrancy Party leaders. So long as the internal battle continues, the Inerrancy Party will not be compelled to deal forthrightly with the one shattering truth that its leaders cannot come to terms with—the simple truth that evangelical-fundamentalist Christianity can never become the most widely accepted faith in the world. The dream is dead, not because of liberalism of whatever variety but because there are too many other forces and conditions that evangelicals and fundamentalists have never had the resources to cope with. Recently Homer Duncan, fundamentalist editor of Missionary Crusader, wrote that of the 4.7 billion people living in the world, 2.7 billion have never heard the name "Jesus Christ." Of the 7000 languages in the world, 5000 are without any Christian Scripture translation. In India, 40,000 people die daily without having heard the name "Jesus Christ." In Afghanistan, a nation of more than 20 million, there is only one Christian in every 500,000 people. In Israel, only one in 60,000 Jews is a born-again Christian.[8]

Lashing out at liberalism and pluralism, blaming them for the failure of Southern Baptists to spread faster than Islam, William Powell writes these revealing words, the words of a man who bought into one of the world's grand delusions. "One of the most heart-breaking days of 1982 was when I went in the World's Fair and entered the building for the display of Muslims. The first thing I saw was a very large and a very high painted column on a scale board stating the Muslims had 800,000,000 members—the largest numbers of any kind of religion—and that they were also the fastest growing religious group!!"[9] The number of Muslims in Indonesia alone is eight and a half times the number of Southern Baptists around the world.

Southern Baptists in particular have been accused of worshiping large numbers and numerical growth. That is an exaggeration, of course, but many Convention ministers do seem to venerate numerical growth. Powell was shocked to learn that Southern Baptists are small potatoes compared with Muslims. Referring to a May 3, 1982, *Time* magazine article, Powell reveals just how shaken he was by the news that by the year 2000, the Muslim population will be 1.2 billion.

Rather than face the cold reality that the postmillennial bubble has popped, Powell issues an irrelevant call: "We must remove the liberals from the SBC payrolls and replace them with those who are 100% committed to the fact that the Bible is the infallible Word of God."[10] He does not seem to see that if all the Inerrancy Party churches pulled out and formed their own missionary Baptist denomination in this century, their effect on the Muslim population would be negligible. A program of convincing Muslims to use birth control more effectively would probably have a better chance of closing the widening gap between Muslims and born-again Christians.

The old-line liberalism of previous generations and the postmillennial resurgence share the grandiose fantasy of turning entire cities and nations to their way of thinking. When introducing his sermon on "The End Times," R. L. Hymers spoke of turning the whole city of Los Angeles to God, meaning to Hymers's brand of religion and his version of God. In his 1985 speech to a group of ministers in Knoxville, Pressler quoted a Houston man of wealth and influence and contended that if Southern Baptists went into theological liberalism, they would see the United States destroyed and the world would fall "back into a period of slavery."

In reality, rarely does a religion sweep whole nations and populations into its orbit by persuasion. Christianity did not become a widespread religion in the Roman Empire until Constantine used the power of the state to carry it throughout the empire and to punish and intimidate its rivals. Kaiser Wilhelm II was close to the truth when he remarked, "We are ourselves Christian by reason of forcible conversion." [11] Islam certainly used the sword and economic pressure to induce infidels to convert to the God of the Qur'an. And the spread of communism is conspicuously not the result of persuasion but of vicious intimidation, military intervention, and the secret police. Without the KGB, that which passes as communism in the Soviet Union would perish within a decade.

The battle among Southern Baptists will continue into the next century because it serves a purpose. It is so serviceable that the Inerrancy Party cannot afford a clear and permanent victory over the moderates. If those who reject inerrancy are forced to leave the Convention, the Inerrancy Party will lose its scapegoat and have only itself to blame for failing to bring about the great revival and missionary triumph. It is in triumph over noninerrancy Baptists that the fundamentalists and evangelicals will meet their most telling and crushing defeat.

14.

The New Current

Thered is a new current moving in slowly but steadily, washing up on the shores of Southern Baptist life. The Inerrancy Party leaders sense it, and they have committed themselves to erecting a seawall against it. It is unlikely that they will stop it. At most they will divert it, and some of the Inerrancy Party people will eventually go with it wittingly or unwittingly. The current is not swift or conspicuously powerful, but it keeps coming, almost imperceptibly. It is the new Puritan revisionism. Fundamentally, the movement challenges cruelties and injustices that have been perpetrated in the name of Christianity.

Outside the Southern Baptist Convention, such defenders of Christian orthodoxy as C. S. Lewis and Stephen Davis have been touched by the outer reaches of the movement. Converted from atheism in 1931, Lewis devoted thirty years of his life to defending the orthodox Christian faith. Like many evangelicals and fundamentalists, he remained hostile to most twentieth-century biblical scholarship. During the last months of his life, he became deeply concerned about "the atrocities (and treacheries) of Joshua." In a letter to philosopher John Beversluis he was frank about the danger of calling the Creator good when He is described as using His power to do evil. Rather than attribute wicked acts to God, Lewis seemed prepared to affirm God's goodness even if it meant giving up the inerrancy of Scripture. "The ultimate question," he wrote, "is whether the doctrine of the goodness of God or that of the inerrancy of Scripture is to prevail when they conflict. I think the doctrine of the goodness of God is the more certain of the two."[1]

Some defenders of inerrancy are quick to argue that individuals cannot know what goodness is unless they go to the Bible to learn it. But, as C. S. Lewis came to see, the Bible itself presupposes some previous understanding of basic goodness.[2] If the assumption is made that the Creator revealed himself through human language, then the words of the language had to possess meanings before the revelation. No one can provide a detailed description of goodness that will cover all situations to the end of time, but that doesn't mean the human species knew nothing about goodness and evil. The Egyptians did not have to wait for Moses to inform them from Mount Sinai that killing was wrong, for they already had a law against murder, a law that Moses himself violated before escaping to the mountain. The definition and application of goodness are never finally finished, even after the arrival of Scripture. The concept must be perpetually improved and refined, which is partly what the revisionist movement is about. Strange as it might seem, hyperfundamentalist Adrian Rogers, ordinarily one of the most uncompromising among the leaders of the Inerrancy Party, has unwittingly yielded to the pull of the movement.

In a 1985 rally at Merriman Avenue Baptist Church, Asheville, North Carolina, Rogers took moral offense at the suggestion that II Kings 2:23–24 says that two bears came out of the woods and killed 42 children as punishment for calling Elisha the prophet a bald head. To be sure, both the King James Version and the Revised Standard Version make it clear that that was what happened. Rogers, however, insisted that those versions had improperly translated the text. First of all, he said, the youths were teenage punks, not children. And the text, Rogers went on, does not say that the youths were killed.

To most scholars, the gist of the story is quite clear. The boys were massacred (split or torn apart) by the bears. The term that Rogers would translate as "teenage punks" is used also in Isaiah 9:6: "For unto us a child is born" (KJV). To be consistent, Kenneth L. Chafin notes, Rogers would have to translate the Isaiah passage to read, "For unto us a teenage punk is born."[3]

The significant point is that fundamentalist Rogers felt a need to go against the most reliable translations, to avoid the conclusion that God would summon bears out of the woods to execute children for calling a prophet "bald head." The evangelical *New Bible Commentary*, equally eager to avoid any unfavorable reflection on God's character, concedes that the bears did kill the lads. But, adds the commentary, the insult that the lads uttered was "a deliberate and deep insult, though its precise nuance is unknown." Finally, the non sequitur conjecture is made that the parents were the ones who really suffered the punishment, "in the conception of the times"—hence, moral relativism.

Why all this exegetical maneuvering? Why does Rogers fly in the face of every major translation of the Bible, including The Living Bible published by the conservative Tyndall House Publishers? Even Rogers, like W. A Criswell and other defenders of inerrancy, has been touched by the new revisionism. They and many scholars who reject inerrancy agree that God did not really cause bears to leave the woods for the purpose of tearing apart 42 boys. They agree on morality; both sides insist that God could not have sanctioned such an atrocity.

But they disagree on the translation of the text. The revisionists who reject inerrancy admit that the majority of translations are correct to conclude that Elisha in the name of the Lord pronounced a curse on the boys and that two bears came out of the woods to rip them apart. They also believe that the biblical text is morally wrong to imply that such retaliation was justifiable or sanctioned by the Lord. Rather than embellish the text as Adrian Rogers has done, they accept its prima facie meaning and then boldly pass moral judgment on it. And they do so for two reasons. First, they are convinced that the full revelation of Scripture cannot allow them to impute such a foul deed to God. Second, they hold that because the concept of God logically entails goodness, it is impossible that God could have sanctioned such an act of savagery.

THE SCANDAL

Despite all the books and articles written on the unity of the Bible and the harmony of the Gospels, there are numerous problems within the Bible. Some of them are severe moral problems. Clark Pinnock's attempt to pass them off as "marginal difficulties" is a bluff unworthy of a scholar of Pinnock's stature.[4] The horrors and atrocities that appear in the Bible cannot be morally justified, as C. S. Lewis eventually came to see. The story of Joshua includes genocide purportedly initiated and led by God. If the wholesale slaughter of an entire people, including children, can be justified in the name of God, then anything can be justified. Joshua's exploits are situation ethics gone berserk. His picture of God is that of a marauding sociopathic killer. Some fundamentalists have concluded that the Nazi program of incarcerating and exterminating six million Jews was divine judgment against a people who had for centuries rejected the Messiah. That view did not originate in a vacuum but actually derived from two fundamentalist and evangelical sources. First, the image of Jews deservedly suffering unbelievable agony in a vast concentration camp called hell is standard evangelical and fundamentalist theology. If the doctrine of everlasting hell means anything for evangelicals, it means that Jews (and most adults of the human race) will be sent to a concentration camp infinitely more horrible than the Nazi camps and from which there is no escape. Hitler's camps were only pale copies of the evangelical archcamp of torture and agony. Evangelical theologicans who use their talents to rationalize such an unimaginable atrocity are morally comparable to those intellectuals who sank so low in perversity as to write elaborate defenses of the Nazi pogroms.

The second source is the evangelical contention that any misfortune that befalls the Jews is the direct consequence of the failure of the Jews to live up to the divine ideal. (The reverse also holds: if the Israelis should take all the territory of the Arabs from the Mediterranean to the Euphrates, their victory would be justified as the fulfillment of divine prophecy, even if it included the extermination of Arab children the way Joshua exterminated Canaanite children.)

Looking back on the whitewash of the purge initiated by Stalin, including his slaughter of at least twenty million Soviet citizens, many former Communists have been shocked at the ease with which they once rationalized such wickedness. Similarly, some former evangelicals and fundamentalists recall the ease with which they once defended the assertion that God had commanded Joshua to exterminate entire populations, including children.

Disillusioned with what he had considered the "beautiful ideal" of communism, Yugoslavia's former vice president Milovan Djilas discovered a fundamental evil in his ideal that many evangelicals and fundamentalists also discovered in their faith. "Nothing so well reveals the reality and greatness of ends," he wrote, "as the methods used to attain them."[5] Max Eastman, once an eloquent defender of Marxism and the Bolshevik Revolution, bitterly denounced some members of the American liberal press in the thirties for their blindness to the massacres and terrors perpetrated by Stalin. He had in mind especially the *Nation* and the *New Republic*, "noted for their liberal thought except where Russia was concerned. As late as September 1938, after more than two years of butchery, the *Nation* was still explaining that the purges resulted from an irresistible popular tide of anti-bureaucratic feeling."[6]

There is, of course, at least one major difference between Stalinism and the evangelical-fundamentalist coalition when it comes to mass torture of those who do not subscribe to their ideology. The Stalinists possessed actual power to carry out their threats, whereas evangelicals and fundamentalists do not. But what they lack as power in their own hands, they make up for in the threat of an eternal reign of terror against all their enemies, or what they label as the enemies of God and Christ. The threat is unmistakable. Incredible torture and torment, they contend, will surely fall upon all who are not of their religious persuasion. Every knee will bow! In short, the evangelical-fundamentalist ideology, no less than that of the Soviet Politburo, justifies sending dissenters to the Gulag or the equivalent.

Evangelical and fundamentalist writers attempted half-heartedly to make their promised eternal concentration camp less offensive to the moral sensibilities of their neighbors, but anything devoted to the endless torment of all non-Christians is a moral offense of unparalleled magnitude. The reality keeps breaking through: "If hell is not fire," says Herschel Hobbs, "it is something infinitely worse."[7] Hobbs is clearly not among the new revisionists.

According to reports coming out of the Soviet Union today, political prisoners are sometimes tortured with such cunning and severity that the victims soon long for death as the more humane alternative. When they slip out of consciousness, their tormentors quickly revive them. The Soviet torturers are so intent on increasing the misery of religious and political prisoners that they will not let them escape through suicide or slip for long from consciousness.[8] Similarly, defenders of the idea of hell for non-Christians make it clear that not even the option of suicide is available to the inmates of hell. With intricate arguments worthy of the Nazi propagandist Dr. Joseph Goebbels, some evangelicals have argued that the entire structure of a moral universe depends on tormenting in hell those who have not embraced the Christian worldview.[9]

The notion of civil rights in hell is not discussed by the orthodox theologians. The inmates of hell are portrayed as stripped of all human dignity, deprived of all meaningful personhood. The despotic government of ancient Babylon held that the victor had absolute authority to do whatever he willed with his captives, and it treated its conquered enemies accordingly. Many biblical scholars think that the

Christian concept of hell developed from the Persian-Babylonian tradition of despotism. In the evangelical-fundamentalist version of hell,
human beings are tortured in ways that not even alley rats would be
made to suffer in a civilized society. Edward John Carnell, a former
president of one of the most prestigious evangelical seminaries, has
written that hell is "the place beyond which nothing more awful can
be conceived."[10]

The numerous attempts to justify the torments of hell are a sad
commentary on the human capacity for rationalizing revenge under
the cloak of holy wrath, and none of those justifications is more perverse than the assertion that those who suffer in hell are there because
they want to be there as a self-inflicted fate. Stalin told some of his
enemies that they had chosen torment simply by not committing themselves to him. The evangelical apology for hell is no less morally
twisted. The Roman emperor Trajan regarded himself as just and merciful when he told Tacitus, governor of Bithynia in Asia Minor, that
Christians brought to trial should be freely pardoned provided they
renounced their religion.[11] Similarly, evangelicals regard themselves as
merciful bearers of good news when they announce that people can
be spared eternal torment provided they renounce what they believe
and embrace the Christian way. In A.D. 112 Tacitus complained that
Christians, according to their neighbors, bore a "hatred against mankind" (Annals XV, 44). The complaint apparently is still justified for at
least one branch of Christianity. Fundamentalist and evangelical eschatology must be classified as hatred unsurpassed. Far from solving
the ancient problem of evil (theodicy), evangelical and fundamentalist
eschatology has embraced an evil beyond compare. It is perhaps an
apocalyptic scenario beyond which nothing more degenerate can be
conceived.

It is standard belief among evangelicals and most fundamentalists
that those who go to hell will someday publicly confess that their torment is perfectly just and that they deserve their endless misery. E. J.
Carnell insisted that in hell unbelievers will willingly confess.[12] In several nations of the world, including the Soviet Union, innocent people
are routinely either induced to confess crimes they have not committed or are intimidated into berating themselves. In the USSR, religious and political dissenters have been sent to psychiatric hospitals,
which the KGB under the late Yuri Andropov turned into tools of the
police state for the purpose of incarcerating and intimidating dissenters. When the World Psychiatric Association threatened to expel So-

viet psychiatry from its membership, the Soviets withdrew to escape international censure for their abuses and connections with the KGB.

To escape the evangelical and fundamentalist threat of eternal incarceration in the future, the unbeliever, like the KGB victim, must recant. He must describe himself not as mentally ill but, in the words of Norman Geisler, as "unworthy of love," "desperately corrupt," "sinful by nature," "evil by nature," and "depraved." [13] By denouncing himself and renouncing his beliefs, he may then and only then gain freedom from the torment that evangelicals insist will most certainly be his lot if he persists as he is. That sadistic mentality led evangelical leader E. J. Carnell to make the chilling confession: "In perfect goodness and justice, therefore, not only can He [the Creator] send some men to hell, but He can send them all." [14] No midnight horror show could begin to equal the macabre and ghastly scenarios that evangelicalism projects for the billions of Jews, Buddhists, Hindus, and all others who do not confess that they are loathsome and depraved and fit only to be tortured unless they renounce their current faith to become Christian believers. No movie has ever sunk to the X-rated depths of evangelicalism's obscene threats of violence. The wild and bizarre scenes of the Book of Revelation contain more mayhem and terror than all the degrading films of carnage produced since the movie industry began. Perhaps that is why fundamentalists worry more about sex in the movies than about violence—they sense a deep kinship with violence. Evangelist James Robison has been trying to come to terms with the anger boiling within him; he has apparently never seen that the theology he preaches rationalizes eternal rage against most of the human race.

In a macabre article one fundamentalist writer in *Fundamentalist Journal* complains that too many preachers are not preaching hell in a loving spirit. "In their zeal to persuade others of their belief in hell, some preachers communicate the impression that they and the Lord delight in the thought of some human beings consigned to eternal punishment. That impression may reflect their own hardness of heart." The writer goes on to urge preachers to change by preaching hell tenderly and with tears in their voices. What he fails to grasp is that some things by their nature cannot be done in a respectful and loving spirit. Like committing rape, sending human beings to hell is so vicious and violent an act that it cannot be done in love. It destroys the very meaning of love. A recent book tries to portray Himmler as less wicked than he was by referring to Himmler's pointless speeches to

his Nazi subordinates, speeches in which he talked of sympathy for
the Jews whom he was about to consign to the death camps. Fundamentalists' tender loving talks on hell are no less morally hollow than
Himmler's sentimental mockery of human decency.[15]

A slippery slope appears when anyone sets out to justify gross evil.
By taking the first step in defending certain atrocities said to have
been sanctioned by God, evangelical apologists risk making it easier
on each successive step to justify still more barbarity in the name of
divine holiness. Thomas Warren, noted Church of Christ fundamentalist, has gone so far as to announce that he could not personally worship a God who failed to perpetuate endless hell for non-Christians. In
essence, his defense of biblically sanctioned atrocities has become a
demand for the eternal vendetta against all who cannot embrace what
he regards as the true religion. To be sure, such sacred words as "holiness," "justice," and "free will" are ritualistically called on to rationalize the vendetta. But behind the theological jargon looms an insatiable
rage set against the majority of the human race.[16] Warren further insists that if God should fail to carry out the threat of endless torture,
"God would not be worthy of worship!"[17] For fundamentalists like
Warren, God is unworthy of their devotion if, in the fierce torture of
his enemies, he cannot outdo the most infamous and fiendish torturers on earth. Warren, Geisler, Paige Patterson, Criswell, Falwell,
and similar champions of inerrancy hold to premises that lead to a
heartless conclusion. The Jews who suffered torment and died in
Auschwitz, Buchenwald, and the other death camps will one day be
raised from their graves for one purpose: to be cast into an escape-
proof cosmic concentration camp more vicious, obscene, and savage
than all the Nazi and Soviet camps combined—a strange outlook for
anyone who professes to be pro-Jewish.

THE INERRANCY HYPOTHESIS AND ITS MORAL COST

Some of those Southern Baptists who reject the inerrancy hypothesis appear greatly relieved about not having to defend the grisliest vision of torture that has ever welled up in the human imagination.
They believe that no hardened criminal mind could have dreamed up
a more degrading scene than that of endless torture for all adults who
do not embrace the true religion. The atrocities of nineteenth-century
Russian prisons, Auschwitz, and the Soviet labor camps, unspeak-
ably horrendous as they were, did not last forever. All the horrors that

Dostoevsky listed in *The Brothers Karamazov* were temporary—except for the imagined torment of those not embracing the true religion. Whatever epistemological advantage they might lose by not subscribing to the inerrancy doctrine, the new revisionists believe they have the greater moral advantage of never being forced to rationalize atrocities in the name of divine justice and holiness.

Indeed, Robert Gundry exposes some epistemological disadvantages in the inerrantists' contention that the biblical accounts of Joshua's battles are perfectly factual records perfectly harmonized:

> Samuel-Kings and Chronicles do not present our only example in the Old Testament of tendentious changes that play loose with the historical facts. According to Joshua 1–12, all Israel conquered all Palestine from Lebanon to the southern desert and ruthlesslessly exterminated the entire population (see esp. the strong language in 10:40–42, describing the central and southern campaigns, and 11:16–23, summarizing all the campaigns—northern, central and southern). Thus in chapters 12ff. the Israelites merely have to settle in their allotments. But Judges mentions—indeed, emphasizes—that the conquest was only partial (see esp. 1:1—2:5). Israel as a united body does not seize the land in a single series of major campaigns, as in Joshua. No, we read about a variety of campaigns conducted by solitary tribes, sometimes by a pair of tribes, with mixed success and failure. Not only did these tribes fail to exterminate all the Canaanites, but also some tribes lived peacefully with them. The large cities (with a few exceptions), the fertile valleys, the seaboard plain, and scattered enclaves stayed in Canaanite hands.[18]

It becomes increasingly clear that the Book of Joshua gives an ideological and exaggerated account, whereas the Book of Judges suggests a picture similar to the skirmishes and battles among Indian tribes in the American West. The revisionists among Southern Baptist ministers, laypeople, and scholars go one step farther to contend that whatever actually happened in the days of Joshua, it is *morally impossible* that the God of love and justice instigated a policy of genocide and racial extermination. Human beings are not cockroaches, and General Joshua was not called to be heaven's Orkin man.

That position does not impose the demands of mortals upon the Creator. Rather, it is the goodness of the divine nature itself qualifying and directing raw omnipotence. Some people worship omnipotence for its own sake, which is not to be confused with worship of God. Might, even infinite might, does not make right. The Creator that is no more than unqualified will cannot be trusted, because such a force would have no dependable character or attribute to trust and therefore could not qualify as God. A power that could send masses to everlasting torment or that could take the lead in wholesale extermination is so lacking in a good nature that it could not be bound even by its own nature to keep promises. What is the cynical deception of gullible devotees compared with atrocities or an unending concentration camp? If the concept of God includes no more than unbounded will, then justification by faith or trust is reduced to a cynical cruelty joke. If there were a hell, Unbounded Will could empty the inhabitants of heaven into hell at his own pleasure and simultaneously declare himself perfectly just in doing so. But he would be just only in a wholly arbitrary sense, with no distinction between just and unjust.

If an omnipotent Creator were supremely evil rather than supremely good, he might cause some people to declare in preaching or in documents that he is good. But that would not make him good. For the Creator to be God, he must *be* good and not merely cause some to *say* he is good. It is conceivable that an omnipotent cosmic sadist could design a world in which he deceives his creatures in order to lead them all into endless torment for his amusement. But such a sinister being would not be good, just, or God, even if he should torture more viciously those who cannot honestly repeat after him that he is supremely good and just.

What some of the new Puritan revisionists among Southern Baptists are trying to say is that any text purporting to reveal the nature of God will not be judged as divine revelation if it falls beneath elementary human decency. Divine goodness may transcend elementary human goodness, but it cannot fall below it.

HELL AND THE GOLDEN RULE

Not all proponents of inerrancy rest as comfortably with the notion of hell as did the medieval theologian Thomas Aquinas, who could also quote Scripture: "The just shall rejoice when he shall see the revenge" (Psalm 57:11). The Revised Standard translation of Psalm 58:10 gives the full force of righteous revenge: "The righteous will rejoice when he sees the vengeance; he will bathe his feet in the blood of the wicked." [19] In an attempt to free the Creator of all culpability for the horrors and terrors of hell, many evangelicals support a modification advanced by one of their heroes, C. S. Lewis. According to Lewis, hell is really the torment that the sinner inflicts upon himself when he ceases to be able to love. Hell is a life without love. Dostoevsky advanced the same view; in the last few years of his life he moved away from orthodoxy toward universalism, the view that hell must eventually be vacated because God is who he is. God cannot be God and go on nursing an endless wrath that is never satisfied. Some interpreters think that the longtime evangelical scholar G. C. Berkouwer has recently become a universalist, too.

Assuming for the moment that there is a hell made up of those individuals so self-centered, arrogant, and incapable of love that their lives are excruciatingly miserable, why should evangelicals also assume that the millions of Jews, Hindus, Confucians, Buddhists, naturalistic humanists, and other non-Christians are less capable of genuine love than themselves? The only answer seems to be that the evangelicals who make that assumption have stipulated their own subjective definition of love. If some people cannot believe that Jesus was the Messiah or that the Bible is divine revelation or believe in various other points on the orthodox chart, then those evangelicals will define them as arrogant and incapable of love. Jewish and Buddhist mothers love their children as dearly as Christian mothers love theirs, but that is of no consequence for evangelicals. If those mothers have not converted to the Christian faith, then literally to hell with them!

In defending hell as not only morally acceptable but morally essential to a universe kept in balance, many proponents of inerrancy have sunk into a bitter cynicism toward humanity. A number of Baptist preachers seem to delight in announcing that all human goodness "is as filthy rags." Carried away with their doctrine of original sin, they insist that their non-Christian neighbors one and all deserve to be tortured day and night forever unless they convert. They take it as a sign of arrogance and pride if their neighbors do not regard themselves as vile. Some preachers harbor a deep-seated resentment against the thought of genuine goodness in anyone who is not within their religious circle. In some cases, it disturbs them to admit that real feelings and acts of moral decency exist anywhere outside the Christian believer's heart—as if they could not establish the greatness of God except upon the natural depravity of the human race. The more rotten humanity is (short of absolute rottenness), the more splendid is the free gift of grace. The same preachers appear to think that humanity owes it to Christ to perceive itself as naturally vile and base in order to give Christ's life and death cosmic meaning.

In the sixteenth chapter of Luke is the little story of the selfish rich man who died and went to Hades. Finding himself in agony, he begs Abraham to send Lazarus to dip the end of his finger in water and cool his tormented tongue. Instead of dispatching Lazarus on the mission of mercy, Abraham calmly explains why the request cannot be granted. The rich man, then, instead of cursing Abraham, thinks of the welfare of his own five brothers and pleads with Abraham to send Lazarus to warn them, "lest they come into this place of torment" (Luke 16:28). Abraham explains why it is impossible to send Lazarus. What evangelicals seldom recognize in this story is the possibility that the rich man has compassion for his brothers. Even though stranded permanently in Hades, he seems to feel a new unselfishness, wishing to help his brothers escape his miserable fate. Yet evangelical writer J. A. Motyer simply cannot bring himself to say anything good about the man. Even the rich man's modest desire to have his parched tongue touched with a drop of cool water is portrayed as the "desire for sensual gratification." Not a word is mentioned about the man's possible concern for his brothers' welfare.[20] Motyer appears to resent anyone's ascribing even a residue of human decency to this damned inmate of Hades.

It is in this context that Bailey Smith's comment about Jews must be understood. In 1980, when still president of the Southern Baptist Convention, this fundamentalist preacher declared, "It is interesting at great political rallies how you have a Protestant to pray and a Catholic to pray, and then you have a Jew to pray. With all due respect, my friends, God Almighty does not hear the prayer of a Jew."[21] His remark was made in Dallas at the August 1980 national affairs briefing for evangelical leaders.

Later, when reports of the remark embarrassed some Southern Baptists and infuriated even more of them, a noted Baptist leader explained to a group of Jews that Bailey Smith did not intend to single out the Jews. Smith, the leader said, believes that God would not hear the prayers of members of his own family if they were not Christians. Another observer asked, "Suppose Bailey Smith had pushed Indians off a cliff and then explained that he would shove off members of his own family, too. Would we accept this explanation as a moral justification?"

Southern Baptist ministers who believe in hell readily quote descriptive phrases that Jesus allegedly applied to hell: "outer darkness," "weeping and gnashing of teeth," "everlasting fire," "everlasting punishment," "the fire that never shall be quenched," "where the worm dieth not," "the furnace of fire," and "wailing." The Southern Baptists who reject the notion of endless torment for any portion of the human race divide on their view of Jesus' attitude toward hell. Some think that as a child of his times Jesus believed in hell just as he likely believed in the flat earth. Without denying that God was revealing himself in Christ, they do deny that every opinion that Jesus held was free of error merely because he held it. It is likely, they say, that Jesus as a carpenter smashed his thumb at times, measured boards incorrectly, and made mistakes in observation, since he was human. And it is conceivable that he held to some crude inherited religious notions, too. If he were indeed fully human and not merely deity pretending to be human, then Jesus would have experienced one of the essential traits of humanness, namely, fallibility. If Jesus had been totally free of all errors and mistakes, he would have been human in appearance only, in which case his temptations were counterfeit and his earthly life a cynical piece of playacting.

A second group of Southern Baptists who deny inerrancy contends that given some of the wondrous things that Jesus taught and his great compassion, he could not have believed in hell. But the Gospel writers, not always able to maintain themselves at the supreme moral heights of Christ, slipped into their traditional ways of thinking and mistakenly attributed to Jesus their own belief in eternal hell. His disciples were doubtless capable of promoting such a vindictive doctrine, these Southern Baptists admit. Did not his disciples urge him to rain fire down upon the Samaritans who had rebuffed him? But Jesus did not heed their call for revenge. Nor did he send bears to attack them. The principle of "Love your enemies" simply does not square with sending even enemies to endless torment, and Christ cannot have subscribed to a dogma that undercuts his moral principles. According to the Southern Baptists who take this line of argument, the writers of the Gospels failed to see that the notion of hell contradicted Christ's Golden Rule. The two cannot logically stand side by side. Evangelicals and fundamentalists are, therefore, accused of paying too high a moral price for their precarious inerrancy theory. At best, they hold to a version of the Golden Rule that is diluted to the point of absurdity. The Golden Rule advances love. Hell advances hatred. The two cannot stand side by side in a theistic universe. Portraying hell as a work of love is to mingle absurdity with perversity.

IF JESUS HAD COMMANDED RAPE

Suppose for the moment that archeologists were to announce that they have discovered an ancient manuscript that seems close in content to the best manuscript copies of the Gospel of Mark. The dating of it has been set at the first century, which makes it the earliest full manuscript of the New Testament. There is great rejoicing over the discovery.

But then Christians are stunned to learn that toward the end of the manuscript Jesus tells his disciples to go into the world and commit rape. After careful examination of the manuscript, the scholars conclude that "rape" seems, unfortunately, to be the correct translation.

Would evangelicals accept the manuscript and the translation as authentic revelation? Clearly they would not. Among the arguments for rejecting it, none would be stronger than the argument that Jesus could not have commanded rape. The very idea is contrary to his entire moral outlook. No one who sincerely taught the Golden Rule could command his disciples to commit rape. Such a violent and vicious act flies in the face of the compassionate Christ.

Those who believe that Christ did not support the idea of tormenting people in hell argue similarly that he could not have supported it. If Jesus was the morally perfect human being on earth, then he could not have believed in torturing people forever in hell any more than he could have supported rape. Just as evangelicals would instantly dismiss as inauthentic any manuscript in which Christ was represented as commanding rape, so some Southern Baptists uncompromisingly dismiss any passage that represents Christ as supporting the idea of hell.

Clearly, Southern Baptists are profoundly divided among themselves. Even though they share such religious terminology as "Jesus," "God," "salvation," "justice," and "regeneration," they are far from sharing the same meanings. They may sing the same hymns together in church, but the hymns do not and cannot mean the same to them all. How long they can continue to sing side by side is the central question facing them as they approach the twenty-first century. Their future will probably depend on how effectively the new revisionists confront the seawall of inerrancy during the next two decades.

15.

Politics and Faith

DENOMINATIONAL SHIFTS AS SOCIAL MOVEMENTS

ust as a thorough medical examination calls on a variety of specializations ranging from dermatology to cardiology, so a thorough examination of a religious movement calls on specializations ranging from psychology and theology to sociology and political economy. The recent upsurge of charismatic Christianity, for example, must be understood as a theological phenomenon, but it is also an economic, social, political, and psychological movement. No in-depth understanding of modern charismatics is possible unless they are seen as the major thrust of a psychosocial phenomenon that might well be labeled Christian hedonism. The label does not imply that they are given to sexual orgies, although emotional orgies are a conspicuous part of the new Pentecostals and charismatics. Heartfelt and demonstrative religion is hedonistic, pursuing happiness in the here and now. The modern emphasis upon faith healing is in its extravagant way the pursuit of pleasure in the present life. One zealous charismatic evangelist recently renounced the religion of "Suffer now but reap joy in the hereafter" as the old religion. For him, the old religion reflected too much of his earlier economic status on the wrong side of the tracks and outside the mainstream of American life. The irrepressible new charismatics are in effect announcing that they are coming in for a larger piece of the happiness pie. Sounding a little like born-again Marxist revolutionaries, some of them make it clear that the whole pie belongs to them as the elect. And they have resolved to "claim it for God!"

For a number of upwardly mobile Americans who are leaving the lower class and moving into the middle class, the charismatic movement serves to legitimate their ascent by giving it a significant place on the Christian theological map. Charismatic literature and charismatic services are full of such ritualistic utterances as "prosperity," "success," "the victory," "health," "Name it, claim it," "happiness," "deliverance," "good feeling in the Lord," "joy in Christ," and "Something good is going to happen to you." Tammy Bakker, noted TV charismatic, embodies this upward mobility and acceptance of hedonism within the boundaries of the Christian culture.[1] Soft-rock music and dancing have been absorbed into the church service or the religious TV show as the new social immigrants cross the tracks of their old life and invade America's establishment.

In times past W. A. Criswell has looked down with righteous scorn upon the theological barbarians who dared to speak in tongues and who dropped the name "Holy Ghost" as if referring cheerfully to a rich relative. Today, when inveighing against his archenemy liberalism, Criswell sometimes concedes that God Almighty himself might be behind the charismatic movement, at least temporarily, until he can wean Southern Baptists away from their wicked affair with liberalism. If God is using unstable charismatics to provoke Southern Baptists to holy jealousy and draw them back into the arms of orthodoxy—thus slamming the door in liberalism's face—then so be it! Unlike the liberals, the charismatics do not doubt sacred Scripture, even though they sometimes misread it outrageously.

For those skeptical of Criswell's theory, there are other explanations. For example, the theory of Christian hedonism explains why the charismatic movement crosses almost every denominational line. According to Christian hedonism, deep in every human breast resides an opportunistic hedonist awaiting the day when the Dionysian yearnings can be satisfied and at the same time legitimated as holy cravings conceived in heaven rather than within the terrestrial id. The resourceful and omnipresent pleasure principle is the driving force, and in the case of the new charismatics, God is opportunistically conscripted to serve it. It is the id who beckons, and it is theology who humbly obeys.

"God's people deserve the best," proclaims Oral Roberts, the Norman Vincent Peale of the charismatics. Jerry Sholes, who worked closely with Oral Roberts for three and a half years, wrote in 1979,

> One of Oral's books, *God's Formula for Success and Prosperity*, is replete with examples of people who did things according to his

suggestions and then succeeded, mostly in financial ways. . . .

Oral's wardrobe is obtained from Brioni and most of the suits he wears each and every day have a price tag of at least $500. He wears $100 shoes and drives $25,000 cars which are replaced approximately every six months. He is a member of Southern Hills Country Club, the most prestigious and elite country club in Tulsa. The membership fee alone is $18,000 (which includes a share of stock valued at $9,000) and, in addition to that, members are charged monthly dues of $130. Oral and his son belong to the ultra-posh Thunderbird Country Club in Rancho Mirage, California. They joined when a membership cost $20,000 each.[2]

When Oral was a young man he heard a voice saying, "Something good is going to happen to you." And it happened!

SOUTHERN BAPTISTS AND THE CHARISMATICS

Recently evangelist James Robison, for several years a favorite among Southern Baptist fundamentalists, left Jimmy Draper's church and burned a number of Southern Baptist bridges when he aligned himself with the rising charismatics. Robison developed his own TV talk show and considered becoming a specialist in casting out demons, which is the charismatic equivalent of traumatic psychotherapy. Described often as a man filled with anger, Robison is convinced that his life and the lives of other Christians are frustrated by personal battles with demons. Most Southern Baptist preachers do not take Satan and his cohorts quite that seriously. Some do not think of the demonic powers as personal beings at all, and James Robison's intimate excursions into exorcism clearly embarrassed a lot of Southern Baptist fundamentalists.

Unless kept under rigid external controls, the role of the exorcist tends to draw power to itself and to generate disruption, competition, and unpredictability among the churches. Personal involvement with alleged demons can consume an enormous amount of the denomination's energy and can drastically alter a church's character, direction, and tone. If a denomination becomes serious in its belief in active demons (rather than latent demons), many of its people will sooner or later come to believe that they have been invaded and possessed by demons. When that happens, a sociological rule of thumb applies: the more church members perceive themselves as possessed by demons, the more political power gravitates to the charismatic exorcists within the denomination. The exorcists become central power figures rivaling the authority of those preachers with different ministries and talents.

The trouble with professional exorcists is that they can generate more strife and dissension than the demons they battle. Practical-minded Baptist ministers in the South learned decades ago that the most efficient way to cast out demons was to cast the exorcist out of their midst. The ministers who tried to keep order and peace in the church learned the hard way that exorcists had a vested interest in raising the level of demon possession within the churches; where there is little demon possession, there is little demand for the services of exorcists.

Preachers who sought to maintain harmony within their congregations needed a theological rationale to help them compete against exorcists and other charismatics. Among Southern Baptists, two cultural or theological developments came to control the social and political threat of the exorcists. First, the Calvinistic doctrine of Once Saved, Always Saved teaches that although there are demons, they have at most a limited influence over the life of the elect. Most Southern Baptist preachers hold that a believer cannot be demon possessed, period. The doctrine of eternal security communicates the message that exorcists are plainly and simply not wanted and not needed in the local churches.

Dale Moody, who has the embarrassing habit of taking a large portion of the New Testament literally, believes in demons. By challenging the doctrine of Once Saved, Always Saved, he unwittingly challenged the theological doctrine that had been binding the demons or, more practically, the troublesome flesh-and-blood exorcists themselves. A number of ministers rightly sense a threat to their power and to the Baptist style of maintaining order within the churches.

The truth seems to be that the early New Testament churches were charismatic, some at times teetering on the edge of chaos. Strife, envy, power plays, treachery, and ideological gerrymandering can be easily detected in the New Testament. By comparison, modern Southern Baptist churches are generally an orderly and well-behaved lot. Or as the noted sociologist Max Weber might have said, Southern Baptist life tends to become rationalized—schematic rather than charismatic.

CR

PRACTICAL AMILLENNIALISM

The second development that helps to cast out the unpredictable exorcists and charismatics is the doctrine of amillennialism. Although it will not sit well with a number of Baptists to hear that their faith has spearheaded the secularization of Western society, the amillennial doctrine may be viewed as one more step in the direction of secularization. It serves as a conceptual device for removing from the universe all excessive supernaturalism. The death and resurrection of Christ, according to amillennialists, bound Satan and his supernatural assistants so effectively that they can be ignored by modern Christians.

A number of Southern Baptists may speak of the influence of Satan on occasion, but they will seldom acknowledge the operation of specific lesser demons in their daily lives. For all practical purposes, demons, like doctors, no longer make house calls on Southern Baptists. Theoretically, demons are still out there, but few Southern Baptists profess to having personal dealings with them. As Professor Paul Brewer has noted, Baptists are disinclined to regard UFO sightings as reports of supernatural visitations, whether angelic or demonic. A visiting anthropologist might conclude that as far as most Southern Baptists are concerned, demons have moved their residence to the primeval forests of Africa, the Amazon, and Southern California. Amillennialism signals to all professional exorcists and similar charismatics that their specialization is not needed. The unpredictable but streetwise James Robison got the message and aligned himself with the charismatics.

BAPTISTS AS A SECULAR INFLUENCE

Whether in the first century, the seventeenth, or the twentieth, theology provides a partial index to intense social tension and secular innovations. The Baptists of the seventeenth century proved to be a dynamic part of secular innovations that stripped away the mystical powers of both priest and church. A century earlier, Luther had helped initiate the process, weakening the imperialism of Roman economics and politics by translating the Bible into the language of the people. In effect, Luther rendered the entire Roman priestly class increasingly irrelevant to Germanic life.

The Baptists, taking many more giant steps forward, had in mind to dismantle the sacramental and sacerdotal monopoly of Rome. The doctrine of soul competency combined with the priesthood of all believers would leave the priestly caste powerless. For centuries, the Roman Catholic Church had taught that there were seven sacraments, which the priests alone controlled on God's behalf. Those who desired access to God were compelled to go through the priests. With a fresh taste for personal dignity and individual liberty, the Baptists of the seventeenth century advanced beyond Martin Luther by declaring baptism and the Lord's Supper to be not salvation-bestowing sacraments but ordinances of Christian celebration to be administered by the believers themselves.

POLITICS AMONG FIRST-CENTURY CHRISTIANS

The history of Christianity is made up of many threads, one of which is the thread of political control—one group seeking to gain control, another seeking to free itself from still other groups. The Apostle Paul apparently spent much of his adult life fighting battles in church politics. When the practice of speaking in tongues, for example, threatened the Corinthian church with chaos, he sought to schematize the practice in five steps (I Cor. 14). In the first place, he instructed those who spoke in unintelligible utterances to provide interpreters to translate the message into ordinary language. It was a stern measure because it took power away from those charismatics who spoke in tongues, giving it to the more socially sensitive and stable individuals who would translate the message for the benefit of the congregation as a whole. What Paul did not explicitly say but what can easily be read between the lines is that the interpreter was authorized to give to the unintelligible utterances whatever meaning he chose. Apparently, Paul trusted the interpreters to translate in accord with Paul's theology.

In the second place, Paul relegated speaking in tongues to the lowest rung of the ladder of divine gifts, thus giving it less prestige. Third, he encircled the tongues phenomenon with a new explanatory context designed to undermine its influence without denying its authenticity. He explained that although no one excelled him in speaking in tongues, he regarded it as largely a private relationship between God and the individual. The better way, he insisted, was to speak intelligibly so that all could understand.

Fourth, apparently conceding that speaking in tongues (or perhaps foreign languages) would continue as a public phenomenon, Paul placed it under another severe restraint by insisting that no more than two or three speakers be allowed to make unintelligible utterances in public, each waiting for his or her turn. That device alone could cut the nerve of tongues-speaking spontaneity. To hold public ecstasy to a schedule is to guarantee its extinction. As if those four restraints might not be sufficient, Paul then told the congregation that if no one in the church could interpret the unintelligible utterances, those uttering them should remain silent. Paul could play political hardball.

In the highly charismatic church at Corinth, he had to deal with another group that threatened to spin out of control. They were the prophets, whom Paul the apostle unapologetically ranked as lower than apostles. A careful reading of I Corinthians suggests that Paul sought to schematize the prophet's role, too. He limited the number of prophets who could speak at an assembly of worshipers and instructed them to speak by turns. He also instructed the other prophets to consider and evaluate the message of the one speaking. That factor alone would have radically changed the social dynamics of prophecy by introducing a check-and-balance system among the prophets.

In the Old Testament, the prophetic rage was an emotional frenzy that could prove embarrassing or even dangerous. The Apostle Paul worried that visitors might leave the Christian churches with the impression that Christian worshipers were mad, because of those speaking in unintelligible tongues or because of a general confusion and disorder created by enthusiastic prophets in ecstasy. Among the Israelites a thousand years before the early Christian churches sprang up, King Saul fell in with a band of itinerant prophets, provoking the question "Is Saul also among the prophets?" (I Sam. 10:11). While he was with the prophets Saul stripped off his clothes to prophesy before the priest Samuel (I Sam. 19:24). What exactly that signified has been debated at length by biblical commentators. One point seems clear, however. The prophecy phenomenon had a chaotic side. Prophets were a threat to anyone who, like Paul, was fighting to hold a church together as a coherent body.

Paul gave a strange little command to the prophets in Corinth, telling them that the spirits of prophets were to be subject to prophets (I Cor. 14:32). Whatever that meant in detail, the overall message was inescapable. Prophets were to settle down and get their public messages in order. "For God is not a God of confusion but of peace" (I Cor. 14:33). In the final analysis, "all things should be done decently and in order" (I Cor. 14:39).

CONTROLLING THE UNPREDICTABLE

The 700 Club's board of directors made an executive decision that there would be no speaking in tongues on the organization's charismatic TV show. The danger inherent in ecstatic speakers of unintelligible utterances, exorcists, and free-lance prophets is their unpredictability. Each group professes to be in direct and unique contact with the Holy Spirit. The Spirit, like the wind, "blows where it wills, . . . but you do not know whence it comes or whither it goes" (John 3:8). Without steady control over those claiming to receive messages directly from the Spirit, the churches would soon be at their mercy. No denomination can long hold itself together unless the potential for widespread confusion and unpredictability in critical areas is limited. Over the decades, noncharismatic Southern Baptist ministers and seminary professors have labored hand in hand to formulate and apply theological doctrines to restrain the disruptive charismatic tendencies in the churches. Why, then, it must be asked, have the leaders of the Inerrancy Party suddenly turned on the seminaries that have served them so well over the years? They have turned because they see the seminary professors as a new source of confusion for the churches and a new fount of unpredictability more insidious than all the potential exorcists and charismatics since the founding of the Convention in 1845!

A NEW WIND THAT BLOWS WHERE IT WILLS

Today it would be impossible for a seminary professor to be elected president of the Convention. But in Memphis, Tennessee, in May 1935 the Southern Baptist Convention elected one of the most distinguished professors at the Southern Baptist Theological Seminary, John R. Sampey, as its president. He defeated the popular fundamentalist minister and orator R. G. Lee. How can it be that in the eighties the same seminary that helped solidify Southern Baptist churches as a denomination and helped supply the denomination with a theology of order and cohesion is now denounced by many as the fount of confusion? Have the professors of that seminary and the other five turned suddenly charismatic? Are they professing to have extraordinary and unique contact with the Spirit that blows where it will? Do they say the Spirit sends them messages unavailable to the ministers and lay-people in the churches? The answer to all three questions is a re-sounding no.

There is nevertheless something that blows where it will, that comes and goes unpredictably, a wind that carries the professors and thousands of Southern Baptist ministers with it. That something is modern historical research into the Bible.

The fundamental requirement of objective research is that those committed to it must follow the arguments and evidence wherever they lead. True scholars cannot waver in their commitment, whether they pursue their work at the seminary or in the pastor's study. Research is not research if it anchors itself against the pull of evidence and argumentation. Scholars cannot be what they profess to be if their inquiry is dictated exclusively by preconceived conclusions. Even new forms of literary criticism must advance arguments to avoid turning the texts into an elaborate Rorschach test. In its heart, scholarly research harbors unpredictability. It is a risky ordeal, a challenge to preconceived belief and preconceived unbelief. The dedicated scholar follows the wind of research because it is his moral duty to follow it.

Anabaptists, charismatics, gnostics, and others who profess to follow the Spirit without mediation have in the past been kept in check by those who insist that every new doctrinal development meet the test of unchangeable Scripture. "Heartening, indeed, it is to know that in an age of confusion and instability, there are certain inalienable and unavoidable truths upon which believers can stand," wrote Charles L. Feinberg in his 1958 preface to *The Fundamentals for Today*. But what will restrain the spread of confusion if there is confusion about the Bible itself? The Inerrancy Party leaders think that biblical scholars who do not subscribe to inerrancy are undermining the only dependable source—the Bible—that could possibly control the threatening waves of doubt regarding what is true and what is right.

It is not surprising that some Inerrancy Party leaders are at least ambivalent about the research methods that come under the heading of higher criticism. On the one hand, Criswell says that as "a scholarly discipline, it is open to use by those who accept the Bible as God's inerrant word and also by those who do not." On the other hand, he says, "Lower criticism is constructive, whereas higher criticism is almost invariably destructive and hurtful."[3] The attempt of the Inerrancy Party to control the Southern Baptist Convention may be seen as a determined effort to gain control of both the professors and the research process itself before they usher chaos into the citadel of Scripture.

New Testament scholar T. C. Smith is writing a book that attempts to trace the political process by which various pieces of early Christian literature were included in the Canon and others were excluded. The Second Epistle of Peter, for example, was included late in the fourth century C.E. because it was presumed to have been written three hundred years earlier by the Apostle Peter. Now an increasing number of New Testament scholars believe that Peter was not the author. The epistle is, instead, a pseudepigraphon, that is, a literary work written by one individual in the name of a famous person of the past. In his commentary on Jude and II Peter, evangelical scholar Richard J. Bauckham is forced to break with his evangelical tradition on the question of the authorship of II Peter.[4] He concludes that the author is unknown and that he used the pseudepigraphical device because he sincerely believed he was mediating the apostolic tradition that Peter represented.

Between 200 B.C.E. and 200 C.E. a number of Jewish pseudepigraphical writings were generated, claiming authorship by such noteworthies as Eve, Moses, Enoch, Solomon, and Baruch. During two of those centuries, Christians produced a number of pseudonymous writings, too, using such names as Paul, Peter, Barnabas, and Clementine. The Shepherd of Hermas and the Epistle of Barnabas appear in one of the earliest collections we have of what purports to be authoritative Christian Scriptures. Biblical scholar W. W. Sloan adds:

> Until the time of Martin Luther in the sixteenth century, all Christian Bibles contained the Apocrypha as a part of the Old Testament. The earliest English translations were made from Latin and included the Apocrypha. However, Luther translated . . . them from the Greek. He placed them between the Old and New Testaments. This became the general style for nearly three hundred years, although the Puritans insisted on having Bibles without the Apocrypha. The Puritans felt that these writings were sensational and on a low moral and religious level. In 1827 the British and Foreign Bible Society printed Bibles without the Apocrypha, arguing that they were seldom read and made Bibles

heavier and more expensive than necessary. Since then this practice has been commonly followed.[5]

T. C. Smith contends that biblical scholars today are better equipped
than were the bishops sixteen hundred years ago to determine what
literature should be accepted as Scripture and what should not.

THE DREAD OF BIBLICAL SCHOLARSHIP

Many Inerrancy Party leaders are more than afraid of scholarly biblical research; they are terrified of it. They predict that the biblical
scholars, if left to their own devices, will generate unprecedented confusion in the churches, confusion that will make the current Convention troubles seem harmless by comparison. How can the church
people possibly bear up under a steady flow of doubts regarding
every book of the Bible? If the foundation of the faith is shifting perpetually, if nothing can be taken as fixed and universally certain about
the Bible, then how can Baptist people expect to remain interested in
the Bible, to say nothing of following its teachings? If the scholars do
not believe that the Gospel of Matthew was written by an eyewitness,
that Colossians was written by Paul, that II Peter was by Peter, that the
Gospel of John was by John, or that the last part of Isaiah was by the
prophet Isaiah, then what portions of the Bible *can* the faithful laypeople believe? If the four Gospels cannot be harmonized, then which
one, if any, is telling the historical truth? If Abraham only imagined
that he heard God commanding him to slay Isaac on the altar, then is it
possible that Jesus only imagined that he was the Son of God sent to
earth to become the sacrifice on the cross? If Smith is right to suggest
that the materials are to be questioned when they represent Jesus as
speaking of eternal hell and damnation, then how can they be relied
on when Jesus is represented as giving the Golden Rule and the Sermon on the Mount?

After reading the story of the woman taken in adultery in John
8:11, Mary Ann Anderson of Southwestern Baptist Theological Seminary wrote these moving words:

These verses describe the incident of the woman caught in the
act of adultery. The scribes and Pharisees brought her to
Jesus. . . . Guilty of violating the seventh commandment, she
was an outcast from her religion. Being involved in an objection-

able situation, she was despised by her community. If she were married, her husband would certainly divorce her. Her family would be forced to shun her. Even the man with whom she had been involved would probably disavow any knowledge of her. (Isn't it interesting that the Pharisees made no mention of the man's complicity in her sin?) Furthermore, punishment for the law she had broken was death. In every dimension, she was ruined.

What Jesus did with her was daring. He demonstrated God's mercy in her behalf. First, He dismissed her accusers by questioning their competency to be her judge. Then, He dealt directly with her. He condemned her sin, forgave her, and restored her. She left a different person.[6]

Despite the stirring power of the story, Paige Patterson's premises force the conclusion that it is not the Word of God, and Paul Pressler straddles the fence as to whether it is infallible revelation or not. If Southern Baptists accept T. C. Smith's challenge to rethink what should go into the Canon of Scripture, then that wonderful story of forgiveness might yet be recognized as a part of authentic Scripture despite the skepticism of Patterson and Pressler. It is both disturbing and exciting to realize that the canon, or standard, for determining what should constitute the Canon of Scripture has never been settled!

THE SEARCH FOR THE FOUNDER OF THE FAITH

Included in the volume Society of Biblical Literature 1984 Seminar Papers is an article entitled "Interpreting Jesus Since Bultmann: Selected Paradigms and Their Hermeneutic Matrix."[7] In it Professor Irvin W. Batdorf of United Theological Seminary, Dayton, Ohio, painstakingly reviews several books written by noted biblical scholars on the life of Jesus. The two impressions that stand out most vividly in this article are that a biography of Jesus appears impossible to reconstruct and that the scholars do not come close to agreeing on an answer to the question "Who did Jesus think he was?"

The Inerrancy Party leaders are understandably angry with the scholars for failing to come up with a unified conclusion about Jesus. Their reaction is similar to the frustration that a patient's relatives feel when a team of medical specialists cannot arrive at a unanimous diagnosis. When physicians reveal that they cannot answer every question

and cure every disease, some patients and relatives turn in despera-
tion to faith healers like Oral Roberts, Kathryn Kuhlman, and Donald
Stewart. When the biblical specialists cannot provide a scholarly consensus on Jesus, some of the laypeople will naturally turn to their
ministers and priests for the answers.

But to whom do the clergy themselves turn? In centuries past, they
could turn to the Bible and from it weave together what they regarded
as a coherent and reliable portrait of Jesus. But it is to the same Bible
that today's scholars turn again and again. Because of their special
training and because of the time they can devote to detailed research,
the professors can study the Bible and its background far more thoroughly than can the typical overworked minister.

Strange as it might seem to some, the professors are often profoundly moved by their research on Jesus. Albert Schweitzer is perhaps the most famous and dramatic example. His attempt to reconstruct a believable account of the earthly Jesus stirred him deeply,
leading him to become a missionary to Africa's primeval forest. In
*The Quest of the Historical Jesus: A Critical Study of Its Progress From Re-
imarus to Wrede*,[8] Dr. Schweitzer demolished the liberal view of Jesus
as the self-sacrificing, postmillennial progressive and democratic-
minded humanist. While the orthodox Christians were rejoicing over
Schweitzer's brilliant critique of the liberal Jesus, they apparently overlooked Schweitzer's equally brilliant exposé of the orthodox failure to
present a coherent portrayal of Jesus.[9]

According to Schweitzer, Jesus expected the Messianic Kingdom to
burst in upon his own generation. Toward the end of his ministry,
Jesus came to believe that he must die and in so doing usher in the
Messianic Age without delay. Jesus was tragically mistaken, Schweitzer explained, but that did not nullify the heroic commitment to love
made by the wondrous Galilean.

WAS THE FOUNDER OF CHRISTIANITY PSYCHOTIC?

"Jesus was either the supernatural Son of God that he claims to be
in the Bible or he was a lunatic." Those are not the words of Albert
Schweitzer but of a number of contemporary evangelicals. During
Schweitzer's lifetime, a group of psychiatrists and others developed
the thesis that Jesus of Nazareth was mentally deranged, a paranoid
suffering delusions of grandeur and bizarre hallucinations. In a little
book translated into English as *The Psychiatric Study of Jesus, Exposition*

and Criticism,[10] Schweitzer argued in reply that to hold to erroneous beliefs about oneself, as Jesus did, is not sufficient reason to be declared psychotic. Jesus was, after all, a man who shared the apocalyptic view of late Judaism. He simply took seriously the worldview in which he grew up.

Schweitzer's position is more sophisticated than can be presented in this chapter, but the point is that biblical scholars, including those who defend the evangelical version of Christianity, have given their best in the effort to present a plausible portrait of Jesus that will meet the minimal test of coherence and also convince the majority of other scholars who have devoted years of their lives to biblical studies. Thus far, no such portrait has emerged.

It is easy to heap frustration onto the biblical scholars, but no one wants more than they to arrive at the truth about what Jesus was like and the truth about the image he had of himself. Their failure to do so is no fault of their own. Regarding some of the writings of the Apostle Paul, the author of II Peter admitted, "There are some things in them hard to understand" (II Peter 3:16). Most of those who have committed their lives to sifting through biblical literature day after day would agree, and then add that there are puzzling passages on nearly every page of the Bible. In some respects, the more one knows about the Bible, the more one realizes that there are vast territories of research that have yet to be explored.

HIGHER CRITICISM AND SOUTHERN BAPTISTS

Paige Patterson is convinced that it was Professor Eric Rust who introduced higher criticism into Southern Baptist life. Glenn Hinson agrees when he writes, "We must remember that historical critical interpretation had barely gotten started even in Southern Baptist seminaries when Eric Rust first began teaching at Southern in 1953."[11] In 1935, the year John R. Sampey became Convention president, Rust took first-class honors in the honors school at Oxford and accepted his first pastorate at Bath, England. In 1942 he received an invitation to become pastor of the large New North Road Church in Huddersfield. Trained in mathematics, science, and theology, Rust has devoted years to developing a Christian theology that pays due regard to scientific research. The founder of Southwestern Baptist Theological Seminary, B. H. Carrol, wrote in 1930 that "the best advocates of science are just as ready to denounce Darwin as I am."[12] Unlike Carrol, Rust is knowledgeable in science and knows that Carrol's remark was as inaccurate then as it is today. Rust would agree with Jimmy Draper that the attempts to harmonize evolution with the Genesis schedule of creation are futile. But whereas Draper rejects the theory of evolution on theological grounds, Rust rejects the Genesis schedule on scientific grounds.

Marvin Tate, Old Testament professor at Southern Seminary, is correct in saying that historical criticism antedated Rust at the seminary. Professor W. O. Carver, who was still at the seminary when I first arrived there in 1953, had used the method, as had William Morton in archeology and Dale Moody in theology, as well as New Testament teachers Henry Turlington, T. C. Smith, and J. Estill Jones. Rust's books gave wider circulation to the historical-critical method among Southern Baptists.

It is clear that the Inerrancy Party wishes to return the seminaries to the first part of the twentieth century, when higher criticism was not practiced among Southern Baptists. Church history has its special ironies. In the seventeenth century, Baptists were a part of the movement to make the Bible available to the people. No longer was it to be the property of a priestly class. Today it seems, on the surface at least, that the interpretation of the Bible has become the privilege of the few, that is, the scholars.

Southern Baptist scholars are exceedingly unhappy with that development. They do not think the people in the pews should be cut off from the fruits or the process of scholarship. Most professors have no desire to maintain a monopoly on research; they are positively eager to take what they have learned and share as much as humanly possible with the Baptist people who have been supporting them for many years. In fact, they feel that they owe it to their fellow Southern Baptists.

It is the leaders of the Inerrancy Party who have tried to cut off the natural interchange between the professors and the people. The Inerrancy Party leaders have created a climate of intimidation that threatens scholars who would reveal to the people what is really going on in the world of biblical scholarship.

Admitting that laypeople would at times be shocked by what they learn, Southern Baptist professors still think it wrong to deprive the people of access to the fruit of biblical research. It certainly seems that the professors have a better appreciation of Baptist history than do the Inerrancy Party leaders. If the principle of the priesthood of believers means anything, it is that no organization of human mortals can appoint itself to stand between the rank and file of Baptists and their right to enjoy every possible means of studying the Bible. That right is only an abstraction if individuals are allowed to study the Bible on their own but are not informed of the tools and methods that the scholars can make available to them. Freedom of choice is empty if the options from which to choose are severely limited.

SCHOLARSHIP, SKEPTICISM, AND FAITH

Harold Lindsell, Paige Patterson, and Eric Rust are skeptics. Rust is skeptical of many of the assertions of Lindsell and Patterson, who in turn are skeptical of many of Rust's assertions. To believe some things, one must disbelieve other things. Scholarship requires both belief and skepticism. If Patterson strongly doubts the documentary hypothesis of the Pentateuch, he is a functional skeptic at that point. If he holds to the hypothesis of inerrancy, he is a believer—in that hypothesis. A scholar may believe in the documentary hypothesis but have doubts about aspects of it. Scholarship is the curious practice of accelerating both belief and doubt. That requires explaining.

A specialist in New Testament literature may advance a new hypothesis for the sake of working on it and testing it. For example, suppose Smith agrees with Draper in accepting the theory that Mark's was the earliest of the four Gospels. That means Smith and Draper believe it. As scholars, they may elect to test their belief—to refine it, to articulate it with greater detail and coherence, and to try to refute it. If they find what appears to be an objection to the theory, then it could be said that they have some doubt about the theory. It does not follow that they have lost belief in it; rather, they are testing it. That is what scholarship requires.

The same can be said about the belief in Jesus. Smith and Draper realize that there are difficulties in the Gospel accounts of Jesus, difficulties that no scholar in the field can ignore. To recognize the problems and to work on them is not to give up the belief that Jesus existed or that he did and said certain things attributed to him in the New Testament. According to Mark 8:29–30, when Peter told Jesus that He was the Messiah, Jesus replied by commanding him to tell no one about Him. Albert Schweitzer called this the Messianic Secret. Jimmy Draper may have an interpretation quite different from Schweitzer's, and Smith may advance a third interpretation. Each scholar believes, and yet each is skeptical of the other's interpretation. In some real sense, the Jesus of Schweitzer is not the Jesus of Draper and Smith, and Draper's is not T. C. Smith's. So, in what sense are these scholars talking about the same Jesus? Carol Draper has one view of her husband, and James Robison has another. Dale Moody will have still another view. It's unlikely that the three views can be made to dovetail into a fully coherent portrait of Draper. In the same way, it is impossible to fit all the views about Jesus into one coherent picture. Smith thinks it is impossible to fit the four Gospel accounts into a fully coherent picture, and most scholars hold that each of the Gospels fails to give a perfectly consistent and coherent portrait.

In journeying through the New Testament, each reader will have to weave together what he thinks Jesus was like and how Jesus saw himself. It is elementary that every passage of Scripture has to be interpreted. The inerrancy theory does not apply to interpretations, nor does it designate one group of Christians as free of error in its interpretations. There is always room for doubt.

Regarding Schweitzer's version of Jesus, Draper will be a skeptic at some crucial points. What each scholar offers is an invitation to look at Jesus from a special perspective, and that is what Southern Baptist scholars can offer the people in the pews—a challenge to look at Christ in the light of different interpretations and from fresh perspectives. For some, accepting the challenge would be exciting, deeply moving, and rewarding. For others, it would be confusing and profoundly disturbing. The rights of each group must somehow be respected and protected in each local church.

The science of physics has spawned a discipline called quantum mechanics. Scientists in this field know that beyond a certain point of observation at the subatomic level, precision of measurement cannot be extended. That does not mean that there are no atoms composed of elusive subatomic particles. Perhaps the study of Jesus is similar. There are limits of precision in the search for the historical Jesus. That is no reason to stop trying to extend precision. Rather, it is simply to point out that so far the results of scholarship have not provided a consensus report on Jesus. There are countless details that cannot be nailed down within any interpretive theory that has been set forth. What is agreed on is that all the efforts to study the life of Jesus have profoundly affected most of those who have devoted years to this study. Their efforts are not pure subjectivism, however, for the scholars find that the research material often forces them to revise their biases and change their interpretations. Some individuals presume that their in-terpretation of the material is the standard. Others cannot agree, they insist, because the biblical materials to be studied and the background documents connected with them have an objective reality of their own that must be respected and patiently worked through.

BAPTIST DEMOCRACY AMID THE CRISIS

As noted above, one group of church members would welcome the opportunity to profit from the fruit of biblical research. Another group would consider such research not an opportunity but an imposition on its freedom. Currently, it seems that the interests of the first group have been sacrificed to the interests of the second, although in some cases the reverse is true. What Southern Baptists need is a political or social mechanism that respects the right of church members to be challenged by biblical scholarship. The same mechanism should equally reinforce the right of church members to be shielded from the results of any scholarly research from which they choose to be pro-tected. In trying to satisfy both groups, Sunday school materials often end up catering to the lowest common denominator.

In 1974 Gene Garman, a graduate of Baylor University and Mid-western Baptist Theological Seminary, was tried and dismissed from membership in the Baptist church in Zion, Illinois. He had issued eight reasons to show why he thought the theory of the Bible's iner-rancy was an unsatisfactory theory. After Garman's expulsion from the church, the pastor contended that Garman was not dismissed be-cause of his view but because of the division he had created among the members by teaching his beliefs.[13]

There are several ways to consider this unfortunate incident. First of all, according to Baptist church polity, a local church can expel from its membership whomever it wishes as long as a majority of the mem-bership or a committee authorized by the membership approves. Sec-ond, expulsion is usually regarded by Baptists as the measure of last resort in any church conflict. Third, the members of the Zion church who did not wish to be exposed to Garman's views on inerrancy had a perfect right to be protected from them. Fourth, they did not have the right to prevent other members from hearing Garman's views at the church if those others wished to hear them.

If the pastor of the church was only trying to assist those members who personally exercised their choice to be protected from hearing

Garman's criticism of biblical inerrancy, then he was in keeping with Baptist polity. But if the pastor was attempting to prevent some of his members from learning about Garman's views, he was using his position to suppress a view that perhaps competed with his own. It may well be that in the remainder of the twentieth century the Baptist polity of congregational democracy will be severely tried at the local church level. It might be wise for Convention leaders and editors of state Baptist journals to offer guidelines and suggestions on ways to maintain peace in the local congregations (and in the associations) while protecting the freedom to discuss the inerrancy issue along with the issue of the future of their Baptist schools and institutions.

It may turn out that the year 1979 was the beginning of the Southern Baptist Convention's divorce. That was the year in which the Inerrancy Party leaders elected their first Convention president, Adrian Rogers. It may be that the divorce will give each party its freedom. Or it may be that, as in many divorces, the lawyers will inherit a windfall. The Inerrancy Party and the Moderate Party agree that Jesus said, "Woe to you lawyers" (Luke 11:52). Most agree also that Jesus said, "Do not resist one who is evil" (Matt. 5:39) and "Make friends quickly with your accuser, while you are going with him to court" (Matt. 5:25). But of course those passages must be interpreted.

And then they must be applied to a twentieth-century incident under twentieth-century circumstances. A once-popular novel by Charles Monroe Sheldon entitled *In His Steps* focused on the question "What would Jesus do?"[14] It would be interesting to know how the leaders and combatants would answer that perplexing question as it applies to their denominational holy war. Would some of them model their behavior in accord with their conjecture of what Jesus would do? Or would they model Jesus after themselves? Perhaps others would give a look of skepticism and confess that they do not know what Jesus would do if he were caught up in this Southern Baptist crisis. In organizing for the June 1986 convention in Atlanta, the Reverend Harold Hunter of Florida made it clear that he expected the members of his church to vote the way he voted if they were elected as voting messengers to the Atlanta convention. "I don't want anyone going from my church that I have any questions about. If they're going to go, they're going to vote like I vote," he said, adding that some might not be certain "what it is to be led by the Spirit of God, but I'm certain. On this issue [of the man to elect as president of the Convention] there is no doubt." At the same organizational meeting of Inerrancy

Party members in Florida, the Reverend Homer Lindsay, Jr., also threw his weight behind the candidacy of Adrian Rogers. "I'm not telling you how to vote, but if you do what God wants you to do, then we'll vote the same way. He's not going to lead you to do one thing and me another."[15]

Apparently, for some Southern Baptist preachers infallibility and inerrancy are not limited to the original autographs of the Bible.

16.

Jesus Loves Everybody,
Especially Winners

ven when James Robison was still in good standing with the brokers of influence within the Inerrancy Party, the Texas TV evangelist was making a number of the brethren nervous. James had developed the habit of taking supernatural intervention in his life to excess. At least that was the way some of his peers saw it. Like Oral Roberts, Jimmy Swaggart, the new Pentecostals, and the charismatics, James Robison frequently uses the phrase "God told me." According to that way of thinking, the preacher's personal revelations are not to be seriously doubted by anyone. Doubting them is like doubting God.

At a recent meeting of ministers' wives in Texas a surprising amount of anger rose to the surface as they discussed the difficulty of disagreeing with their husbands the way married couples normally disagree. Some of the wives felt themselves in a double bind. On the one hand, they were intelligent human beings who could think and pray. On the other hand, disagreeing with their husbands was like disagreeing with the Lord God Almighty Himself.

Old-line American evangelicals of the B. B. Warfield tradition have remained skeptical of every charismatic and Pentecostal upsurge among the churches. According to the Warfield tradition, the gifts distributed to the first-century churches ceased before the century ended, as did divine revelation. Warfield and his followers, as well as John Calvin before him, drew a hard and fast line between inspiration and illumination. Since the authors of Scripture alone were inspired, they alone were infallible. Subsequent to the first Christian century, believers could receive only illumination, never inspired revelation. Illumination is always refracted through and corrected by revelation set down in Scripture. The claims to illumination are therefore always subject to challenge on two accounts. First, do the claims violate Scripture? If so, they cannot be true illumination. Second, do the claims violate the laws of logic or elementary common sense and wisdom? If so, then at the least they need to be looked at with a cocked eyebrow. According to the Warfield school of thought, it might be that God has given James Robison sufficient illumination to lead him to begin construction of a multimillion-dollar complex in the Dallas-Fort Worth metroplex. Or it might be that James has confused his enormous ambition with the voice of the Holy Spirit, the way a lot of Southern Baptist ministers think Oral Roberts has been doing habitually.

For some reason, those Southern Baptists who think they are guided by the Spirit in most everything they do speak more of hearing or feeling divine direction than of seeing visions. Among Baptists, visions are unpopular. It was Oral Roberts who said he saw a vision of a 900-foot-tall Jesus on the afternoon of May 25, 1980. Distraught about the financial difficulties of his unfinished City of Faith, Oral was suddenly swept by an unusual feeling:

> I felt an overwhelming presence all around me. When I opened my eyes, there He stood . . . some 900 feet tall, looking at me. . . . He stood a full 300 feet taller than the 600 foot tall City of Faith. There I was face to face with Jesus Christ, the Son of the Living God. I have only seen Jesus once before, but here I was face to face with the King of Kings. He stared at me without saying a word; Oh! I will never forget those eyes! And then, He reached down, put His hands under the City of Faith, lifted it, and said to me, "See how easy it is for me to lift it!" [1]

When the vision vanished, Oral, his eyes now filled with tears, spotted a young man nearby and related to him what he had just experienced. To this day, Oral is not clear in his own mind about the true identity of the young man. Was he a human being or was he an angel? What Oral remains certain about is his vision of Jesus and the divine reassurance that the financial payments would come through for the City of Faith. [2]

Upon hearing his account of the 900-foot Jesus, a number of Southern Baptist ministers smiled and allowed that it was all just another one of Oral's tall tales. One fundamentalist minister denounced Oral's appeal letters as "hucksterish tactics" and added, "I have that Oral

Roberts appeal on my desk right now. . . . It's unbiblical, unfunda-
mentalist, and anti-Christian."[3] A Methodist pastor in Iowa wrote an
open letter that was particularly galling to Oral. "Now, I understand
from very reliable sources that Jesus has been talking with you again,
and the theme running through those chats has been money. . . . Oral,
you're a United Methodist, and just between us, I would appreciate
the benefit of your counsel. . . . Could you please give me the area
code and unlisted number to you-know-who? I feel cheated."[4]

Carl McIntire, fundamentalist of the vintage and style of J. Frank
Norris, said Roberts had gone berserk. "No decent Christian," McIntire reportedly added, "believed that Christ was nine hundred feet
tall."[5] Oral Roberts has often stated that he challenges people to stretch
beyond their capacity, but a number of Southern Baptist ministers
balked at the idea of Oral's challenging Jesus Christ to stretch to 900
feet tall.

Oral's vision uncovered a prejudice among noncharismatic fundamentalists: hearing the voice of God or a ministering angel is acceptable to them, but seeing visions is not. In fact, Baptists seem rarely
to consort with angels. Billy Graham wrote a book on those secret
agents from heaven, but even he finds little personal use for their services. Smarting under J. I. Packer's criticism of those who profess to
experience visual representations of God, Jimmy Swaggart has tried
recently to disclaim any visual content to his professed visions from
Heaven. If the president of the Southern Baptist Convention revealed
that he had regular visitations from talkative angels, he would likely
have a visitation from a committee of the trustees urging him to at
least test the angels. The brethren would suggest that he consider the
possibility that he was either the dupe of Satan or the victim of bad
hamburger.

The prejudice against visions among Baptists is of sociological interest that need not be explored here. Presumably, if Jesus could walk
through closed doors (John 20:19–20) and lift off Planet Earth via a
cloud (Acts 1:9), he could make himself appear 900 feet tall. It is a
theological question as to whether a glorified body has a fixed dimension, anyway. So, I began to wonder what all the fuss was about. My
conclusion is this. The idea of Jesus coming down to Tulsa, Oklahoma,
to visit Oral about his City of Faith placed a double strain on the
imagination. To extend the image to a 900-foot Jesus seemed to turn
the questionable into the embarrassingly ridiculous. An exceedingly
competitive man, Oral just could not remain content with an ordi-

nary, run-of-the-mill vision. With outrageously big bills to pay, he needed an outrageously big Jesus. And it worked.

James Robison had to admit that God does not speak to him in good Texas English but through urges, feelings, and other behind-the-skin areas not open to public investigation. When James reports the communiqués, he freely embellishes them, leaving the impression that God addresses him by his first name. What divides ministers among Southern Baptists as much as anything else is the degree to which they believe that most of their personal acts and decisions come under the direct guidance of Heaven. Several jokes among many ministers indicate their awareness of this division. One old favorite is about a minister who receives a call to a better church. A better church usually means a larger congregation, a pulpit with wider influence, and more financial benefits for the minister. The minister, upon receiving the call, asks his wife to phone for a moving van and to start packing while he goes to the upper room to pray and to ask God if he should accept the call to this new and better field of service.

At one end of the continuum stand those ministers who appear to believe they have divine guidance and sanction for all their decisions, from selecting the right car to designating which oil well to sink money into. At the other end of the continuum stand those who believe that common sense and tested experience based on the general revelation of nature and history should guide most day-by-day decisions. Whenever ministers of the latter group hear one of the clergy speak as if most of his decisions were divine in origin, they are likely to regard him as either sincerely deluded or lying through his teeth.

Ford Oil and Development, Inc., stands ready to receive the money of devout believers who feel led by the Lord to buy stock in oil well drillings in Israel. One fundamentalist oilman assured charismatic Southern Baptist TV host Pat Robertson that within a matter of days his drillers would tap into "the largest oil field ever discovered." Getting as excited as a hungry coyote chasing a jackrabbit, Pat exclaimed, "I just thank the Lord and pray for this project because it could revolutionize the fulfillment of Bible prophecy." Unfortunately, the devil was up to his old tricks again and created an endless string of troubles for the drillers until, hopelessly stuck 21,428 feet below the Holy Land, the drills stopped and the spot was at least temporarily abandoned. Despite the prayers of investors and the visions of the fundamentalist wildcatters, the $13 million site named Asher-Atlit No. 1 is only one of many dry holes drilled in Israel by oilmen who had bet their bottom dollar and other believers' dollars, too, on the expectation of miracles.

Faithful to the end, Harris "Koop" Darcy, a Houston geologist who sank about $100,000 in Asher-Atlit No. 1, insists that despite the junk in the hole, which makes it physically impossible to save the well, God is going to start it flowing in his own good time. Harold "Hayseed" Stephens of Weatherford, Texas, thinks his fellow believers have got it all wrong. The way he reads his Bible, the largest oil deposit in the Holy Land is not in the tribal lands but in the ancient valley of Siddim.

The Reverend Jim Spillman may just be slicker than Holy Land oil itself, for he has found a way to pump money straight out of the faithful. Speaking at a three-day Bible Prophecy Conference in Lakeland, Florida, Spillman sold copies of *The Great Treasure Hunt*, which offers whiz-bang, Scripture-riddled evidence that treasures lie in the tribal lands of Asher, Zebulun, Issachar, Ephraim, and Manasseh. Paul the Apostle spoke of being a "fool for Christ," but somehow the fundamentalist wildcatters have made sincere believers into fools of the type that the apostle could not have imagined.[6]

CHRISTIAN HEDONISM

A movement is developing among Southern Baptists that might be described as Christian hedonism, but it is more accurate to call it a "Jesus will help you get to the top" movement. The emphasis is upon competition and taking advantage of opportunities and circumstances. Jesus is seen as the chief capitalist and as a rewarder of faithful capitalists who come after him. The Lord Jesus likes to see his investors make a spiritual killing. He calls the elect to be winners, to come out on top of the heap, not the bottom. True, he said, "Blessed are you poor" (Luke 6:20), but he really meant what Matthew reported him as saying: "Blessed are the poor in spirit" (Matt. 5:3). All in all, this movement is a sharp this-worldly turn in modern Christendom. Ideally, the Protestant Reformation gave all a chance to read the Bible for themselves, assuming they could read in the first place. The new Christian hedonism goes one step farther to give everyone a shot at the material things of this world. No longer are money and wealth something that spiritually minded believers should feel uncomfortable with, for capitalism is itself a part of the divine economy. In Europe, Christian hedonism took the form of socialism, purporting to give everyone a piece of the pie. In America, Christian hedonism has as its John 3:16, "God Helps [Only] Those Who Help Themselves."

Self-help books and help-yourself cassette tapes are selling like hotcakes in the United States. Leaders of the new Christian hedonists, recognizing a good thing when they see it, have begun to cash in on it. Jesus would have it that way. Why leave a good thing like this for the devil's crowd to exploit? If during the fifties the liberals and moderates challenged the competitive spirit and the get-ahead ethic of American Christian materialists by opposing racial segregation, the new fundamentalist materialists are certain that God wants especially Christian true believers to think mink! Setting a good example, W. A. Criswell receives a salary of $90,000 from his church and has made serious and shrewd inroads into the real estate business. Each year his church dresses him in a new wardrobe fit for leading the rapture parade. Meantime, as long as the Lord tarries, they make W.A. accept a new car every year, whether he wants it or not. As befits a man poor in spirit, W.A. confesses that he does not even think about wealth.

Contemporary Christian hedonism must be seen as a movement to help legitimate those rising from lower middle-class economic status to upper middle-class status, and beyond. It tells them they are okay if they accumulate filthy lucre. After all, it's not money itself but the love of money that is the root of all evil (I Tim. 6:10). True, the author of the inspired Epistle to the Hebrews wrote, "Keep your life free from the love of money" (13:5), but that can't mean that we have to keep free of money itself. Actually, one way for Christians to avoid yearning after money is to have so much of it that they do not need to yearn.

Another way for Christian materialists to prove they are free from the love of money is to give a healthy percentage of it to God's ministers and ministry. Speaking the language of both Zion and another apostle born out of due time, Adam Smith, the TV preachers in particular give their supporters to understand that contributing money to their television ministries is really not giving it away but spiritually investing it. It is more blessed to give than to receive, but it is even more blessed to invest for the heavenly future by helping TV preachers bear their crosses and financial burdens. "But thou shalt remember the Lord thy God: for it is he that giveth the power to get wealth" (Deut. 8:18 KJV). Help Jimmy Swaggart declare war on Satan, and in return he will send you a free cross and dove lapel pin. In addition, your seed-faith investment will earn the highest dividends.

Testimonials are a major tool for the modern preachers of the Fifth Gospel, the Gospel of Success. Whereas the Hall of Faith in the eleventh chapter of the Epistle to the Hebrews pointed to great martyrs of the faith to inspire the early Christians, the modern TV preacher Bob Schuller points to twentieth-century saints like Tony Orlando, Hugh

O'Brian, Cherry Boone O'Neill, Tom Landry, and that paragon of two-fisted, give-'em-hell Christian meekness, John Wayne. It is the John Wayne style of meekness that the new Christian Pelagians admire.

To help the meek to inherit the real estate God wants them to have, Dallas evangelist Robert Tilton will for $100 sell them a dozen inspiring cassette tapes, which he says are worth several times that. "Jesus wants to bring you into your inheritance," Tilton announces, holding up his packaged Biblical Success Course. "I'm not just a guy who lives in a post office box. I'm an ordained minister." And that is the gospel truth. He lives in one of Dallas's most exclusive havens of the wealthy. Having personally climbed high up the ladder of material success, he promises to give his customers "power to create wealth." It's all on the tapes, for a hundred bucks.

Sitting at a table at a banquet and indoor rally starring evangelist James Robison and the brilliant Texas lawyer Racehorse Haynes, sociologist Charles Glasgow leaned over and whispered to me, "You're watching a rising entrepreneur at work." Growing up a Baptist and attending the Midwestern Baptist Theological Seminary in Kansas City, Dr. Glasgow had for years observed ministers like Robison in action. James Robison did indeed represent the American entrepreneur who, starting out small, has climbed the ladder to material success. Robison once explained why he did not need to go to seminary. Would a successful engineer stop his work to go off to engineering school? From Robison's point of view, seminary could teach him little. He is living evidence that neither college nor seminary is essential to climbing to the top of the heap in the Gospel of Success business.

COMPETITION

Christian materialists in America tend toward capitalism partly because they see life as hard competition, even as battle. In a battle somebody has to win and somebody has to lose. Since Jesus does not want his followers to be the losers, the Reverend Robert Tilton challenges his audience to learn quickly how to climb to the top. He loves to quote Proverbs 13:22: "A good man leaves an inheritance to his children's children, but the sinner's wealth is laid up for the righteous." As a high school student in the late forties I ordered a copy of V. P. Kaub's *Jesus: A Capitalist* and read *Christian Economics*, an ultra-conservative publication. It was from *God, Gold and Government* that I learned that Jesus favored the gold standard. Later, I read other books declaring that Jesus was a socialist at heart. But I was never convinced by either side. When Jesus fed the five thousand, he did not get a promissory note from the customers. Nor did he seem interested in nationalizing the wine or donkey industry of his homeland. As a youth I found comfort in reading from my Scofield, "But seek ye first the kingdom of God, and his righteousness; and all these things shall be added unto you" (Matt. 6:33 KJV). I had read often that God would supply our need (Phil. 4:19) and that there was no point in worrying about tomorrow's supplies since the Father who clothed the lilies and grass of the field and fed the birds of the air would watch after his human family. But I knew there were adults and children whose survival needs were scarcely met. Unlike some Christians I knew, I could never bring myself to think that all who lost out materially in the world were lazy bums or that those who prospered over their neighbors were morally better or worse than their fellow mortals. I remained a capitalist because neither socialism nor communism seemed credible. I was a Baptist and a small-time capitalist, but I could never assure myself that Jesus favored or disfavored the gold standard.

The modern Christian materialists are to be saluted for their this-worldly outlook. They are looking out for themselves. Love yourself as your neighbor. Unfortunately, their religion does not speak to the problems of perpetual world hunger and population sprawl. There does not seem to be a religion on earth that has anything of practical worth to say about those two problems. Maybe that is too much to expect. Maybe that is why serious premillennialists talk about the world's ending soon. They see that their religion has run up against obstacles that cannot be overcome. Providence seems preoccupied or even absent at times, as though the God of Elijah has taken a vacation. So, the premillennialists switch to another channel, only to find that the story is even more pessimistic there.

The new Christian materialism can be seen as a modern response to modern conditions. In essence, it says that since it is impossible to meet the basic needs of food, shelter, and health for a large percentage of the world's population, let's do the next best. Let's look out for our own kind, giving now and then a drop in the bucket to help others. At least we can make ourselves as happy as possible and fulfill our own potential. What else can be expected of us? Besides, there is the Soviet Union, an evil empire named Gog. We have to spend most of our money to keep it from intimidating us and the rest of the world. Jerry Falwell's new Liberty Foundation is committing to the Star Wars defense system, not to a sustained Peace Corps or Vista. If the world cannot be saved for Jesus Christ, then the new Christian materialists are certainly not going to worry perpetually about world hunger. Perhaps someday God and capitalism will feed the world, but that is only a part of the postmillennial dream that may have perished once and for all. After all, life is a competition. Some will win and rise to the top. Others will lose. So, to those who have ears to hear (and have been born in the right country), see you at the top! Jesus loves everybody, especially winners.

THE NEW RICH

It is not by coincidence that the grandfather and most influential personage of the Inerrancy Party, W. A. Criswell, is the senior minister of one of the largest and wealthiest churches in the nation. Billionaire H. L. Hunt was a member there for many years. The prophet of profit, Zig Ziglar, teaches a Sunday school class there. Though Paige Patterson and Jimmy Draper are not rich, they are Criswell's protégés, and he is reasonably well pleased with them. Richard Land is at the Criswell Center with Patterson. There is no question that the First Baptist Church of Dallas, with its 26,000 members and annual budget of $12 million, has wittingly or unwittingly spearheaded the Christian hedonism movement among Southern Baptists. Evangelist Billy Graham, who for some obscure reason transferred his church membership to the Dallas church many years ago even though his home was and is a thousand miles away in North Carolina, laid the foundation for Christian hedonism among Southern Baptists. Billy felt compassion for the wealthy. Somebody had to minister to them. Jesus loves the rich as well as the poor. Why discriminate against those who have large bank accounts? Billy himself had the initiative to inherit valuable property on the edge of Charlotte, North Carolina, and sell it for a profit worthy of Joseph of Arimathea, one of the moneyed who is reputed to have played an important role among the first Christians.

The new Christian hedonists will not appreciate being classified as hedonists, because for centuries priests and preachers have ritualistically thundered against hedonism. The word "hedonism" is taken from a Greek word meaning pleasure, and there are several versions of ethical hedonism. Only one version emphasizes pleasure at the moment without regard for painful consequences in the future. Others stress long-term pleasure for both oneself and other people. Christian hedonism may be described in a preliminary way as simply the ethic or morality of pleasure within a Christian and caring framework.

For centuries Christian theologians and preachers extolled the virtue of suffering and pain. Great numbers of their fellow Christians were suffering disease, poverty, and severe deprivation with little hope of improving their earthly lot. Hence, it made sense to make a virtue out of bearing one's suffering and deprivation courageously and free of pointless bitterness. Some Jewish rabbis and Christian preachers and priests treated unavoidable suffering as not only a virtue but also a means of gaining eternal salvation. Perhaps their motives were noble, for they did enhance the value of suffering by giving it meaning in the cosmic scheme of things. But the strategy backfired. Instead of easing suffering, the new theological twist turned pain and self-torment into a goal, leading believers to think they could not gain entrance to heaven unless they earned it by suffering. Over the centuries, that way of believing contributed to the buildup of untold private torment, as people sought out new ways to suffer on earth so they could escape damnation in hell. That miserable outlook spawned generations of dedicated masochists in the name of Christianity and made it practically impossible for the Christian clergy to calmly consider the merits of a Christian hedonism.

The Protestant Reformation had a good chance of casting off the old chains of churchly masochism. In many ways, it paved the way for Christian hedonism by establishing one resolute point. The suffering of Jesus on the cross was the only suffering required for salvation, so any suffering by believers added nothing to the ledger of salvation. A later hymn summarized the point crisply: "Jesus paid it all."

With the advance of medical research and technology along with the spread of affluence in America, Christian hedonism was bound to flower in the fullness of time. It is revealing that the Inerrancy Party leaders who criticize Convention educators most severely for altering the face of Christianity tend to be the same preachers who are most successful at introducing Southern Baptists to the Gospel of Success. By focusing on the educators, the preachers of success draw attention away from the greater alteration that they themselves are accomplishing among their fellow Southern Baptists. But Zig Ziglar and the ministers of the gigantic, affluent churches within the Convention have not knowingly set out to alter the face of Southern Baptist Christianity. Far from it. They will join Paige Patterson in declaring that they are dedicated to preserving the faith once delivered to the saints.

Despite all the misdirected speeches against humanism, many of the new Christian hedonists are opening the doors to the humanistic ethic. Perhaps a word should be said about humanism. Hyperfundamentalist Tim LaHaye has given the erroneous impression that all ethical humanists are socialists if not communists, along with the reckless innuendo that humanist parents actually want their teenage children, or at least their neighbors' children, to destroy their lives on drugs, to engage in promiscuous sex, and to run the risk of getting pregnant. Those wild charges are all a smoke screen. The truth appears to be that through their use of pop psychology and, more substantially, a heavy indebtedness to self-realization psychology some of the new fundamentalist hedonists have opened the gates to traditional humanistic morality. In haranguing at length and sometimes invectively against what they call humanism, they do protest too much.

FOR WHOM THE SABBATH?

Zig Ziglar has an interesting film for churches and other groups in which he stresses the development of one's human potential. The self-realization or self-fulfillment ethic in its most consistent form advances the view that moral rules and laws are instrumental rather than ends in themselves. That is, they are instrumental in the development of the potential of every individual. That is precisely what the humanistic ethic is about, and perhaps nowhere in all literature can a more sparkling and succinct statement of it be found than in the New Testament. "The sabbath was made for man, not man for the sabbath" (Mark 2:27).

Like traffic laws, some moral rules serve to bring order out of the chaos of human desires. The humanistic goal is not order for its own sake, not man for the sabbath, but the fulfillment and pleasure gained when the conflict of desires is controlled and transformed into a more or less steady flow of satisfaction. Far from saying, "Do it if it feels good no matter what the consequences," humanism is a moral philosophy that studiously cares about the consequences of human acts. Just as some dangerous drivers have to be taken off the streets, so some human desires have to be restrained or redirected to satisfy the other desires. Humanistic morality, then, is a highly practical venture and is essential to self-realization.

The revolution of the new Christian hedonism lies in its message that suffering and poverty are neither a means of salvation nor a state that the deity prefers for his creatures. Christian hedonism teaches the new affluent Baptists—the modern heirs of the old Puritans—to celebrate life with more enthusiasm. The boldly materialistic aspect of the movement is grounded in the honest admission that without material means—money—considerable individual freedom is lost in a highly mobile and complex society such as the United States. Instead of feeling guilty about having the means to develop their potential and talents, the Southern Baptist hedonists are learning to enjoy money within a legitimated framework. The danger threatening their movement is that it will turn into a Baptist Yuppie Club of narcissistic self-indulgers, people who imagine that they have earned all their good fortune and that those at the bottom of the heap deserve to be there either because God did not see fit to endow them with comparable talents or because they have not tried to help themselves.

FALSE PROFITS AND FALSE PROPHETS

Earlier I suggested that Southern Baptist ministers can be classified according to how strongly they feel that every aspect of their lives is guided directly by the deity. Oddly enough, those ministers who readily invoke the authority of God to validate their decisions also present the thickest walls of skepticism when opposing ministers do the same. Like competing shamans, each will declare that he has consulted the deity in prayer and will appear righteously indignant if his opinion is met with a cool reception. In the June 1985 Convention in Dallas I overheard supporters of Charles Stanley thank God for giving their man the victory and turning back the threat of Satan. Later that day I was in the Convention press room when the losing presidential candidate, Winfred Moore, appeared. I could not help wondering if the soft-spoken minister of the First Baptist Church of Amarillo felt that he had been the tool of Satan in opposing Stanley.

Invoking the authority of the deity is like crying wolf. If done too often, its effect is diminished. There is a group of Southern Baptists who cannot comfortably live with ambiguity in certain areas. They need to feel that almost all their beliefs and actions have the stamp of divine approval and that anyone holding contrary opinions lacks divine approval. In the sixties, for example, one group of integrationists could not imagine that busing children to school might not be Heaven's only way to implement the goal of desegregation. All who opposed

busing were labeled bigots, even if they had demonstrated their commitment to the principle of integration in a variety of other public and
detectable ways.

The habit of invoking the authority of God in defending decisions
and lifestyle infuses the invoker with an unshakable confidence. It
also tends to shut down rational discussion. The more one invokes
the deity to justify one's opinions, the more one is inclined to charac-
terize as satanic those who profess rival opinions. The everyday world
of decisions becomes only a shadow of supernatural wars carried on
in a supernatural arena.

BAPTISTS AND FAITH HEALERS

Pat Robertson of the 700 Club is a Southern Baptist who is also
something of a faith healer, which places him in a minority among his
fellow Baptists. Most Southern Baptists have learned to live with the
uncertainty and ambiguity of the world of disease. Regularly, the majority of Convention ministers visit the afflicted and infirm in hospitals and offer prayers for recovery. They do not belong to the "Name It,
Claim It" group of new Pentecostals who have convinced themselves
that God will heal all on earth if only the prayers of the faithful are
sufficiently strong. One reason that Southern Baptists and the old
Pentecostals have rejected the "Name It, Claim It" movement is quite
clear. Diseases are a part of the empirical, observable world of space
and time; claims to physical cures can be empirically tested.

There are so-called faith healers who are tricksters, and there are
others who are cruel racketeers. James Randi, one of the most informed professional illusionists in North America, is currently working on a book to expose some of the con artists in the faith-healing
enterprise. Southern Baptists face a challenge from the mounting
claims of charismatics and new Pentecostals. Time is on the side of the
vast majority of Southern Baptists, because the sun of reality will
sooner or later burn away much of the charismatic fog, but the capacity for each generation to lose itself in a new charismatic fog cannot be
overrated. The faith-healing service itself is an interesting study in the
role of pretense; the entire auditorium becomes a stage for what the
participants temporarily take to be a cosmic drama—or at least a dress
rehearsal for the holy drama—in which the deity descends to work
miracles and fill the faithful with new hope.

Southern Baptist ministers on the whole are quite aware of the charlatans in the faith-healing business. I was not aware of just how lucrative faith healing was until I began a somewhat intensive study of it recently. After years of resisting the temptation to attach pecuniary motives to faith healers, I have decided that there are some exceedingly cynical faith-healing evangelists who are out primarily for a buck and whose concern for the less fortunate scarcely exists.

More than a decade ago, when I wrote my first book, *The Billy Graham Religion*, I received criticism on one point that took me wholly by surprise. I was accused of failing to expose Billy Graham as a man driven by greed. My response then and now is quite simple. I do not think Graham is in the business principally for the money. Nor do I think Criswell or most other Southern Baptist nouveaux riches are in it solely for the money. The possibility does exist that the new moneyed and especially the new apostles of the Gospel of Success will fall innocently into the habit of imagining that their affluence is a sign of their spiritual superiority, with their money as an external sign of internal grace.

PROVIDENCE AND THE GREAT LOTTERY OF LIFE

Christianity, Judaism, and Islam have in common, roughly, the belief that the universe is governed by a Supreme Mind who is just in his treatment of his creatures and so powerful that he does not fail to accomplish his purpose. In short, the universe is under the perpetual control of Divine Providence. That belief has been challenged relentlessly by the conspicuous existence of unfairness and injustice in the world. Many theologians in the past have acknowledged the inconsistencies forthrightly and then called upon the doctrines of heaven and hell to explain that by and by all injustices will be overcome in a just and perfectly harmonized universe.

Appeals to the next life have in the twentieth century lost some of their luster. To market their religion in a highly competitive and pluralistic world, Christians have been forced to meet more of the demands of the market. Promises of a better deal in the next life must be accompanied by manifest and sustained material improvement on this present planet. It was not coincidence that modern capitalism and Protestantism emerged simultaneously in the West. They both represented the weakening of monopolistic and imperialistic controls and the opening up of new markets. As new religious options began to appear, the customers won more freedom to select from the religious market. It took decades for revolts within Protestantism to develop, resulting in a radical increase in the options on the religious market. For more than three centuries the Baptists have been a major contributor to the free market in religion and to the free market in economics. (In 1888 a Baptist named John D. Rockefeller contributed to the building of New York Hall at Southern Seminary in Louisville.) So it is not surprising that a number of Southern Baptists now seem bullish on capitalism.

Unfortunately, millions of Protestants are far from prosperous, and the new Christian materialism poses a temptation for the prosperous to cut themselves off unwittingly from the unprosperous. Instead of receiving inspiration and realistic help from their prosperous siblings, those Baptists near the bottom of the heap could be made to feel that they are deficient in faith and morally inferior.

That returns the discussion to Christianity's emphasis on Providence and to the difficulty of squaring a loving Providence with the world's rampant misery. A world under the guidance of a caring Heavenly Father ought to appear quite different from a world that moves by impersonal patterns and by nontheistic evolution. In the evolutionary framework, not only individuals but whole species end up at the bottom of the heap. If the deity wants everyone on top of the heap, why are so many at the bottom?

Southern Baptist ministers have often criticized faith healers for leaving the unhealed to feel that something is profoundly wrong with them spiritually and morally. The faith healer's message to the afflicted goes something like this: "Does our Heavenly Father take pleasure in anybody's physical suffering or physical impairment?" The answer of course is no. "Did not the Lord say, 'Ask and you shall receive'? And doesn't the Lord command us to ask in faith and promise us that if we have the faith of a mustard seed, we can move mountains? And do you believe that the Lord wants this mountain moved out of your life, this disease removed from your body?" The Christian can only answer yes. But if he is not healed, whose fault is it? Is God to blame?

Having failed to receive the blessing of restored wholeness, infirm Christians understandably begin to doubt their own faithfulness. They see themselves as weak in faith instead of courageous. And despite striving and praying to strengthen their faith, they often develop an image of a crippled spirit to match their crippled body.

The new preachers of prosperity may have unintentionally sent out the message that the less fortunate Baptists are failures in life and inferior as persons until they climb to the top of the ladder. The faith healer's reasoning applies to the poor man too: "Does God our Creator take pleasure in the poverty and failure of any of his human creatures? Did not the Lord say, 'Seek and ye shall find'? Did he not promise the faithful that he would supply all their needs according to his riches in glory? Are his favors not boundless? Then God cannot be blamed for your failure to claim your earthly inheritance, can he? God wants you to be a winner, Brother. God wants you at the top. If you're still near the bottom, don't blame God."

Christian theology has never developed a decent explanation of why life has so much fierce competition and why there is so much disparity of fortune and misfortune among human beings. John Calvin came up with the notion that God had an eternal hankering for variety. Divine sovereignty was manifested through great disparity among mortals, variety being the spice of God's manifest glory. Some of Adam's heirs were elected for eternal joy and some for eternal ruin. If everyone ended up on top, creation would be so drab and dull as to be a poor reflection of God's sparkling glory. It did not take too long for John Calvin's heirs to begin thinking that the Creator had foreordained some people to be at the top and others at the bottom of the social and economic ladder. Dutch Calvinists took the idea with them to South Africa and gradually decided that God had elected the black race to remain at the bottom as Ham's descendants.

That kind of reasoning pervaded the American South in the nineteenth century, and for many decades most Southern Baptists believed it was firmly grounded in Scripture. But in recent times a rival theory has emerged to explain the disparity among earthly mortals. It may be called the footrace theory. Everybody in the world begins with the same opportunities at life's starting line. God is impartial and gives everyone equal opportunity. After the race starts, some people put more effort into the race and end up ahead of the others, while slackers end up at the rear. If anyone is trapped at the rear, it is his or her own doing. The protégés of Norman Vincent Peale, following this glib explanation, have no realistic recommendations for helping the truly down and out. Instead they exhort one another with such clichés as "You can do whatever you want to do. You can reach whatever goal you wish to reach. God has given you all the resources you need. The rest is up to you alone."

In eighteenth-century England the noted Christian theologian and philosopher William Paley wrote several books and articles on the reasonableness of Christianity. Three of his books profoundly influenced a young ministerial student at Cambridge in the nineteenth century. The student's name was Charles Darwin. From *A View of the Evidences of Christianity* Darwin drew the idea of God as the Master Contriver and Architect who attained his goals by establishing the "great lottery of life," in which many individuals draw a blank, that is, a losing ticket.

Instead of imitating Calvin and his theological cousins, who postulated that the Creator had rigged every particle and detail in the overall scheme of things, Paley advanced the view that God had deliberately created a chance element in the distribution of goods and resources among human mortals.[7] God did not, therefore, foreordain that Mr. and Mrs. Jones would be presented with an armless or blind infant. Instead of asking why God had elected them to suffer or asking what sins they had committed to deserve so severe a punishment, Mr. and Mrs. Jones may explain that they simply drew a losing ticket in the lottery of life. Another couple might have drawn it instead. Neither God nor the unfortunate couple are to blame.

Most Christians have never had a broad explanation of human misfortune at the individual level. They have tried all sorts of theories and combinations of theories—from original sin to moralistic scenarios—but they are all like frayed flags flapping in the wind. The twentieth century has not treated kindly the idea of Divine Providence. The postmillennial vision that pictures the Christian gospel pervading the whole planet and gradually transforming the kingdoms of this world into the Kingdom of Christ has fallen against harsh realities. Famine, drought, disease, violence, a plurality of beliefs—all serve to remind Christians that Providence seems to have a precarious hold on the reins. Faced with so many setbacks, premillennial fundamentalists have reaffirmed a neo-Manicheanism that tries to translate all the troubles of contemporary human life into a black-and-white cosmic war between the two greatest of supernatural powers, God and Satan.

One of the distinguishing characteristics of members of the Inerrancy Party is the quickness with which they invoke the Satan hypothesis to explain the world's problems. Within the Moderate Party, some members believe in a personal Satan and some do not, but even those who do are reluctant to apply the explanation to everything that threatens them. When Pat Robertson, for example, complained that Satan had stirred up a hurricane in the Atlantic and aimed it at his TV station in Virginia, some of the moderates who believe in a personal

Satan would not accept that God had turned the weather over to his archenemy.

THE ULTIMATE WAR

Within the Inerrancy Party are many who see not only human life but the entire universe as embroiled in perpetual battle. They see everything in terms of the ultimate war between two and only two forces, the heavenly force and the demonic force. For some, the battle is so real that at least temporarily the demonic force can wrest power from the heavenly, taking over the weather and creating a hurricane to obliterate Pat Robertson's TV station. Pat Robertson is an example of a man who believes that he personally possesses cosmic influence through his prayers. In the case of the hurricane, he holds that his timely prayer aided the heavenly force in recovering control over the weather. This is Star Wars theology, and Southern Baptists are strongly divided over it. One side regards it as literal truth; the other side regards it as mythical projection at best, dangerous lunacy at worst.

The violence that fundamentalism seems to justify in the form of extermination, everlasting hell, and apocalyptic mayhem is difficult for many people to understand. How can such atrocities be a part of one's religion? It helps to realize that even fundamentalist missionary programs come under the war model. In many ways, missionaries are, like Jonah, ambassadors of the Lord sent ahead of God's army to warn the enemy to accept the terms of surrender or suffer the rack. In a war model one learns little from one's enemies. One conquers them while telling them that it is a war of their own liberation.

ORGANIZED COSMIC CRIME

Fundamentalist theologians tend to regard Satan as the chief mobster in organized cosmic crime and wickedness. He is portrayed as a supernaturally clever executive with hosts of demons at his disposal. Inexplicably, fundamentalists bestow this godfather of evil with an extended and special freedom to play havoc with most of the human race. Some fundamentalists go to great lengths to explain that the Creator respects the civil rights of the chief mobster so much that he cannot lock him up until after he has swept most of the human race into everlasting torment and made it necessary for the Creator to incinerate the planet in an upsurge of holy wrath. Most fundamentalists oppose the American Civil Liberties Union's concern for the rights of a variety of people, but they seem, paradoxically, to think it necessary to give Satan every conceivable liberty to do evil, even though fundamentalist theology states that the chief mobster's fate has already been sealed. In short, he is free to commit unspeakable crime after crime but not free to convert. It is a clear case of obscenity without socially redeeming qualities.

Meanwhile, the fundamentalists are called on to fight in the cosmic battle by seeking to take earthly power from those they see as the servants of the enemy. They want that power for themselves as the true representatives of righteousness on the planet.

SURVIVAL OF THE FITTEST

Some fundamentalists, in the midst of their relentless opposition to Darwin and his version of evolution, have advanced a social Darwinism of their own. It may be that fundamentalist Darwinism is the foremost social movement in the United States in the eighties. To help goodness survive as the fittest in this cosmic war, the righteous must come together in mutual aid. The result is the Inerrancy Party. The Southern Baptist holy war may be viewed in part as an attempt by the Inerrancy Party to lay hold of denominational resources that can help to win the great struggle, resources that, they insist, belong essentially to them in the first place.

In the eighties and probably the nineties the super churches, with their thousands of members and the charisma of their ministers and their ready access to the electronic media, will likely increase their influence as the power of the traditional denomination decreases. The two will often stand in direct conflict over money and influence. Individuals who shift their allegiance to the jumbo churches will often do so with the belief that they are revolting against bureaucracy in religion. It will take another decade, perhaps two, for the moderates to establish their own super churches. Eventually, the truth will dawn on many of the people in the pews that the jumbo churches spawn their own bureaucracies. J. Frank Norris, fighting against the Southern Baptist Convention's growing bureaucracy in the previous generation, built a new bureaucracy with himself as dictator. Rival preachers with their own charisma finally broke away from Norris, founded their own jumbo churches, and became new warlords in the battle against the enemy.

The Southern Baptist holy war today is in limited respects a battle between the fundamentalist jumbo churches and those whom they define as the enemy within the Convention. It is also a fight over the vast material resources that Southern Baptists have accumulated over the years. Even more, it is over theology and divergent worldviews. Not until the present decade have so many Southern Baptists realized just how far apart their two major worldviews are. There is no way those worldviews can be harmonized.

17.

Fundamentalism in America

undamentalist ministers today are largely secular and modern in outlook regarding electronic communications. In other areas nostalgia pulls them back to an imagined time when they had more political clout and when most things worth explaining fit neatly into supernatural categories. The dreaded disease AIDS has become a delicious godsend to many fundamentalist preachers, who like to believe that sin must face divine judgment in the here and now. Even though most American parents would not want their children to become homosexuals or fundamentalist preachers, they would be reluctant to regard either as deserving of AIDS as divine punishment. But contemporary fundamentalist preachers harbor a desperate longing for a supernatural world that makes them the primary brokers and mediators of power. Charles Stanley and James Kennedy (a fundamentalist Presbyterian who was a hit at the June 1985 Southern Baptist Pastors' Conference) insist that AIDS is divine judgment and that preachers are God's mediators appointed to pronounce the judgment. What that implies about finding a medical cure for AIDS is unclear. Perhaps physicians and researchers will come under divine judgment if they attempt to sever a divinely established link between homosexuality and AIDS?

In 1847, when the Scotch physician Dr. James Young Simpson advocated the use of anesthesia in obstetrical cases, the Protestant clergy raised an immediate storm of protest. Pulpit after pulpit rang with warnings that Dr. Simpson's use of chloroform was contrary to Scripture. Texts were cited to prove that the use of chloroform was a deliberate attempt to interfere with the divine curse visited upon women in childbirth. Because of Eve's role in Eden, her female heirs were destined to suffer pain in pregnancy and childbirth (Gen. 3:16). In 1591 a lady of rank, Eufame Macalyane, sought relief from pain during the birth of her two sons. For daring to thwart the curse of God on pregnant women, Mrs. Macalyane was roasted alive on the Castle Hill of Edinburgh.[1]

In 1885 smallpox broke out in Montreal. The Abbe Filiatrault, Catholic priest of St. James's Church, proclaimed from his pulpit, "If we are afflicted with smallpox, it is because we had a carnival last winter, feasting the flesh, which has offended the Lord; it is to punish our pride that God has sent us smallpox." Consistent with his belief, Filiatrault, joined by other priests, exhorted the faithful to take up arms rather than submit to vaccination. As a result, a heavy toll was taken on the Catholic population, whereas Protestants and others who submitted to vaccination suffered comparatively little loss of life. They regarded the Catholics as superstitious. The Catholic clergy, clinging to their power and their worldview, urged devotional exercises, repentance, and religious processions to persuade Heaven to withdraw the killing disease.

The clergy's resentment of the medical profession's power in the Middle Ages expressed itself in the early thirteenth century at the Lateran Council, where physicians were forbidden to initiate medical treatment before calling in ecclesiastical counsel.[2]

In the Old Testament, the priest Samuel convinced a number of Israelites that priestly blessings were essential ingredients of the army's power against the enemy. Some members of the clergy class have always sought to extend their power by making themselves necessary to the interplay of sociopolitical forces. That is largely what official prayer time in the public school is about—an extension of the pulpit into the classroom.

Today many Southern Baptist ministers, far from seeking to extend their political power, find that they have more than enough work to do in ministering to the needs and crises of the people who have called them to serve the churches. In times past, the clergy maneuvered for invitations to offer prayers at sociopolitical functions. Today, many busy ministers complain that too much of their time is eaten up by perfunctory prayers at this and that gathering. They look upon such rituals as a carryover from the days when prayers were an ingredient in the balance of power among seekers of political influence.

Those who interpret fundamentalism as a rejection of modernity fail to see that fundamentalists have embraced a great deal of modernity with open arms. Most fundamentalist preachers did not oppose the space program, advances in high-speed transportation and high-speed ballistics, or the booming microelectronics and computer industry. Instead of denouncing television, fundamentalist preachers learned to use it. Fundamentalists did, however, oppose the motion picture industry for several years, since they could not use it to widen their own influence. Hollywood and the film industry were regarded as one of Satan's most successful ventures because they often exhibited views and values that clashed with fundamentalism. Only in recent years have Christian soap operas appeared on Pat Robertson's TV station, their purpose being to inject a fundamentalist message that would reinforce the fundamentalist worldview.

Technology is a tool for both good and ill in every worldview. In the eighties fundamentalist Christianity has come to terms with much of the technological revolution. But before the Depression, it joined Catholicism in opposing birth control devices. The current antiabortion campaign is another round in the fundamentalist fight to return women to the position that the fundamentalist worldview has required. As a high school student in the late forties I read *The Home—Courtship, Marriage and Children,* by one of the leading fundamentalist evangelists, John R. Rice. In the chapter on birth control, Rice argues that since God is in control of giving and withholding conceptions, it is a sinful interference with God's efforts to use birth control devices. I quote from Rice's dated book to illustrate how much of the fundamentalist worldview has been eroded by the spread of birth control information:

> "There is no need for birth control when in the early child-bearing period a woman would normally have a child only every two years or more. . . . Since God Himself gives life as He chooses and does not give babies except as He makes it possible to care for them, . . . in most cases it is obvious that birth control is neither necessary nor desirable."[3]

Today fundamentalism must reconsider where the supernatural ends and science and technology begin. In one generation most fundamentalist preachers have accepted the role of technology in several areas previously reserved for direct divine control. Oral Roberts, with his emphasis upon direct divine healing, believes he can strike a compromise with the powerful medical forces of Western culture rather than challenge them head-on. Stated bluntly, in a showdown between medicine and faith healing, the faith healers would lose power and influence with all but the lower economic class, which has never been able to afford the benefits of medicine in the first place. Indeed, they can no longer afford the big-time faith healers. Roberts's resolution of the dilemma came in the form of what can only be described as an obsession to build the City of Faith: Against every sort of rational advice from his friends, Roberts poured almost all his energy into the project. Why?

Unless he could somehow link faith healing with the entrenched and powerful medical profession and its countless institutions and agencies, the faith healing to which Roberts had devoted most of his life would simply remain as an isolated phenomenon. Faith healing has never been a part of the middle class. The City of Faith is his attempt to legitimate faith healing and give it medical respectability. Even though he has considerable charisma, Roberts was worldly enough to see that unless faith healing was institutionalized and wedded to other institutions that are already legitimated, it would remain at best a poor and embarrassing relative in middle-class America.

There is one American institution that fundamentalist leaders have tried to challenge head-on—the public school system. In many ways the technological revolution is only a minor threat to fundamentalism; the real challenge is education. No institution in America poses more threat to fundamentalism than public education. James Robison once stated that the schools should teach nothing that conflicts with his faith. The recent attempts of some fundamentalist leaders to intimidate biology teachers into inserting a fundamentalist version of Genesis 1 and 2 into biology textbooks have finally alerted educators to the relentless threat of fundamentalism. Some fundamentalist leaders have made it clear that they wish to abolish the public schools. The voucher plan being supported by the White House encourages the creation of private schools so that fundamentalist children will not have to attend public schools. If school bills are not passed in local communities, the public schools will eventually disappear. In Ireland the flames of religious conflict are fed by a system of denominational schools that is largely designed to prevent the understanding of rival worldviews.

A number of Southern Baptist ministers within the Inerrancy Party have given serious thought to establishing their own schools to compete with the public schools. The jumbo churches are more likely to succeed in such ventures. If they succeed on a wide scale, a number of Southern Baptist children will be shuttled into intellectual ghettos. It is at first surprising that the fundamentalist leaders have not challenged the public schools to offer elective courses in creationism or in other subjects favoring the fundamentalist worldview. If a positive approach were taken—namely, to broaden the curriculum—fundamentalists might actually enrich public school education and contribute to open debate in the classrooms. The 1963 Supreme Court decisions in Abington v. Shempp and Murray v. Curlett make it clear that the academic study of religion and related topics in the public schools is perfectly compatible with the Constitution, especially with the First Amendment. I suggest that many fundamentalist leaders have failed to pursue such an alternative because they do not want their views studied in a truly academic environment. They want not so much to be represented well at the public schools as to undermine public education's academic environment.

Members of the Moderate Party and members of the Inerrancy Party would do well to find a way to prevent the drive to shut down the voice of the other. They need to make certain that both are well represented in the Sunday school literature and other pieces of denominational literature. That would of course increase theological discussion within Southern Baptist churches, a frightening idea for leaders who would like to give the impression that Southern Baptist waters are smooth and that controversy among the sheep is an exception, not the rule. Their outlook is taken from PR texts, certainly not from the New Testament, which is filled with debates and controversies. The truth is that churches can thrive as well on controversies carried out decently and in order as on theological pabulum.

It may be that Southern Baptist leaders have lost their nerve. It may be that each side not only distrusts the other but also distrusts its own ability to present good reasons for the hope that lies within. If that is the case, then the time has come for Southern Baptists to turn their controversies into legal battles. The legal battles will not be as interesting or as enlightening as the theological battles, but they will at least throw lawyers and newspaper editors into a state of ecstasy.

18.

The Great Divorce

ne of the most insightful interpreters of Southern Baptist history is Dr. Walter B. Shurden, Callaway professor of Christianity at Mercer University in Macon, Georgia. He contends that the current emotional climate among Southern Baptists will not permit a rational divorce of the two parties, which is doubtless true. But is he correct to add that the two warring parties need one another? The answer depends upon what they want. If their goal is to hold themselves together as the largest Protestant denomination in the nation, they do need each other. If that goal is unimportant, then they might find that a divorce is to their mutual benefit.

Jerry Falwell insists that a merger between Moral Majority, Inc., and the Southern Baptist Convention is a structural impossibility, even though the 1984–86 president of the Convention, Charles Stanley, was a founding member of Moral Majority. Falwell is correct: Moral Majority and the Liberty Foundation are not religious denominations but a political coalition run mostly by ministers. Falwell is a leader within the Baptist Bible Fellowship, a fundamentalist denomination of more than three million members that originated in 1950. If the Southern Baptist Convention splits, it is conceivable that some deal will be made to merge the Inerrancy Party churches with the Baptist Bible Fellowship.

More likely, each party will initially go its separate way if either pulls out of the Convention. In time, the churches of the Inerrancy Party might seek an alignment with the General Association of Regular Baptists (organized in 1932), the Conservative Baptist Association (organized in 1947), or some other body of fundamentalist Baptists. A

loose confederation of fundamentalist and evangelical Baptist denominations could emerge, with the Inerrancy Party churches becoming a dominant part of it after forming themselves into a new convention. It is even possible that a number of evangelical-fundamentalist
churches will seek membership in two Baptist denominations, in dual
alliance.

It is conceivable but unlikely that the moderates will as a new denomination seek structural unity with the American Baptist Convention. There would be little point to such a merger since it is already
possible for any local Southern Baptist church to have dual membership. If the Broadway Baptist Church of Fort Worth, for example,
chose to belong to a newly founded Southern Baptist Moderate Convention and to the American Baptist Convention, nothing could prevent it from doing so. And if the First Baptist Church of Amarillo
chose to belong to the Southern Baptist Moderate Convention without seeking membership in the American Baptist Convention, nothing
could prevent it from taking that option. If a Southern Baptist Moderate Convention were formed, the energy and money required to make
it succeed would likely prevent most of its churches from seeking
dual membership in the American Baptist Convention. However, the
American Baptist retirement fund appears in some ways to offer ministers a better retirement plan than the current Southern Baptist plan,
a factor that should be given considerable weight.

TOO RICH TO DIVORCE

As suggested in the first chapter, Southern Baptists may be too rich
and too powerful to divorce. They have an enormous amount to lose
in a divorce proceeding, assuming such a divorce is legally possible.
Not only do they have buildings and agencies at the Convention-wide
level; they also have institutions and in-depth programs at the state
level. The legal problems alone are overwhelming to consider. In Kentucky, which one of the warring parties will gain control and owner-
ship of the Baptist colleges? Who will get Samford University in Alabama? Carson-Newman College and Union University in Tennessee?
Mars Hill College in North Carolina? The Baptist childrens' homes in
several states? The Baptist hospitals? The list goes on and on. In the
Annual of the Southern Baptist Convention are six pages of small
print listing the names and addresses of directors of associational
missions alone. Will each director be forced to take sides in a struggle

for power at the associational level? (In each state there are normally several Baptist associations.) Ten and a half pages list the ordained chaplains among Southern Baptists. All in all, 447 pages of the annual are devoted to the names and addresses of Southern Baptist ministers of various specialities and of ordained denominational workers. How many of them will be shuffled and lost through the cracks in the long and drawn out divorce process? How will a traumatic organizational split and realignment affect the marriages and family life of Southern Baptists? Paige Patterson says that no one can predict the organizational outcome of the current Southern Baptist battle. It is still harder, even impossible, to predict the effect on the emotions and personal relationships during the years required to accomplish a split and during the readjustment years thereafter. In most divorces there is a bitterness that does not easily dissolve, and the emotional wounds heal slowly if at all.

The richness of Southern Baptist life lies not in money and property alone but in its heritage. A heritage, like a cell, grows and sometimes divides—no matter what its content and ideology. That is why each side in the Southern Baptist battle can solemnly cite quotations and prooftexts from the same heritage. In some respects each party is a true heir of its tradition for the simple reason that no tradition is a static entity that passes unchanged from generation to generation. It is inevitable that individuals select from their past the threads that they judge to be the essence of their heritage. Internal disagreement is unavoidable, and self-contradiction will remain a permanent ingredient of every tradition. To insist that one's religious tradition must expunge all theological error before its members can justify committing themselves to it is to lock that tradition into the harness of perfectionism and to hitch it to the wagon of holiness epistemology.

If the Southern Baptist Convention does split, a peaceful settling down will not follow. New and more bitterly contested disagreements will likely break out within each separate party. A 79-year-old woman who has been a Southern Baptist since her twenties made this comment: "If we split up, there'll just be that many more of us Baptists." Cells will beget new cells. Currently, there are more than 33 million Baptists of various sorts around the globe.[1] To what extent the new Baptist cells will resemble the old ones and their contemporaries remains anyone's guess. Religious and social movements are notoriously difficult to predict.

ANOTHER ALTERNATIVE

The marriage counselor often advises the quarreling couple to lay their complaints out on the table. They are encouraged to express their views and feelings frankly. Each is urged to listen carefully to what the other has to say. The counselor's assumption is that sharp disagreements have a better chance of resolution if the points of disagreement can be well articulated and heard in good faith. Despite the enormous number of books, journals, magazines, tracts, and publications that Southern Baptists turn out every month, the two sides in the fierce controversy are not communicating as well as they must if they want to resolve the deepest differences between them.

If, as some inerrancy proponents insist, the disagreement is at least one third theological, then what is to prevent Southern Baptists from creating a new publication devoted exclusively to discussing their theological differences? As noted in chapter two, Southern Baptists seem pathologically afraid to do this. One group fears being repressed and intimidated in their jobs; the other group fears the risk of educational exchange.

Paige Patterson said that at the New Orleans Seminary his evangelical teacher Clark Pinnock came out victorious in confronting professors who held different viewpoints. Patterson went on to say that he would not fear competition of ideas at the seminaries. His so-called parity plan appears, however, to undermine intellectual competition and diversity within each seminary. Does he wish to guarantee Baptist professors in each seminary the freedom to present their views without the threat of being fired? Clearly not. Does he wish to have his own view ably represented in the seminary *in free competition* with other views of inspiration? The answer again seems to be no. On more than one occasion Patterson has suggested that the opponents of inerrancy would be reluctant to confront the defenders of inerrancy in a debate on the floor of the Convention. But how does he know that? Has he tried hard to initiate the debate? To be sure, the debate would be superficial. An emotion-laden convention packed with thousands of people is scarcely an environment where the messengers can follow involved arguments calmly and carefully, and the convention simply cannot provide enough time for the issues to be rationally and systematically discussed. If Patterson is serious about a debate of genuine substance rather than of flash and showmanship, then he would do well to call for at least two years' exchange in an official Convention publication that would be sent into the homes of as many Southern Baptists as possible. But Patterson seems to be one of those who are reluctant to participate in an orderly and rational debate over a reasonable period of time.

Now, why do Pressler, Criswell, and Patterson appear so afraid of free competition of ideas within the classrooms of higher education? Is it because they fear they cannot hold their own? Is it because they can't answer point by point the charge that their view is logically reducible to an atheism that has "might makes right" as the foundation of its ethics? Is Pressler willing to give a straight answer in print to the specific question of whether he wants to prohibit biology teachers who adhere to the theory of evolution from teaching at Baylor University? When I asked that question, Pressler asked which view of evolution was meant. I told him he was free to specify any view he wanted—just tell the reader plainly which views of evolution he would prohibit from being taught at Baylor—but Pressler chose not to specify or to pursue the issue further.

Is it possible that one party in the Southern Baptist battle is unwilling to present its views in an orderly, point-by-point exchange in print? Are Richard Land and Paige Patterson prepared to accept T. C. Smith's challenge to exchange views, replies, and rejoinders in a book or series of articles for Southern Baptist laypeople to read? If Land charges that William Hull, former dean of the faculty at Southern Seminary, has a faulty view of the Bible, is Hull willing to engage Land in a series of articles on the topic of biblical authority? Why have the moderates delayed in pressing for an open and orderly debate in print?

In decades past, laypeople could read that kind of informed exchange for themselves in Baptist state papers. The scholarly debate in the early fifties between Clyde Francisco, Old Testament professor at Southern Seminary, and Moody on the translation of Isaiah 7:14 could well serve as a model for current Baptists who think it important for the laypeople to share in the benefits of theological scholarship. It may be, as the leaders of the Inerrancy Party have long contended, that a large number of professors, ministers, and denominational workers have a lot to hide concerning what they think about the Bible. If that is the case, the inerrantists ought to welcome the opportunity to draw them out and expose them in a published debate.

It may be, on the other hand, that the inerrantists have a deep fear of facing and answering in print specific criticisms of their doctrine and its implications of extreme moral relativism. If so, then Smith is correct: the opponents of inerrancy should draw them out, and challenge them to reply point by point so that the laypeople can follow the arguments carefully and judge for themselves. The means could easily be found by both parties to underwrite a Convention-wide, biweekly publication devoted to such an exchange of views for at least two years. Or the state journals could be made available, but only if the leaders of both parties are really willing to risk laying their views on the line and to respond to the objections that they inspire. If they are not, then at best the Southern Baptist Convention will go on as an increasingly miserable marriage in which wild charges are hurled back and forth.

When a large percentage of faculty members of Southwestern Baptist Theological Seminary voluntarily signed a statement in support of seminary president Dilday, Pressler could not believe that they had acted voluntarily. Without stating in print how he had arrived at his conclusion, Pressler charged that Dilday had manipulated the faculty. At a Christian Life Commission seminar a Bible translator and critic of inerrancy, Robert Bratcher, instead of focusing on what he regarded as severe problems with the theory of inerrancy, offered an unjustifiable and immoderate personal attack on the motives of the proponents of inerrancy. "Only willful ignorance," Bratcher said, "or intellectual dishonesty can account for the claim that the Bible is inerrant and infallible." Bratcher and Pressler are only human, and under trying conditions men and women of goodwill are tempted to engage in personal attacks rather than debate the issues. Such attacks will increase in number and bitterness if Southern Baptists persist in talking across each other rather than engaging in systematic debates. If the Inerrancy Party leaders refuse this direct challenge, they will lend credence to the charge that their real concern all along has been not theology but power. There is little to lose but much to gain in a series of scholarly theological exchanges between the two parties.

And there is always time for the parties to go their separate ways if all else fails.

Epilogue

TO THE VICTOR BELONGS THE SPOILS

At the Atlanta convention of June 1986 the difference between the presidential vote for Adrian Rogers of Tennessee and the vote for Winfred Moore of Texas was roughly eight percent. Even though Moore lost his bid for the presidency, he contended that the 54 percent of the 40,000 representatives attending the Atlanta convention did not necessarily reflect the predominant will and thinking of the 14.4 million Southern Baptists. The moderates had unquestionably prevailed at the Texas Baptist Convention in the fall of 1985. In the bid for the presidency of the Tennessee Baptist Convention of 1985–86, James McCluskey defeated the candidate that Adrian Rogers actively supported. The success that the Inerrancy Party has accumulated for almost a decade at the national convention has not been generally enjoyed at the state and local levels. Nevertheless, the Inerrancy Party's impressive national triumphs will continue to strengthen its position on the boards that oversee the SBC agencies.

That is not to predict a sweeping purge in the eighties. A few individuals will perhaps be fired on ideological grounds. James M. Dunn, executive director–treasurer of the agency known as Baptist Joint Committee on Public Affairs, is under heavy fire. Other key individuals will retire or resign to be replaced by fundamentalists of the Inerrancy Party. The process will take time, but it will eventually have a profound effect across the entire Convention. Therein lies one of the moderates' major sources of negotiating strength. Dr. Jack Prince pointed out to me the irony and humor of the approaching reversal of arguments used by the two warring parties. The more fundamentalism becomes the ruling theology of the Convention agencies, the more the Inerrancy Party rank and file will begin to speak movingly of cooperation and love, while the moderates will speak of withholding money because they cannot support what violates their conscience.

Former Convention president Jimmy Draper said in June 1986 that even though his candidates won in Dallas and Atlanta, he was not happy. He explained that the Convention had worked itself into a win-lose system rather than a win-win. Draper doubtless realizes that without the moderates' money, the SBC institutions and agencies would have to be severely cut back or eliminated. In 1985 Draper himself threatened to withhold his church's cooperative program money if his candidate, Charles Stanley, failed to be elected. The threat that moderates might in time withhold money if they perceive themselves as not well represented in the agencies is as real as the threat coming from the Inerrancy Party.

The appeal of dual alliance lies in its offering the local church an opportunity of sending the major portion of its contributions to the denomination that reflects more faithfully its own orientation. Instead of perceiving themselves as a congregation that withholds its money, church members may regard themselves as responsible stewards guiding their gifts and offerings in the direction that more fully harmonizes with their local church's convictions and mission. In addition, instead of feeling the powerlessness of a captive alien in their own denomination, they can by dual alliance increase their control over their destiny.

Whereas Draper seems unhappy even though his candidate won in 1986, Adrian Rogers, the winner, seems elated with his victory and appears to be in no mood for reconciliation or compromise. Despite the fact that he would not today be the new president had only five percent more of the vote gone to his opponent, Rogers boasted, "I don't believe by any stretch of the imagination that the division [within the Convention] is 55-45. I believe it is more like 90-10." Although Rogers stretched his imagination much farther than did the moderate candidate, the hard reality seems to be that Southern Baptists could continue to be an embattled and embittered two-party denomination for years to come unless they elect a mediating president by 1988. In his 1986 address to the annual Pastors' Conference, Rogers demonstrated that he is a fundamentalist at the extreme end of the continuum. "I wouldn't give you a half and a hallelujah for your chance of heaven if you don't believe in the virgin birth," he exclaimed. Apparently, it did not occur to him that a high percentage of Southern Baptists were baptized as youths without knowing what a virgin was. He offers no room for honest disagreement on what he regards as the fundamentals. If a fellow minister, a seminary professor, or a deacon has doubts about the virgin birth, Rogers sees it as not a difference of intellectual judgment but a flaw of character.

With Rogers in office, the Peace Committee that was established at the Dallas convention will count for almost nothing. The Baptist holy war has only begun. The moderates are down but not out. Doubtless the Convention institutions will continue to survive for at least a decade. By then, the pendulum could swing back. In the meantime, hyperfundamentalists like Rogers are looking for people to fire and to intimidate through threat of firing. According to one report, Rogers will try to persuade the governing boards and agencies to require all Convention employees to sign a document affirming their belief in the Bible's inerrancy. If the moderates yield like lambs going to the slaughter, the hyperfundamentalists will have a field day.

WITHOUT MIXTURE OF ERROR

If Paul Pressler, Paige Patterson, and Harold Lindsell were to hold uncompromisingly to their version of inerrancy, it is unlikely that even Clark Pinnock could be hired at one of the Southern Baptist seminaries as an inerrantist. That is despite Pinnock's well-earned reputation as a defender of biblical inerrancy and evangelical Christianity. There was a time when Patterson looked upon Pinnock, his former professor, as a champion of the authority and inerrancy of Scripture. In *The Bible in the Balance* Lindsell charges that Pinnock has gone "in retreat from the strong stand he took in his earlier book *Biblical Revelation* published by Moody Press in 1971."[1] The charge rests in part on Pinnock's assertion that in the sermon recorded in Acts 7, Stephen made a few statements that are historically inaccurate. Luke, in recording the sermon, did not correct the inaccuracies but faithfully recorded what he believed he heard. Pinnock's point apparently is twofold: first, Stephen's sermon was an early Christian sermon, and like many other sermons over the centuries it communicated the gospel message even though it was not free of all error; second, Luke, not Stephen, was inspired to write the Book of Acts, and therefore Luke would have been in error to present Stephen's sermon with the errors removed or doctored. The situation may be compared to the disciples' seeing Jesus but mistaking him for a ghost. Pinnock's position, I take it, is that Mark and Matthew do not affirm the disciples' mistake but rather record it. For Pinnock, the Bible is inerrant "in all that it affirms," (a phrase that Lindsell seems to object to mightily), and the Bible does not affirm the errors within it pages merely by containing or recording them faithfully. I am surprised that Lindsell should fail to grasp that point. When Pinnock says, "Job cites the errant opinions of liars," he does not say that Job endorsed the opinions.

I will admit that there are problems with Pinnock's view and most certainly with Lindsell's. However, one little sentence in the Baptist Faith and Message Statement is not going to settle even the growing dispute as to which version of inerrancy or infallibility is to be the final word. I think I could show easily that neither Pressler nor Paige Patterson can affirm with consistency or without qualification that the Bible has "truth, without any mixture of error." Some inerrantists not only have treated the Baptist Faith and Message Statement as if it were itself an inerrant summary of Christian truth but also conspicuously want to use it as an instrument for removing fellow Southern Baptists from their jobs. Taking potshots at seminary professors is one thing. Getting down to the serious business of engaging them in a detailed and systematic debate for fellow Baptists to see in print is another.

DOWN BUT NOT OUT

"It's all over."

That is what one of the few and rare liberals among Southern Baptists said to me the day after Adrian Rogers was elected president of the Convention in June 1986. Using the word "they" to refer to the moderates, he observed that they were not well organized and had no forceful leadership.

Similar talk could be heard among Republicans when Lyndon Johnson whipped Barry Goldwater in the U.S. presidential election. "The Republican Party is finished," an assortment of pundits announced. Recently, some have suggested that the Democratic Party has breathed its last breath.

Judge Paul Pressler is right. Southern Baptists are a two-party system. Both parties are vital and well. Neither has an overwhelming majority. That is the clear lesson from the Dallas and Atlanta conventions. Eventually, those of the Moderate Party will elect their president if, but only if, they resolve to fight back with new and fresh ideas, a more effective organization, and hard work, which is the only way a party can win in a two-party or multiparty system.

If and when the moderates win a national election, there will doubt-less be those among them who see their triumph as heaven's triumph, the way Charles Stanley saw his victory as God's victory. Moderates tend, however, to refrain from portraying their opponents as agents or dupes of the Devil. To exercise such restraint is in part what it means to be moderate and a member of the Moderate Party.

According to the June 14, 1986, issue of the *Dallas Morning News*, the Reverend Greg Dixon, minister of the 8000-member congregation calling itself the Indianapolis Baptist Temple, placed Texas attorney general Jim Mattox on his hit list for Jesus. In the tradition of self-proclaimed witches and witch doctors, Dixon tried to put a biblical hex on Mattox, A Southern Baptist and Baylor graduate who made a legal decision unfavorable to Dixon's vested interest in a school in Texas. As a staunch believer in the inerrancy of Scripture, Dixon holds that God caused every word of the Psalms to be written and preserved for a purpose. As a man who readily blends his own purposes with those of heaven, Dixon quoted from Psalms for the purpose of intim-idating Jim Mattox: "Let his children be fatherless, and his wife a widow" (Psalm 109:9 KJV).

Most of the various translations of the passage agree that it carries a murderous intent, contrasting sharply with passages that exhort be-lievers to love their enemies and to pray for their enemies rather than against them. Not willing to dictate the precise method of execution for the attorney general, Dixon asked only tht God remove Mattox from this life "by whatever method, whether it be illness or whether it be by death, whatever pleases God."

Dixon is not a Southern Baptist. It is rare for Southern Baptist min-isters to indulge in such excess because they are so organized from the bottom up that a moderating effect generally prevails among them. If they are planning to attend the local pastors' conference during the week or month, they will be less likely to make outlandish statements that might elicit critical remarks or teasing from fellow ministers. If the current war among Southern Baptists is to subside, much of the calming influence will emerge from ministers who meet to share prob-lems, stories, and fellowship once a month or every week.

MONEY AND JOBS

It is basically money, jobs, and a labyrinth of legal battles that keep the Southern Baptist Convention from splitting in twain. It is unfortunate for the feuding sides that no simple and efficient way exists for them to divorce and go their separate ways. Perhaps it is time, nevertheless, to think the unthinkable, that is, to form not another Peace Committee but a Divorce Arbitration Committee that will report back to the annual convention with recommendations in 1989 or 1990.

That is one suggestion. In the long run, I think, it is the best of several options, none of which will resolve the conflict painlessly. The truth is, the animosity between the leaders of the two sides will likely increase during the next decade. The president of the Criswell Center for Biblical Studies, Paige Patterson, deeply resents the Southern Baptist Theological Seminary as it is today. He resents that 42 percent of the Seminary's $12 million annual budget comes directly from the Southern Baptist Convention. "It's the same situation as before World War II," Patterson is quoted in the June 5, 1986, issue of the *Atlanta Journal*, "when we shipped scrap metal to the Japanese and they shot it back at us." Such inflammatory rhetoric breeds distrust and suspicion. Like Pressler, Paige Patterson appears to want to perform surgery, and that is precisely why the moderates see him as their enemy.

Which in one respect is unfortunate. Paige Patterson has come up with one of the most fruitful proposals to resolve the war, or at least the battle over the seminaries. One aspect of his proposal would tear the Convention to shreds, which is what blinded me for a long time to its genuinely creative aspects. I would like to turn to those more fruitful aspects. As noted earlier, Dr. Patterson suggested dividing the seminaries into two groups. Three of the six schools would require their faculty members to subscribe in writing to the hypothesis (or doctrine) of the inerrancy of the Bible. The other three would give their Baptist professors, in writing, the genuine freedom to pursue their scholarly work and to teach according to the dictates of their religious convictions and their research; a faculty member could not be fired or intimidated by a group of Baptists who happen to disagree with what he or she teaches. Ideally, the teacher would not teach merely his own views in the first place but would provide students a spectrum of religioius and scholarly opinion.

All six seminaries should receive money from the Cooperative Program. It is here that Patterson's proposal has been amended, for he insisted that he could not in good conscience give money to the three seminaries that teach views to which he cannot subscribe. Two responses can be made to that. First, those who do not want *any* of the seminaries to bow down to the inerrancy requirement would have to compromise, too, in order to go along with the amended proposal. In short, they would go contrary to one level of their conscience in order to follow what they judge to be a higher level. No human conscience is a perfect harmony of voices.

Second, Patterson and his colleagues in inerrancy will continue to compromise one level of their conscience in deference to another level no matter what alternative they adopt in the decades to come. To remain a part of the Southern Baptist Convention is to compromise. To leave it is to compromise. To imagine that there is an alternative that does not violate one level of conscience in favor of another is to fall into the holiness delusion of imagining oneself to be able to reach a state of moral perfection on earth.

The two groups of seminaries, three in each group, could supplement one another academically. At the same time, they would compete with each other. Patterson's unamended proposal would have them vying for money by allowing negative designation, a device for eliminating some of the seminaries from the Cooperative Program.

The amended proposal would allow all six of the seminaries to benefit from the Cooperative Program. They would continue to compete with one another for students, and the three seminaries committed to the inerrancy doctrine would compete academically with the other three. It seems, therefore, that of the three lines of competition—for students, for academic superiority, and for money—Patterson would have to give up only one, namely, direct competition for money in each local church, if he and his Inerrancy Party followers could accept the amendment to his proposal. Indirectly there would still be some competition for money on the amended proposal. If one of the seminaries should cease to attract students, it would in time cease to receive Cooperative Program funding.

THREE NEW SOUTHERN BAPTIST SEMINARIES

Instead of creating a bitter and long furor over Fort Worth's Southwestern Baptist Seminary (the largest in the world), the following spin-off from Paige Patterson's proposal might work as a genuinely creative compromise. First, let Southwestern remain as it is, with no inerrancy requirement but free, at the same time, to bring in some professors who do hold strongly to inerrancy. In short, Southwestern will enjoy the same academic freedom that Southern Seminary will enjoy. Second, let the Criswell school in Dallas become the seventh SBC seminary to receive Cooperative Program money. The argument that the new Dallas seminary would be only forty miles from the Fort Worth seminary is irrelevant. The gap between Southern Baptists is not spatial.

Third, let the inerrancy seminary in Memphis and the inerrancy seminary in Florida become the eighth and ninth seminaries to receive Cooperative Program money. They, too, could require an inerrancy statement to be signed by faculty and administration. This plan would give the Inerrancy Party much of what it wants without tearing apart Southwestern. If eventually the inerrancy schools attract more students and therefore more money, so be it. If Southern Baptists continue to grow, they will need new seminaries. In summary, the inerrantists would gain five of nine seminaries—New Orleans, Golden Gate, Mid-America, Rice, and the Criswell Seminary. If each of the two warring parties will consider what it gains rather than what the other gains, the above 5-4 plan will perhaps appear to be a reasonable solution.

A LESS DRASTIC OPTION

Another option looms on the horizon, a plan and strategy suggested to me by Inerrancy Party faithful Jim Stroud, who has talked at length with Paige Patterson and Paul Pressler. I introduced myself to the Reverend Stroud after learning that he had said, "They accuse us of trying to take over the seminary, but all we want is to have our position represented [at Southern Seminary]." President Honeycutt admits that there are no true fundamentalists on the Southern Seminary faculty. (Actually, Professor Lewis Drummond is an inerrantist at Southern Seminary, but he is more an evangelical than a hyperfundamentalist in the image of Adrian Rogers.) Jim Stroud's strategy for a realistic resolution of the Baptist battle has the ring of plausibility for two reasons. It makes on behalf of the Inerrancy Party a demand that the moderates can probably live with even if they do not like it, a demand stated in straightforward language without the inflammatory rhetoric that suggests a purge. It also offers hope that a new leadership within the Inerrancy Party can understand what the moderates require as their justifiable right. (As will be seen shortly, this right applies equally to the inerrantists.)

Regarding the demand of the Inerrancy Party, Stroud makes it clear that he and his fellow advocates of inerrancy have been denied places on Convention boards and agencies. Furthermore, they have been denied positions on the seminary faculties. There is no point in trying to deny Stroud's charge. Nor is there any point in suggesting that a satanic conspiracy was at work in keeping the inerrantists out of key positions. The practical point is this. Now that the Inerrancy Party has won at the national level, although not uniformly at the state level, it is to be expected that inerrantists will be appointed to positions in the seminaries and in the Convention agencies if they are qualified for the positions. Let there be no misunderstanding. This means giving preferential consideration to qualified inerrantists. And it means not using the world "qualified" to block inerrantists from positions.

Regarding the principal demand of the moderates, the following point is crucial. Moderates want a work environment in which their denominational officers and workers are not intimidated with the threat of being fired if they deviate from the inerrancy ideology and theology. Let there be no misunderstanding here. This means that the Inerrancy Party members will have to be considerably more tolerant of diverse views expressed in the schools and in the denominational literature than they have been. At the same time, the inerrantists will gain something crucial through this principle of toleration. They gain the right to have their own views presented with greater clarity and more thoroughly than before. That will, of course, cause some of the moderates to wince. But tolerance is, after all, a two-way street.

Jim Stroud seems to reflect the thinking of those inerrantists who are truly conservative in the historical sense of the term. "I have great respect and admiration for Southern Seminary and its tradition," he told me after the Atlanta convention. "I would have no interest in firing seminary faculty members. What many of us want is to have our position well represented at the seminaries." This is the same Jim Stroud who went to a meeting of the trustees at Southern Seminary and demanded the right to be heard. (The man should be given an A+ for spunk.) His purpose in going to the trustees was to persuade them to fire Glenn Hinson from the faculty because of his use of higher criticism in interpreting the Bible.

At the seminary an interesting thing happened. Stroud and Hinson had a long, private talk. Neither convinced the other that his particular view of the Bible's authority was correct. (That would take years, not hours.) But each gained an appreciation of the other's integrity and Christian commitment.

In my own interview with Stroud, I could sense the man's inner conflict. He articulated it with astounding honesty, saying that he was deeply troubled by the very thought of firing a caring person like Professor Glenn Hinson, who clearly does not subscribe to the inerrancy hypothesis. I believe that ministers like Jim Stroud are earnestly trying to understand the importance of academic freedom, which is far more than the freedom to agree with either the inerrantists or the noninerrantist. They understand some of the profound differences that separate the Southern Baptist Theological Seminary from the Jimmy Swaggart Bible School.

It appears that the Inerrancy Party will continue to carry the day at the national conventions. As Stroud noted, "This increases the responsibility of us inerrantists." If the Inerrancy Party can, therefore, put forth a presidential candidate who is sensitive to the claims of both parties, the Convention might be able to gain a time of relative peace, especially if the president can be reassuring instead of inflammatory. The moderates, on the other hand, must graciously accept that the inerrancy position has won the right to be better represented in the Convention agencies. The moderates must understand also that a large number among the very conservative feel that they have been unfairly denied their share of jobs on the faculties and in the agencies.

Stroud, sounding much more conciliatory than the hard-line leaders of the Inerrancy Party, insists that conservatives of his kind wish to see jobs go to inerrantists as the positions open up in the normal ways—retirement, death, and job change. Moderates can live with that. What they cannot live with is the thought that their professors will be deprived of academic freedom, without which teachers are reduced to serving as intellectual whores and the schools are turned into vulgar propaganda mills. If Adrian Rogers truly did say, as he is reported to have said, that the seminaries should be trade schools, he must be led to understand that he is out of step with millions of Southern Baptists on both sides of the conflict. The seminaries and their traditions of educational responsibility were not built in a day, and moderates will not without a bitter fight watch the anti-intellectuals strip the schools of their academic achievements.

Perhaps no one has stated the moderates' position more graphically and succinctly than the self-educated Winfred Moore: "We don't want to take our institutions of higher learning and build a chain-link fence around . . . them, and put the students behind the . . . fence and let them growl at the world as it goes by. We've got them there to teach them, to train them to go out into the world and change the world. They've got to be taught to think. That's what they're there for."

It seems to me that life would in the long run be simpler for Southern Baptists if the two parties bit the bullet and tried to split. But that is asking a lot from individuals who live on the short run. A divorce between the parties is not inevitable. Both the inerrantist Jim Stroud and the moderate Jack Prince (who first urged me to talk with Stroud) contend that a mellowing effect will prevail as the Inerrancy Party leaders sense the terrible responsibility that has fallen on their shoulders. I do not see the mellowing effect coming but rather foresee the Inerrancy Party leaders driving hard to take full control of every Convention agency possible.

THE MORMONS ARE COMING

There is something ridiculous about Southern Baptists' turning on one another when the Church of Jesus Christ of Latter-day Saints has geared up not just to catch the Southern Baptists but to pass them within another generation. Within fifteen years the Mormons, who currently are less than one fourth the number of Southern Baptists, will reach the 14 million mark. The theory that the forsaking of strict orthodoxy and inerrancy will cause church rolls to decline falls before the phenomenal growth of the Mormons, whose theological deviation from Christian orthodoxy is beyond calculation. In the year 2030 (the Mormon Church's bicentennial) there will be 90 million Mormons if the present growth rate continues. Already "the LDS Church has become the largest private video network owner in the world, with the added capability of tying into any cable system in North America."[2] Eventually, Mormons will send up their own commercial satellite.[3]

Meanwhile, a group of Southern Baptists is trying to decide whether to fire James M. Dunn from the Baptist Joint Committee on Public Affairs.

Notes

CHAPTER 1: A NOISE OF WAR IN THE CAMP

1. Russell Dilday, "What Kind of Convention?" *SBC Today,* 2:11 (March 1985), p. 7.
2. James T. Draper, Jr., *Authority: The Critical Issue for Southern Baptists* (Old Tappan, NJ: Fleming H. Revell Co., 1984), pp. 104f.
3. Grand Rapids: Eerdmans, 1981.

CHAPTER 2: THE POWER AND THE MONEY

1. Perry Deane Young, *God's Bullies* (New York: Holt, Rinehart and Winston, 1982), pp. 214f.
2. Ibid., pp. 217–219.
3. Robert G. Torbet, *A History of Baptists* (Philadelphia: The Judson Press, 1950), p. 437.
4. *The Cooperative Program at Work Around the World, 1985: 60th Anniversary* (Nashville: Stewardship Commission), p. 13.
5. Jack D. Sanford, "Where Does the Money Go?" *Baptist and Reflector,* 151:44 (November 6, 1985), p. 4. This article appears as a guest editorial.
6. Keith Parks, "Foreign Mission Board," *The Cooperative Program, 1986* (Nashville: SBC Stewardship Services), pp. 15–19.
7. William Powell, Sr., in *The Southern Baptist Journal,* 13:2 (April 1985), p. 12.
8. Clayton Sullivan, *Called to Preach, Condemned to Survive* (Macon, GA: Mercer University Press, 1985), pp. 70f.

CHAPTER 3: INERRANCY AND THE BIBLE

1. James Barr, *Fundamentalism* (Philadelphia: Westminster Press, 1977), p. 335.
2. Larry Jonas, "Steps to the Top," *West Coast Review of Books,* Vol. 11, no. 4, (July-August 1985), pp. 36–37.
3. Joe T. Odle, "The Bible and Baptist Literature," in William A. Powell, *The SBC Issue and Question* (Buchanan, GA: Baptist Missionary Services, 1977), p. 164.
4. Edward J. Young, *Thy Word Is Truth* (Grand Rapids: Eerdmans, 1957), pp. 73, 86f.
5. C. H. Dodd, *The Authority of the Bible,* rev. ed. (London: Nisbet and Co., 1938) pp. 226f.
6. Ibid., pp. 239–241.

CHAPTER 4: STEPPING INTO THE BAPTIST WORLD

1. Herschel Hobbs, *Studies in Hebrews* (Nashville: Sunday School Board, Southern Baptist Convention, 1954), p. 52.

2. Ibid., p. 55.

3. Ibid., p. 52.

4. Ibid., p. 54.

5. Evangelicals are sometimes justified in regarding James Barr as an epistemological babe in the woods. While his work *Fundamentalism* (Philadelphia: Westminster Press, 1977) offers poignant insights into the fundamentalist-evangelical ambivalence regarding professional biblical scholarship, it reveals an equal amount of ambivalence regarding the epistemological question of impartiality (p. 131). He should have conceded to the bombastic fundamentalist K. A. Kitchen that translators and interpreters do not approach their work in a neutral state of mind. All exegetes carry their biases with them when they enter through the door of research. What Kitchen might have learned from Karl Popper, however, is that objective inquiry requires an openness to criticism and a commitment to revise or exchange our most precious biases when they have been filled with holes.

6. Bernard Ramm, *Special Revelation and the Word of God* (Grand Rapids: Eerdmans, 1961), p. 102; A. T. Pierson, "Testimony of the Organic Unity of the Bible to Its Inspiration," *The Fundamentals for Today*, ed. C. L. Feinberg (Grand Rapids: Kregel Publications, 1961), pp. 178–184.

CHAPTER 5: EVERY CONTEXT HAS A CONTEXT

1. Stephen T. Davis, *The Debate About the Bible: Inerrancy Versus Infallibility* (Philadelphia: Westminster Press, 1977), p. 15. J. W. MacGorman in *Layman's Bible Commentary: Romans, 1 Corinthians* (Nashville: Broadman Press, 1980), pp. 75–76, provides readers a sample of traditional context gerrymandering. Scholars like MacGorman and Davis know that context gerrymandering cannot be avoided. The best scholars keep track of the price paid for each shift of context and the price paid also for the status quo.

2. Grand Rapids: Academic Books, Zondervan Publishing House, 1984.

3. *Zondervan 1984 Display Preview*, p. 6.

4. "Millennium," *Baker's Dictionary of Theology*, eds. E. F. Harrison, G. F. Bromiley, and C.F.H. Henry (Grand Rapids: Baker Book House, 1960), p. 353.

5. See Samuel G. Craig's introduction to B. B. Warfield, *Biblical and Theological Studies*, ed. S. G. Craig (Philadelphia: Presbyterian and Reformed Publishing Co., 1952), pp. xxxviii–xli.

6. Personal communication, March 1, 1985.

7. Boston: Beacon Press, 1985.

8. The orthodox Christian hierarchy labeled this document the Gospel of Pseudo-Matthew. Cited in D. L. Dungan and D. R. Cartlidge, *Sourcebook of Texts for the Contemporary Study of the Gospels*, 4th ed. corrected (Missoula, MT: Scholars Press, 1974), pp. 36f.

9. Ibid., p. 38.

10. Elaine Pagels, *The Gnostic Gospels* (New York: Vantage Press, 1981), pp. xv–xvii.

11. Ibid., p. 90.

12. Morton Smith, *Jesus the Magician* (San Francisco: Harper and Row, 1978), pp. 1–2.

13. Grand Rapids: Eerdmans, 1982.

14. Cited in Dungan and Cartlidge, *Sourcebook of Texts for the Contemporary Study of the Gospels*, pp. 33f.

15. Leslie R. Keylock, "Evangelical Scholars Remove Gundry for His Views on Matthew," *Christianity Today*, 28:2 (Feb. 3, 1984), pp. 36–38.

16. Robert Gundry, "A Response to 'Matthew and Midrash,'" *Journal of the Evangelical Theological Society*, 26:1 (March 1983), p. 54.

17. Ibid., pp. 49f.

CHAPTER 6: THE RESURGENCE OF CONSERVATIVE CHRISTIANITY

1. *The Fundamentalist* (March 20, 1936), p. 4.

2. C. Allyn Russell, *Voices of American Fundamentalism: Seven Biographical Studies* (Philadelphia: Westminster Press, 1976), p. 28.

3. Patsy S. Ledbetter, "Crusade for the Faith: The Protestant Fundamentalist Movement in Texas" (Ph.D. dissertation, North Texas State University, Denton, Texas, 1975), pp. 232–234.

4. Ibid., p. 235.

5. Ibid., p. 236.

6. Ibid., p. 255, citing transcript in Copeland paper.

7. Ibid., pp. 255f.

8. C. Allyn Russell, *Voices of Fundamentalism*, p. 237.

9. Quoted in Ralph Roy, *Apostles of Discord: A Study of Organized Bigotry and Disruption on the Fringes of Protestantism* (Boston Press, 1953), p. 354.

10. Ibid., p. 355, citing *Gospel Witness and Protestant Advocate* (1947).

11. Ibid., p. 356.

12. Ibid., p. 357. In the past, fundamentalism tended to separate into splinter groups. Edward Dobson portrays his group as centric Fundamentalism and labels a rival group as "the lunatic fringe of Fundamentalism." One characteristic of the latter group, says Dobson, is its tendency to call other Fundamentalists "by derogatory names"—as if the phrase "lunatic fringe" were not derogatory. See "Fundamentalism Today: The Lunatic Fringe," *Fundamentalist Journal*, 3:4 (April 1984), p. 10.

13. Harold Lindsell, *The Battle for the Bible* (Grand Rapids: Zondervan Publishing House, 1976), p. 197.

14. Nashville: Broadman Press, 1969.

15. Under one volume these writings have been compiled, reorganized, and edited by Charles L. Feinberg, *The Fundamentals for Today* (Grand Rapids: Kregel Publications, 1961).

CHAPTER 7: THE CRISIS OF SOUTHERN BAPTIST EDUCATION

1. Harold Lindsell, *The Battle for the Bible* (Grand Rapids: Zondervan Publishing House, 1976), p. 104.

2. Zig Ziglar, "Has Baylor Strayed from the Bible?" *Waco Tribune-Herald* (August 2, 1984), p. 5A.

3. Kenneth W. Underwood, *Protestant and Catholic: Religious and Social Interaction in an Industrial Community* (Boston: Beacon Press, 1957), pp. 148–156.

4. Sidney Hook, *Heresy, Yes—Conspiracy, No* (New York: The John Day Co., 1953).

5. "An Interview with Judge Paul Pressler," *The Theological Educator*, special issue 1985, p. 23. This issue is under the title "The Controversy in the Southern Baptist Convention."

6. Ibid., p. 20.

7. (Garden City, NY: Doubleday and Co., 1986), p. 131.

CHAPTER 8: TOWARD A MODEL FOR SOUTHERN BAPTIST
COLLEGES AND SEMINARIES

1. Max Morris, "Seminary Destroys Minister's Faith in the Bible," *Christ for the World* (Nov. 1977).
2. Quoted in Lisa Ellis, "Baylor Faculty Teacher Under Cloud of Controversy," *Dallas Times Herald* (July 5, 1984).
3. Robin Horton, "African Traditional Thought and Western Science," *Africa*, 37 (1967), pp. 50–71, 155–187.
4. Lynn Ridehour, "Academic Freedom at Liberty Baptist College," *Free Inquiry*, 4:1 (Winter 1983/84), pp. 16–18. If various points of view could be presented at Liberty University with the clarity and thoroughness found in the presentation of fundamentalism by Ed Dobson and Ed Hindson, Liberty University could boast of having become an education center of outstanding quality. These two LU professors have written an insightful book titled *The Fundamentalist Phenomenon: The Resurgence of Conservative Christianity* (Garden City, NY: Doubleday, 1981). Despite the vast distance of opinion between us, I have found their work enlightening and helpful.
5. James T. Draper, Jr., *Authority: The Critical Issue for Southern Baptists* (Old Tappan, NJ: Fleming H. Revell Co., 1984), p. 105.

CHAPTER 9: RELATIVISM AMONG SOUTHERN BAPTISTS

1. Thomas S. Kuhn, "Reflections on My Critics," *Criticism and the Growth of Knowledge*, eds. I. Lakatos and A. Musgrave (Cambridge: Cambridge University Press, 1970), p. 277.
2. Maurice Bucaille, *The Bible, the Qur'an and Science: The Holy Scriptures Examined in the Light of Modern Knowledge*, trans. A. D. Pannell and M. Bucaille (Indianapolis: American Trust Publications, 1979), pp. 124f.
3. James Orr, *Revelation and Inspiration* (Grand Rapids: Eerdmans, 1953), p. 153.
4. Harold Lindsell, *Battle for the Bible* (Grand Rapids: Zondervan Publishing House, 1979), p. 169.
5. Jacket of Lindsell's book *The Bible in the Balance* (Grand Rapids: Zondervan Publishing House, 1979).
6. Orr, *Revelation and Inspiration*, pp. 150f.
7. *The Bible in the Balance*, p. 280.
8. *Ibid.*, p. 221.
9. *Ibid.*
10. Norman Geisler, *Christian Apologetics* (Grand Rapids: Baker Book House, 1976), p. 226.
11. *The Bible in the Balance*, pp. 55f.
12. Stanley Milgram, *Obedience to Authority* (New York: Harper and Row, 1969); Martin Ebon, *The Andropov File* (New York: McGraw-Hill Books Co., 1983).
13. *Khrushchev Remembers*, trans. Strobe Talbott (Boston: Little, Brown and Co., 1970), p. 4.

CHAPTER 10: WORLDS APART

1. Gordon Clark's book review of Bernard Ramm, *After Fundamentalism*, in *Fundamentalist Journal* (June 1983), p. 53.
2. Dale Moody, *The Word of Truth*, pp. 198–238.
3. Bob E. Patterson, ed. (Nashville: Broadman Press, 1979).
4. Orson Pratt, *Divine Authenticity of the Book of Mormon* (Liverpool: R. James, 1850), p. 1.

5. Sandra and Jerald Tanner, "Absolutely No Middle Ground," *Salt Lake City Messenger*, 47 (July 1982), pp. 7f.

6. Cited in A. D. White, *A History of Warfare of Science With Theology in Christendom*, Vol. I (New York: Dover Publications, 1960), p. 126.

7. Ibid., p. 127.

8. Robert Gundry, "A Surrejoinder to Norman Geisler," *Journal of Evangelical Theology*, 26:1 (March 1983), pp. 110f.

9. Cited in William A. Powell, *The SBC Issue and Question* (Buchanan, GA: Baptist Missionary Services, 1977), p. 58.

10. Maurice Bucaille, *The Bible, the Qur'an and Science: The Holy Scriptures Examined in the Light of Modern Knowledge*, trans. A. D. Pannell and M. Bucaille (Indianapolis: American Trust Publications, 1979), pp. 122f.

11. Ibid., p. 120.

12. Ibid., p. 149.

13. Ibid., pp. 140–153, 159.

14. Ibid., pp. 162f.

15. Ibid., p. 169.

16. Ibid., p. 187.

17. Ibid., p. 125.

18. Ibid., p. 119.

19. Herschel Hobbs, *Studies in Hebrews* (Nashville: Sunday School Board, Southern Baptist Convention, 1954), p. 121.

20. James T. Draper, Jr., *Authority: The Critical Issue for Southern Baptists* (Old Tappan, NJ: Fleming H. Revell Co., 1984), p. 59.

21. Joseph F. Green, *The Bible's Secret of Full Happiness* (Nashville: Broadman Press, 1970), p. 100.

CHAPTER 11: THE GOLDEN CALF

1. Vol. I (Grand Rapids: Zondervan Publishing House, n. d.), p. 23.

2. Vol. I, trans. James Maring (Grand Rapids: Eerdmans, 1951), pp. 157f.

3. Ibid., p. 160.

4. Nashville: Broadman Press, 1961.

5. I owe this crucial point to Professor Paul Brewer of Carson-Newman College, Jefferson City, Tennessee.

6. This distinction I have taken from Dr. Leroy Garrett's interesting study, *The Stone-Campbell Movement: An Anecdotal History of Three Churches* (Joplin, MO: College Press Publishing Co., 1983), pp. 8–11.

CHAPTER 12: THE STATUS OF SOUTHERN BAPTIST WOMEN

1. *The Criswell Study Bible*, ed. W. A. Criswell (Nashville: Thomas Nelson, Publishers, 1979), pp. 1414f.

2. P. K. Jewett, *Emil Brunner's Concept of Revelation* (London: Clarke, 1954).

3. P. K. Jewett, *Man as Male and Female* (Grand Rapids: Eerdmans, 1975), p. 119.

4. Harold Lindsell, *The Battle for the Bible* (Grand Rapids: Zondervan Publishing House, 1979),p. 119.

5. Jack Weir, "Biblical Inerrancy and Infallibility: A Philosophical Analysis" (presented to the faculty of Hardin-Simmons University, 1985).

6. *The Criswell Study Bible*, p. 1413. For an insightful hypothesis as to why Paul accommodated his teaching to patriarchialism despite the antipatriarchialism of Galatians

3:28, see Daniel P. Fuller, "Paul and Galatians 3:28," *Theological Student Fellowship Bulletin*, 9:2 (Nov.-Dec. 1985), pp. 9–13.

7. Raphael Patai, *The Arab Mind* (New York: Charles Scribner's Sons, 1973), p. 27.

8. New York: Harper and Row, 1976.

9. Geoffrey Furlonge, *Palestine Is My Country: The Story of Musa Alami* (New York: Praeger, 1960), pp. 4f.

10. See Patai, *The Arab Mind*, p. 29.

11. *The Criswell Study Bible*, pp. 1413–1415, 1454–1456.

12. Ibid., p. 1413.

13. "Women in Baptist History," (unpublished lecture), p. 4.

14. Ibid., p. 12.

15. *The Criswell Study Bible*, p. 1413.

16. Ibid., p. 1414.

17. In some ways the phrase "the new Puritans" is a more accurate description than "the new revisionists." Unfortunately, the former has developed a secondary negative meaning that does not apply to these Southern Baptist reformers within the Moderate Party. Dr. Gene Garrison, minister of the First Baptist Church of Oklahoma City, does not believe the word "Puritan" describes accurately those who wish to allow for ordination of women among Southern Baptists. "We don't need a wholesale reformation or purging of the denomination," he says. "We only wish to allow to continue what has long been a tradition among us Southern Baptists." With Bruster, Mynatt, and Professor Leon McBeth, Garrison is eager to point out that ordaining women is not a recent turn among Southern Baptists.

As noted earlier, the new Puritans or revisionists are to be distinguished from those more radical restorationists who do wish to make a sweeping purge under the assumption that it is both possible and imperative to turn twentieth-century churches into first-century churches. The new Puritans, while as uncompromising as the restorationists, have a less utopian outlook. But they are Puritans in the positive sense that they consciously seek a moral reform (in contrast to a political purge) of their denomination when it would deny women the right to seek their calling. Their tactic is primarily persuasion rather than excommunication or sectarian separation.

18. Hans Sebald, *Witchcraft: The Heritage of a Heresy* (New York: Elsevier, 1978), p. 166.

19. Ibid, pp. 191f.

20. *The Case for Orthodox Theology* (Philadelphia: Westminster Press, 1959), p. 55.

21. In 1886 a physician wrote an article entitled "Sex" in the *Western Recorder* (state Baptist paper of Kentucky) to protest the higher education of women for several reasons. He "wanted to save some silly woman from mortification she would suffer from placing herself before the public." Furthermore, he was deeply worried that higher education for women would seriously threaten the "healthful procreation of our race" (*Western Recorder*, Jan. 7, 1886, p. 2, cited in Blevins, "Women in Baptist History").

22. C. Allyn Russell, *Voices of American Fundamentalism* (Philadelphia: Westminster Press, 1976), pp. 62, 117.

23. C. Brownlow Hastings, "Ordination," *SBC Today*, 2:10 (February 1985), p. 9.

24. *The Criswell Study Bible*, pp. 1413f.

25. Ibid., pp. 1456, 1443.

26. Ibid., p. 1414.

27. New York: Summit Books, 1981.

28. Fortunately, evangelical scholars on the abortion question have begun to do the careful work that fundamentalists have failed to do. Robert N. Wennberg, *Life in the Balance: Exploring the Abortion Controversy* (Grand Rapids: Eerdmans, 1985), reaches a new height in carefully reasoned conclusions and sensitivity to the various twists of this complex issue.

29. Her paper, "Organizational Conflict in a Divided Denomination: Southern Baptists and Abortion," presented at the annual meeting of the Society for the Scientific Study of Religion, Savannah, Georgia, and the conference on Religion and the Political Order, Hilton Head Island, South Carolina, Oct. 1985.

CHAPTER 13: THE GREAT BEAST LIBERALISM

1. Statement made in Denton, Texas, in January 1985 at a conference on Bold Mission Thrust.
2. Nelson Keener, "To Obey Is Better Than to Evangelize," *Fundamentalist Journal*, 3:4 (April 1984), pp. 65f.
3. Ed. Hamid Algar and trans. R. Campbell (Berkeley: Mizan Press, 1984).
4. *World Aflame* (New York: Pocketbooks, 1965), p. 2.
5. "An Interview With the Lone Ranger of American Fundamentalism," *Christianity Today* (Sept. 4, 1981), p. 25.
6. "Shrine Under Siege," *The Link*, 17:3 (August/September 1984), p. 3. Published by Americans for Middle East Understanding, Inc., in New York.
7. Ibid., p. 2.
8. Homer Duncan, "The Fields Are White," *The Southern Baptist Journal*, 13:1 (Jan./Feb. 1985), p. 20.
9. "God Help Us," *The Southern Baptist Journal*, 13:5 (Sept./Oct. 1985), p. 21.
10. Ibid.
11. Cited in Harrison E. Salisbury, *Without Fear or Favor* (New York: Times Books, 1980), p. 130.

CHAPTER 14: THE NEW CURRENT

1. John Beversluis, *C. S. Lewis and the Search for Rational Religion* (Grand Rapids: Eerdmans, 1985), pp. 156f, citing letter of July 3, 1963.
2. Ibid.
3. Kenneth L. Chafin, "Who Is the Liberal?" *The Call* (May 1985), p. 3.
4. Clark Pinnock, Forward to Stephen T. Davis, *The Debate About the Bible* (Philadelphia: Westminster Press, 1977), p. 12.
5. *The New Class: An Analysis of the Communist System* (New York: Frederick A. Praeger, Publishers, 1957), pp. 152, 163.
6. W. L. O'Neill, *The Last Romantic: A Life of Max Eastman* (New York: Oxford University Press, 1978), pp. 183f.
7. Hershel Hobbs, *Fundamentals of Our Faith* (Nashville: Broadman Press, 1960), p. 146.
8. See Sidney Bloch and Peter Reddaway, *Psychiatric Terror: How Soviet Psychiatry Is Used to Suppress Dissent* (New York: Basic Books, 1977), p. 201.
9. Robert Anderson, "Sin and Judgment to Come," *The Fundamentals for Today*, ed. C. L. Feinberg (Grand Rapids: Kregel Publications, 1961), pp. 330–32.
10. E. J. Carnell, *A Philosophy of the Christian Religion* (Grand Rapids: Eerdmans, 1960), p. 380.
11. T. A. Burkill, *The Evolution of Christian Thought* (Ithaca: Cornell University Press, 1971), p. 11.
12. *An Introduction to Christian Apologetics: A Philosophical Defense of Trinitarian-Theistic Faith* (Grand Rapids: Eerdmans, 1948), pp. 303, 309.
13. Norman Geisler, *Ethics: Alternatives and Issues* (Grand Rapids: Zondervan Publishing House, 1971), pp. 149f.
14. *An Introduction to Christian Apologetics*, p. 343.
15. "You Said It," *Fundamentalist Journal*, 3:4 (April 1984), p. 6; Jonathan Bennett "The

Conscience of Huckleberry Finn," *Vice and Virtue in Everyday Life*, ed. Christina H. Sommers (New York: Harcourt Brace Jovanovich, 1985).

16. Thomas Warren and Wallace Maston, *The Warren-Maston Debate on the Existence of God* (Jonesboro, AR: National Christian Press, 1978), pp. 44–46.

17. Ibid., p. 45.

18. Robert H. Gundry, "A Response to 'Matthew and Midrash,'" *Evangelical Journal of Theology*, 26:1 (March 1983), pp. 51f.

19. Thomas Aquinas, *The Summa Theologica*, Supplement to the Third Part, Q 94, Art. 3.

20. J. A. Motyer, "The Final State: Heaven and Hell," *Basic Christian Doctrines, Contemporary Evangelical Thought*, ed. Carl F. H. Henry (New York: Holt, Rinehart and Winston, 1962), p. 291. Abraham in the story justifies sending no one from the dead to the rich man's five brothers by saying that he foreknows that the brothes will not heed the message. After all, they have not heeded Moses and the prophets. What the author of the story apparently did not wish (or think) to explore was the theological implication of Abraham's reply. If it is pointless to send someone with a message from the dead because it is foreknown that the message will not be heeded, was it not also pointless to have sent the same message through Moses and the prophets to them if the Creator foreknew that the message would not be heeded? Would it not be pointless and cynical to bring into existence those whom the Creator infallibly knew will end in utter torment and misery? Who benefits if billions of individuals are brought into existence when the Creator foreknew infallibly that they would live forever in hell? Who would want to benefit from it? In *The Fire That Consumes* (Houston: Providential Press, 1982), Edward Fudge, who is a member of the Evangelical Theological Society, argues that the Bible does not teach that hell is everlasting torment. Clark Pinnock says that evangelicals have not answered Fudge's thesis.

21. *Newsweek*, Nov. 10, 1980, p. 76. Bailey Smith's words were delivered in his public address before the Religious Roundtable 1980 in Dallas, Texas. Grace Halsell's latest book, *Prophecy and Politics* (Westport, CT: Lawrence Hill and Co., 1986), develops the thesis that dispensational fundamentalists like Smith tend to view Jews as pawns in an apocalyptic cosmic drama called Christian Zionism.

CHAPTER 15: POLITICS AND FAITH

1. Tammy Bakker with Cliff Dudley, *I Gotta Be Me* (Harrison, AR: New Leaf Press, 1978); Margaret Poloma, *The Charismatic Movement: Is There a New Pentecost?* (Boston: Twayne Publishers, 1982); Eve Simson, *The Faith Healers: Deliverance Evangelism in North America* (St. Louis: Concordia Publishing House, 1977).

2. *Give Me That Prime-Time Religion* (New York: Hawthorn Books, 1979), pp. 130, 132f. Copyright 1979 by the Oklahoma Book Publishing Co.

3. *The Criswell Study Bible*, ed. W. A. Criswell (Nashville: Thomas Nelson, Publishers, 1979), pp. 1535, 1537.

4. *Jude, 2 Peter: Word Biblical Commentary 50* (Waco, TX: Word Books, 1983).

5. *A Survey Between the Testaments* (Patterson, NJ: Littlefield, Adams and Co., 1964), p. 35.

6. "Jesus: The Model Neighbor," *Royal Service* (September 1985), p. 5.

7. (Chico, CA: Scholars Press), pp. 187–215.

8. Third edition (London: Adam and Charles Black, 1954).

9. Dr. Harold H. Oliver, Boston University School of Theology, called this point to my attention more than a decade ago.

10. Trans. Charles R. Joy (Boston: Beacon Press, 1948).

11. E. Glenn Hinson, "Eric Rust, Apostle to an Age of Science and Technology," *Science, Faith and Revelation*, ed. Bob E. Patterson (Nashville: Broadman Press, 1979), p. 24.

12. *Inspiration of the Bible* (New York: Revell, 1930), p. 18.
13. T. C. Smith, "The Canon and Authority of the Bible," *Perspectives in Religious Studies,* 1:1 (Spring, 1974), p. 43.
14. Philadelphia: Universal Book and Bible House, 1947; New York: The Christian Herald Bible House, 1920.
15. Cited in Al Shackleford, "Conservative Leaders Ask Rogers to Run," *Baptist and Reflector,* 151:49 (Dec. 11, 1985), p. 3.

CHAPTER 16: JESUS LOVES EVERYBODY, ESPECIALLY WINNERS

1. Oral Roberts, "I Must Tell Somebody," *Abundant Life* (Sept. 1980), pp. 10–13. Also see "Oral Roberts Meets Big Jesus," *Oklahoma Observer,* Tulsa (Nov. 10, 1980), p. 10.
2. David Edwin Harrell, Jr., *Oral Roberts: An American Life* (Bloomington: Indiana University Press, 1985), p. 415.
3. Ibid.
4. "Share Jesus' Area Code, Oral Urged," *Tulsa World* (Feb. 13, 1983), p. 12-A.
5. Harrell, *Oral Roberts,* p. 416.
6. George Getschow, "Biblical Petroleum," *Wall Street Journal,* Aug. 22, 1985, reprinted in *Creation/Evolution Newsletter,* 5:5 (Sept./Oct. 1985), pp. 18–19.
7. Edward Manier, *The Young Darwin and His Cultural Circle* (Boston: D. Reidel Publishing Co., 1978), chap. 5.

CHAPTER 17: FUNDAMENTALISM IN AMERICA

1. A. D. White, *A History of the Warfare of Science With Theology in Christendom,* Vol. II (New York: Dover Publications, 1960 [1896]), pp. 62–63. According to Genesis 3:19, God cursed Adam by compelling him to earn his food by the sweat of his face. But male preachers air condition their offices, cars, and homes without considering that they are thereby nullifying the Genesis curse.
2. Ibid., pp. 37, 60–61.
3. Wheaton, IL: Sword of the Lord Publishers, 1945, pp. 162, 183.

CHAPTER 18: THE GREAT DIVORCE

1. James Leo Garrett, Jr., "Who Are the Baptists?" *The Baylor Line,* 47:3 (June 1985), p. 11. Leon McBeth of Southwestern Baptist Theological Seminary understands the structure and history of the SBC. In my opinion, if Southern Baptist leaders in the current battle wish to come to some realistic compromise short of delivering themselves into the eager hands of lawyers, they would do well to sit down with someone like Leon McBeth at the negotiation table. His 1986 paper "Convention Representation" ought to be widely distributed within the Convention.

EPILOGUE

1. Harold Lindsell, *The Bible in the Balance* (Grand Rapids: Zondervan Publishing House, 1979), p. 190.
2. John Heinerman and Anson Shupe, *The Mormon Corporate Empire* (Boston: Beacon Press, 1985), pp. 55.
3. Ibid., p. 56.

Index

port for presidential candidacy of Pat
Robertson, 4
Drummond, Lewis, 6, 248
Duncan, Homer, 173
Dunn, James M., 241, 251
Durham, G. Homer, 125

Easter Enigma (Wenham), 54
Eastman, Max, 178
Eccles, John, 123
Education: free marketplace model, 80–
81; hothouse model, 77–80; Moderate
Party view, 251; objective inquiry and,
99–101, 102–103; openness to criti-
cism, 102–103; purpose of, 98–99;
threat to fundamentalism, 232–233;
value of dogmatism, 103; value of in-
doctrination, 103; versus indoctrina-
tion, 77–83, 86, 100–102
Edwards, Jonathan, 67
Egypt, 144, 168
Elisha, 176–177
Elliott, Ralph, 136
Embryology, 127. *See also* Science
Enoch, Book of, 110
Ephesians, Epistle to, 153–154
Epicurus, 129
Estes, Joseph R., 22
Eternal security. *See* Apostasy; Salvation
Ethics and Poetics (Aristotle), 43
Evangelical Council for Financial Ac-
countability, 17
Evangelical Theological Society, 59
Evangelism, 68–70, 93–96, 167
Eve. *See* Adam and Eve
Evil, 180
Evolution, 5, 43, 70, 76, 113, 122–123,
203, 227
Evolutionary naturalism, 39–40
Exorcism, 191–193, 196

Faculty. *See* Seminaries
Faith healing, 189, 201, 221–223
Falwell, Jerry: abortion, 70, 75, 159; adultery of friend, 10; attack on Christians
for involvement in politics, 73; capital
punishment, 70; charges of fraud and
deceit, 17–18; contributions to Star
Wars defense system, 216–217; defense
of biblically sanctioned atrocities, 182;

education and, 102; humanism and, 78;
merger between Moral Majority and
SBC, 235; money received from tele-
vision ministry, 22; Moral Majority,
Inc., 4, 165; noncreedal conservatives,
70; postmillennialism, 57; purposes of
United States, 170
Feinberg, Charles L., 197
Filiatrault, Abbe, 230
Financial success. *See* Capitalism; Materi-
alism; Prosperity
Finney, Charles, 93
Fite, Harley, 147
Flanders, Jack, 79–80, 86
Flew, Antony, 102
Ford Oil and Development, Inc., 212–213
Foreign missions. *See* Missionary move-
ment; Southern Baptist Convention:
Foreign Mission Board
Forwood, Frank, 121
Fosdick, Harry Emmerson, 73
Francisco, Clyde, 41, 239
Free will, 53–54
Freeman, William, 93
Friedan, Betty, 158
Fruitland Bible Institute, 4
Full Businessmen's Fellowship Inter-
national, 93
Fuller, Charles E., 107
Fuller, Daniel, 108–109, 113, 114
Fuller Theological Seminary, 107, 169
Fundamentalism: and medical profes-
sion, 229–232; anti-intellectualism, 75;
associated with political right wing, 71;
basic definition, 74; belief in inerrancy,
76; charges of liberalism, 74–76; early,
67–68; evolution in public schools, 70,
76; millennium position, 57; modern
era, 68–74; need for own schools,
232–233; prejudice against visions,
210–212; resurgence of, 167; social Darwinism, 227–228; technology and, 231;
use of invective, 73
Fundamentalist, 73
Fundamentalist Army, 60
Fundamentalist Baptist Missionary Fellowship, 72
Fundamentals, 75, 76

Galatians, Epistle to, 142, 144, 155
Galileo, 125

curriculum, 8, 91; Lindsell's proposal, 105; Patterson-Land proposal, 3–4, 104–106, 238–239, 246–247; president's role, 27–30; purposes of, 93–99; rejection of inerrancy, 115; Rogers' view as trade schools, 250; study of ancient Greek, 49–51; trustees' role, 26–30

Semler, Johann, 112

700 Club, 4, 22, 196, 221

Sexism. See Women

Shakarian, Demos, 93

Shannon, Harper, 95

Sheldon, Charles Monroe, 207

Shepherd of Hermas, 198

Shields, T. T., 73

Sholes, Jerry, 190–191

Shupe, Anson, 57

Shurden, Walter B., 235

Simpson, James Young, 229–230

Single Adults Want to Be the Church, Too (Wood), 156

Skinner, B. F., 78–79

Slavery, 130, 131, 135–136, 150

Sloan, W. W., 198–199

Smallpox, 230

Smith, Adam, 214

Smith, Bailey, 1, 186

Smith, Chuck, 171

Smith, J. Harold, 93

Smith, Joseph, 109, 124–125

Smith, Noel, 73

Smith, T. C., 29, 65, 90, 169, 198–199, 200, 203, 239, 240

Social Darwinism, 227–228. See also Darwinism

Socialism, 213

Society of Biblical Literature, 32

Socrates, 154

Sophocles, 154

South Africa, 224

Southern Baptist churches: in foreign countries, 24; influence of Moderate Party, 26; money to state convention, 21; rural areas, 121; super churches, 121, 227

Southern Baptist Convention: Annuity Board, 21, 23; Christian Life Commission, 26; Committee on Boards, Commissions, and Standing Committees, 7, 26; Committee on Committees, 4, 7, 26; conflict, 1–2; Cooperative Program, 18–22, 246–247; debate on differences,

238–239; Education Commission, 26; embezzlement in 1928, 19; Executive Committee, 22, 26; finances 18–23, 25; Foreign Mission Board, 12, 19–20, 22–25; Home Mission Board, 20, 22, 165, 166, 169; Inerrancy Party strategy for control of, 6–8; legal difficulties of split, 236–237, 246; likelihood of split, 235–236; new coalition, 121; Peace Committee, 243; president's powers, 7, 26; Radio and Television Commission, 23, 26, 164, 169; Sunday School Board, 23, 124; Women's Missionary Union, 23, 142, 145

Southern Baptist Foundation, 23

Southern Baptist Journal, 7, 132

Southern Baptist Moderate Convention, 236

Southern Baptist Theological Seminary: Abstract of Principles, 12, 13; beginning of higher criticism of Bible, 202; faculty departures and firings, 6, 9, 12–13, 25, 29; faculty views of McCall, 27–29; female enrollment, 145; Max Morris as student, 95; respect for, 249; trustees' role, 26–30

Southern Baptists: gap between laypeople and faculty, 91; laypeople denied biblical scholarship, 203–204; membership statistics, 1

Southern Baptists for Life, 160

Southwestern Baptist Theological Seminary: abortion study, 70; addition of inerrancy faculty, 247–248; faculty support for president, 240; theological spectrum in classroom, 10; trustees view of SBC conflict, 3

Soviet Union. See Russia

Sparkman, G. Temp, 86

Speaking in tongues, 194–195

Spurgeon, Charles, 59, 93, 142, 166

Stalinism, 178–181

Stanley, Charles, 144, 220

Stanley, Charles: career experiences, 4; Moral Majority member, 235; SBC president, 7, 26, 168, 220, 242, 245; view of AIDS, 229; view on divorce, 155; women's role, 144, 150–151

Star Wars defense system, 216–217

State conventions, 20–22, 26

Stephens, Harold "Hayseed," 213

Steps to the Top (Ziglar), 33